T0301410

Entrepreneurial Universities

Collaboration, Education and Policies

Edited by

João J. Ferreira

Associate Professor, University of Beira Interior and NECE – Research Unit, Portugal

Alain Fayolle

Distinguished Professor of Entrepreneurship and Director, Entrepreneurship Research Centre, EMLYON Business School, France

Vanessa Ratten

Associate Professor of Entrepreneurship and Innovation, La Trobe University, Australia

Mário Raposo

Full Professor of Marketing and Strategy, University of Beira Interior and NECE – Research Unit, Portugal

Cheltenham, UK • Northampton, MA, USA

© João J. Ferreira, Alain Fayolle, Vanessa Ratten and Mário Raposo 2018

All rights reserved. No part of this publication may be reproduced, stored in a retrieval system or transmitted in any form or by any means, electronic, mechanical or photocopying, recording, or otherwise without the prior permission of the publisher.

Published by
Edward Elgar Publishing Limited
The Lypiatts
15 Lansdown Road
Cheltenham
Glos GL50 2JA
UK

Edward Elgar Publishing, Inc.
William Pratt House
9 Dewey Court
Northampton
Massachusetts 01060
USA

A catalogue record for this book
is available from the British Library

Library of Congress Control Number: 2018935748

This book is available electronically in the **Elgar**online
Business subject collection
DOI 10.4337/9781786432469

ISBN 978 1 78643 245 2 (cased)
ISBN 978 1 78643 246 9 (eBook)

Typeset by Servis Filmsetting Ltd, Stockport, Cheshire
Printed and bound in Great Britain by TJ International Ltd, Padstow

Contents

Contributors

Sharmaine Sakthi Ananthan, London School of Science and Technology, UK.

Sandro Battisti, Bruno Kessler Foundation, Italy.

Vitor Braga, Institute Polytechnic of Porto, Portugal.

Mauricio Camargo, Université de Lorraine, France.

Fintan Clear, Brunel University, UK.

Gertrudes A. Dandolini, Universdade Federal de Santa Catarina, Brazil.

Ana D. Daniel, University of Aveiro, Portugal.

Alain Fayolle, Distinguished Professor of Entrepreneurship and Director, Entrepreneurship Research Centre, EMLYON Business School, France.

Sara Fernández-López, Universidade de Santiago de Compostela, Spain.

João J. Ferreira, University of Beira Interior, Portugal.

Stéphane Foliard, Jean Monnet University, Saint-Étienne, France.

Ayantunji Gbadamosi, University of East London, UK.

Ferran Giones, University of Southern Denmark, Denmark.

Eduardo Giugliani, Pontifical Catholic University of Rio Grande do Sul, Brazil.

Maribel Guerrero, Newcastle Business School, UK.

Andrea-Rosalinde Hofer, OECD, France.

Gabi Kaffka, University of Twente, the Netherlands.

Tariq Khan, Brunel University, UK.

Kari Kleine, University of Southern Denmark, Denmark.

Jacek Lewicki, SGH Warsaw School of Economics, Poland.

Nnamdi O. Madichie, University of East London and London School of Business and Management, UK.

Carla Marques, University of Trás-os-Montes and Alto Douro, Portugal.

Sonny Nwankwo, Nigerian Defence Academy, Nigeria.

Mariana Pita, University of Aveiro, Portugal.

Sandrine Le Pontois, University of Grenoble Alpes, France.

Rafael Prikladnicki, Pontifical Catholic University of Rio Grande do Sul, Brazil.

Mário Raposo, University of Beira Interior, Portugal.

Vanessa Ratten, La Trobe University, Australia.

Lucía Rey-Ares, Universidade de Santiago de Compostela, Spain.

David Rodeiro-Pazos, Universidade de Santiago de Compostela, Spain.

Moses Rodrigues, Federal Deputy, Brasilia, Brazil.

Ademar Schmitz, Universidade do Sul de Santa Catarina, Brazil.

Kavita Panwar Seth, Brunel University, UK.

João A. de Souza, Universidade Federal de Santa Catarina, Brazil.

Silke Tegtmeier, University of Southern Denmark, Denmark.

Paolo Traverso, Bruno Kessler Foundation, Italy.

David Urbano, Universitat Autònoma de Barcelona, Spain.

Andreia Vitória, University of Aveiro, Portugal.

Urszula Wiśniewska, WSB University, Poland.

Guillermo A. Zapata-Huamaní, Universidade de Santiago de Compostela, Spain.

1. Introduction: the role of entrepreneurial universities in society

João J. Ferreira, Alain Fayolle, Vanessa Ratten and Mário Raposo

INTRODUCTION

Universities are increasingly becoming more entrepreneurial in their outlook and the way they integrate into society. This comes from the competitive pressures universities are facing in the global economy. More emphasis is being placed on the knowledge and service economies, which is impacting upon how universities are seen in communities. In the past universities were viewed more as teaching institutions, but this has changed, with research and development also being emphasized in terms of regional competitiveness. Therefore, the role of universities has adapted to be more entrepreneurial, as there are multiple stakeholder considerations.

Local, state and federal governments are interested in universities because of the role they play in economic growth and social cohesion. However, the different levels of government are interested in universities in different ways depending on their goals and objectives. Local governments, particularly those around the geographical area of a university, are interested in how the university contributes to the living conditions of citizens in an area. This means that housing, recreational and tourism considerations are important for local governments which gain monetary and reputational benefits from universities. At the state level there are similar considerations but there is a more group mentality on how universities are managed. Thus, there is competition amongst universities at the state level in terms of rankings and student income. At the federal or country level universities offer an indicator of the educational levels or capabilities within the global economy.

Formica (2002: 167) states that entrepreneurial universities 'embed entrepreneurship in academic culture in order to achieve economic returns from the knowledge generated through research projects, empowered teams of teachers, students and business people, face-to-face and electronic relationships, and networked enterprises emerging from their spin-off activity'. The goal of entrepreneurial universities is to provide an environment that promotes risk taking and innovative activity. The key feature of entrepreneurial universities is to explore new ideas by utilizing the curiosity about potential business opportunities.

There is more pressure on universities to transform themselves to integrate new technology and business practices. In order to propel students into the new economic landscape, universities are incorporating more entrepreneurial initiatives on campus. This forms part of the changing academic landscape that incorporates a more interactive style of teaching and research (Ferreira et al., 2016). Universities need to integrate entrepreneurial ideas and beliefs into their organizational structures (Clark, 1998). This is a complex process involving testing and reformulating suggestions about entrepreneurial practices (Ratten and Ratten, 2007). To do this the ideas need to be worked out and incorporated in the university. Often a willingness to change is part of this process, as it provides a way to embrace new behaviours (Suseno and Ratten, 2007). By unifying organizational members under the vision of being entrepreneurial they can work together in a progressive way. Zhou and Peng (2008: 638) define an entrepreneurial university as 'the university that strongly influences the regional development of industries as well as economic growth through high-tech entrepreneurship based on strong research, technology transfer and entrepreneurship capability'. This definition is adopted in this chapter, as it focuses on a holistic view of entrepreneurial universities and the place they have in society.

This chapter is structured as follows. First, the development of the term 'entrepreneurial universities' in the literature is discussed. Second, the important role universities have in society is discussed with reference to the increased integration of entrepreneurship in educational systems. Third, the growing influence of technology and knowledge transfer at universities is stated. Next, community interaction and entrepreneurial universities is discussed. The chapter then provides an overview of chapters in the book. A final section draws conclusions.

ENTREPRENEURIAL UNIVERSITIES

Entrepreneurial universities can include a range of activities, from licensing and patenting agreements to the creation of new companies (Siegel et al., 2007). There has been a shift in the way entrepreneurship is understood at universities, with a flurry of cross-disciplinary programmes being started around entrepreneurship. Traditionally entrepreneurship was considered in terms of the monetary income a university received from outside business activities that mostly arose from scientific discoveries. However, this conceptualization of entrepreneurship has changed, to include partnership arrangements with other education providers and housing arrangements on campuses. This diversity in entrepreneurship is reflected in the building and construction going on at universities.

Previously universities would focus on their onsite students and visitors, but with information technology advancing there has been an increase in online courses. Thus, the branding of universities has changed to suit the market needs. There has also been related merchandise using the university brand that is most evident in North American universities, particularly those with well-known sports teams. The changing nature of universities has meant that there has been some debate about how to encourage entrepreneurship at universities, whilst regulating it. This has resulted in informal technology transfer occurring, with university employees working with industry. Link et al. (2007) suggests that academics are motivated to engage in informal technology transfer due to potential monetary gains. Whilst linking industry to university research is important, there have been some people using these connections as a way to avoid disclosing potentially lucrative arrangements.

Heinonen and Hytti (2010) state that there is an academic revolution in the changing of universities into socio-economically engaged institutions. Thus, the modification has resulted in a dynamic interaction of universities in terms of their teaching, research and service. There is more awareness of the additional services a university offers to society, such as land for leisure activity and being a source of knowledge dissemination. In addition, there has been a change in the way entrepreneurship is taught at universities: previously this was only available at business schools, but it is now being embedded in other faculties. This has been a source of irritation for many entrepreneurship scholars who view entrepreneurship as a discipline similar to that of engineering or medicine that needs to have academically qualified professionals teaching the subject. However, universities have increased the use of qualified entrepreneurship scholars by promoting interdisciplinary subjects that link with business schools.

The rise of entrepreneurship at universities is timely, as it coincides with growing interest in solving problems in creative ways. Heinonen and Hytti (2010: 283) state that entrepreneurial universities focus on 'the close collaboration between academia, industry and government, and on the contribution of tertiary level education to society and the economy'. 'Entrepreneurship' at universities is a buzzword that is increasing in popularity due to its linkage with innovation and creativity. This is due to universities being integrated in the social fabric of their community. The global economic landscape has placed more emphasis on entrepreneurship, which universities have capitalized on by promoting more entrepreneurial activities.

Gianiodis et al. (2016: 610) state that 'while an entrepreneurial university facilitates innovation and regional economic benefits, it also enhances scientists' reputation'. This stems from increased opportunities made available to scientists working for an entrepreneurial university. Universities produce market-relevant knowledge that helps to fill existing gaps in the marketplace. Part of the process for knowledge creation is innovation, which enables wealth creation. Martin and Turner (2010: 274) state that 'innovation is currently seen as the remedy for a range of ills, not only for economic development, but also societal issues'. Thus, innovation provides a way for the entrepreneurial university to achieve its goals and objectives within society.

Sporn (2001) highlights how efficiency and effectiveness are being encouraged through entrepreneurship at universities. There are different forms of entrepreneurship at universities that focus on interaction with student body communities through alumni and fundraising initiatives. Sporn (2001) suggests there are several ways to build more adaptive universities. First, the environment needs to be responsive to change. This can occur by placing more emphasis on resource allocation to ensure adequate funding for entrepreneurship projects. Second, the missions and goals need to focus on entrepreneurship. To do this it is useful to reward actions that are in alignment with an entrepreneurial culture at the university. There needs to be the use of entrepreneurial language in the mission statement as a way to signal to the community that the university values innovative thinking. Third, the culture needs to take an entrepreneurial approach to life on campuses. This can be exemplified by new processes that shorten product life cycle times in terms of getting ideas into the marketplace. Fourth, the structure of the university needs to be more conducive to cross-disciplinary collaboration. This might involve more of a matrix structure in which people can discuss ideas at any level of the organization. Fifth, management needs to focus on entrepreneurial decision making. This can include the use of information technology to harness the resource potential of ideas. Sixth, governance mechanisms that respond to decisions in a timely manner can help to facilitate the flow of ideas. This is important to engaging with different stakeholders in a productive manner. Seventh, leadership needs to be committed to the process of adaptation. This can include communicating new thought processes and standards of behaviour.

Universities are important parts of the knowledge economy and are trying to be more entrepreneurial in outlook. To do this they are focusing on having an entrepreneurial management style that encourages interaction with the environment. There is a vast amount of research on entrepreneurial universities, due to their educational and business role in society. However, there is a need for more research on the changing nature of entrepreneurial universities, particularly from an interdisciplinary perspective, which is the purpose of this book.

Entrepreneurial universities can be explained as a way to stimulate engagement with industry through strengthening the commercialization of innovation. Thus, it is important to understand the contextual factors influencing the success of entrepreneurial universities. Universities are changing their organizational structure to more hybrid forms that can interact with new technology innovation. More universities have tried to emulate Stanford by focusing on entrepreneurship. This has enabled the status of universities that associate with entrepreneurship to be valued as more prestigious. To facilitate entrepreneurship there needs to be the use of networks as a way to coordinate the flow of resources. This can enable the use of entrepreneurial capabilities to disseminate important information and knowledge.

The traditional goal of universities was to disseminate knowledge to the global community. This occurred through university and industry engagement that often centred on research exchange. Entrepreneurial universities can renovate economies by promoting leading-edge arts, science and technology research (Etzkowitz, 2010). Universities have become more entrepreneurial internally with their processes and collaborative efforts, but also through external partnerships. This change in orientation towards entrepreneurship has enabled more collaborative initiatives around business development.

CHANGING ROLE OF UNIVERSITIES IN SOCIETY

Universities are supporting more proactive and engaged responses to solve problems or help society. This involves universities collaborating with a range of entities in a way that they have not done previously. To facilitate entrepreneurship there needs to be an organizational culture at universities that is flexible and open to change. Disseminating knowledge helps in evaluating the reality of moving forward with certain innovations. To encourage more entrepreneurship, universities are marketing themselves as sources of knowledge. This signal to the market changes past perceptions of universities as bureaucratic structures resistant to change.

Many universities are public universities funded by governments, but there has been a change towards more self-funded programmes and initiatives in education. This has resulted in universities looking for ways to gain revenue and be less reliant on government funding. To achieve this, public–private partnerships that combine the use of university resources with those of private businesses are being encouraged. This helps to increase market efficiency at universities, but there has been a debate about how to do this whilst maintaining the reputation of universities. Universities are increasingly trying to integrate views from industry in their programmes in order to maintain their market competitiveness.

Jessop (2017) discusses how the increased interest in entrepreneurial universities is a result of the trend towards capitalization, commercialization and financialization. Universities are part of their regional innovation systems, due to the way they disseminate knowledge and contribute to its development. Brown (2016) suggests that universities are good for business, but also good instigators of business creation. This is due to universities playing an important role in national and global innovation policy through the impact they have on knowledge systems.

There has been a process of academic capitalism that has changed the way universities are viewed. Universities play an important role in entrepreneurial ecosystems by encouraging networks and the sharing of information. Some universities have focused on visionary policies that aim to solve future needs. Brown (2016: 190) states that 'entrepreneurial ecosystems depict the actors (for example, entrepreneurs, universities, business incubators) and inter-relationships (links between entrepreneurs and venture capitalists, university–industry linkages) which shape the nature of regional entrepreneurship'. An example is the Yale endowment fund, which substantially increased due to investment returns and increased integration of technology initiatives in partnership with commercial entities.

D'Este and Perkmann (2011: 318) state that 'rather than concentrating on "blue-skies" research, academics are seen increasingly to be eager to bridge the worlds of science and technology'. This involves a sense of ambidexterity, in being able to do research but then commercialize it. Academic entrepreneurs are able to combine multiple skills that enable a better way to access market potential. This can be conducted through disseminating knowledge in a way that provides a gain to the university. The convergence of both research and practice is an important way in which universities contribute to the economy. There is a hybrid nature to the way research outputs are communicated to communities, as some knowledge will apply to academics and some to practitioners. In addition, there are more incentives for universities to engage with their communities in an entrepreneurial manner. This involves providing personnel exchange between academia and industry to enable knowledge dissemination.

Advocates for entrepreneurial universities view them as an important way to harness the business potential of knowledge coming from academic partnerships. Universities are increasing their ambitions to be the producers and disseminators of knowledge in the global economy. This involves taking ownership of the way knowledge is utilized in a university setting. D'Este and Perkmann (2011) view entrepreneurial science as using scientific knowledge in an innovative way, normally involving business applications.

Universities are essentially knowledge businesses, as they manage information in a productive manner. The arrangements made for facilitating knowledge exchange involve universities working with the community in a collaborative way. This can involve interaction amongst different entities of the university to advise on the potential of ideas. Hence, knowledge can accrue over a long time period, and it evolves based on societal demand. In order to evaluate risk there should be an understanding about how knowledge might be used.

In entrepreneurial universities, people are active participants in the ideation process that results in business creation. The logic of entrepreneurship in universities stems from the ability of knowledge to make a difference to society. Moreover, there are practical considerations deriving from the ability of people to focus on entrepreneurship. These include communicating research findings to another setting, thereby further facilitating knowledge dissemination. This enables the public to gain information about scientific discoveries in a transparent way. In order to encourage new behaviours, individuals need to have academic freedom to pursue ideas. This involves focusing on the overall benefit of an idea based on an evaluation of its potential. Thus, knowledge can undergo a life cycle whereby it is generated, then disseminated, and the comments fed back into further innovation. This means there needs to be information communicated about how to reach out to the community in order to provide more improvements.

TECHNOLOGY AND KNOWLEDGE TRANSFER AT UNIVERSITIES

Technology can be transferred at universities through human capital, licences and research (Brown, 2016). In addition, the spin-off firms from technology invented at universities have been a major source of commercialization. These spin-offs are sometimes bought by large companies as a way to gain access to cutting-edge research. Successful spin-off inventions from university technology transfer include Gardasil, a vaccine for cervical cancer that was developed at the University of Queensland, Australia. This vaccine has been a source of large royalty payments to the university.

There are also student start-ups at universities that encourage new ideas to be commercialized.

Gur et al. (2017: 1) states that an '"entrepreneurial university" is the third mission attached to the higher education institutions in addition to their role in research and education'. This is due to universities being part of regional innovation systems diffusing innovation within a region by encouraging collaboration. Universities play a role in engendering entrepreneurship within regional innovation systems. Policy decisions are often made from knowledge originating from universities and related institutions.

More universities are focusing on their position in the international economy for competitiveness reasons. There has been a growing popularity of entrepreneurial universities as a way to combine private and public initiatives. In the global economy there is a need to spread knowledge rapidly, due to its role in knowledge-intensive industries. Due to the knowledge spillover effects universities have on individual countries, it is important to flag up universities' path-breaking teaching, research and service activities. This is due to universities being primarily concerned with the generation and dissemination of knowledge.

Universities are a source of innovation networks due to their ability to disseminate information. However, there have been criticisms of universities for being too remote and not in touch with the business community. This perception has started to change in the marketplace, with more effort by universities to engage in their community. Kirby (2006) suggests that there are a number of strategic actions that universities can promote to encourage entrepreneurship. The most important way is through encouragement and support. This helps to build an entrepreneurial ecosystem at universities that encourages innovation and risk taking activity. There is 'hard' support that is tangible and can be measured more easily than 'soft' support. Hard support includes computers, buildings and infrastructure that facilitate entrepreneurship. There has been a trend towards more science parks and incubators that can teach people how to be entrepreneurs.

Soft support involves intangible help such as training and mentoring that is needed for entrepreneurship. Often the soft support is utilized in conjunction with hard support as a way to facilitate and maintain business ventures. Endorsements in the form of senior university staff being engaged in entrepreneurship are useful. This helps to endorse entrepreneurial behaviour as being important at universities. Incorporation involves starting entrepreneurship programmes at the university as a way to foster entrepreneurial activity. Implementation refers to setting targets about the number and range of entrepreneurship initiatives occurring at the university. These can be communicated through marketing and information dissemination methods. Promotion refers to advertising about entrepreneurship that can include rewards and recognition. Business plan competitions or start-up days are ways in which universities can promote the entrepreneurship occurring at their universities. Organization means facilitating a cross-disciplinary research and teaching initiative on entrepreneurship. These different types of functions of entrepreneurial universities are part of the way they interact with the community.

COMMUNITY INTERACTION AND ENTREPRENEURIAL UNIVERSITIES

Entrepreneurial universities are a way to encourage organized interaction amongst members of a community in order to come up with novel ideas. This contrasts with the previous view of universities as being interventionist and autocratic in decision making processes. Entrepreneurship is a dynamic process and there needs to be awareness in the marketplace about how it develops. Some see entrepreneurship as being linked to a certain individual or maverick, whilst others view it as a collaborative project. Thus, it is becoming more generally accepted that a supportive environment is needed for entrepreneurship as a way to provide a trigger for innovative ideas. This helps to create synergistic relationships that advance current thinking and provide ways to grow the economy.

Entrepreneurial universities are anchor institutions that have mutual interdependencies with other members of a community. The presence of entrepreneurship at a university is viewed as a positive way to engage in the ideation process. Universities are at the heart of geographic networks due to their magnetic ability to attract talented individuals and companies. This helps to develop a source of intellectual capital for innovation that can lead to the creation of new business ideas. In addition, universities have a particular benefit to knowledge, service and manufacturing industries due to the spillover effects of information disseminated from their campuses.

Kirby (2006) suggests there are seven main reasons why universities have not been considered as entrepreneurial. First, the impersonal nature of relationships means that there can be a lack of communication amongst people at universities. This impacts upon the ability of people to have conversations about ideas. Second, the hierarchical structure means that it is hard to make quick decisions. This limits the ability to be responsive to market needs. Instead of quickly reacting to opportunities, there can be many levels of approval needed to make things happen at universities. Third, there is a need to adhere to rules and procedures, which slows the time taken to make decisions. Fourth, there is a sense of conservatism that focuses on maintaining the status quo. This is reflected in the types of people employed at universities and their willingness to engage with outsiders. Part of this is the organizational culture existing at universities that has tended to limit risk taking. Fifth, the need for immediate results has decreased the ability of universities to focus on long-term opportunities. This means that strategic decisions requiring long-term investment are not made. Sixth, the lack of entrepreneurial talent means that the people employed by universities are unwilling to change. This deters innovation and proactive thinking about future trends. Seventh, there are inappropriate compensation methods in terms of rewarding entrepreneurship.

Due to the increased automation of industries many of the jobs done now will not be available in the future. Hence, universities play a key role in educating and training people for future work positions. A difficult challenge for universities is how to encourage entrepreneurship but at the same time maintain high economic standards. Culkin (2016: 11) states that there is 'potential for universities to play a thought leadership role in shaping the development of skills in their regional economy'. This is important given the changing nature of the labour market and the increased need for competitiveness in the global economy. This has resulted in changing views of curriculum and assessment at universities. More assignments and experiential forms of assessment are being utilized as a way to foster real-life problem solving. This is a break with past practices of exams and assessment that encouraged rote learning.

Entrepreneurship provides a way to prepare students for the future by providing them with practical skills. Entrepreneurial universities have an opportunity to encourage progressive thinking in a supportive environment. This enables the embracing of innovative education and research strategies that lead to scientific discoveries. In order to move society forward there needs to be an acknowledgement of the transformative role of education. More entrepreneurial leaders are required to do this by shifting the way innovation is viewed in society.

OVERVIEW OF CHAPTERS

Chapter 2 titled 'The role of university–business collaboration in entrepreneurship education programmes' by Ana D. Daniel, Andreia Vitória and Mariana Pita discusses the importance of entrepreneurial communities. The chapter highlights the role of impactful teaching methodologies in promoting industry engagement. This is an important consideration for non-business students who can learn about entrepreneurship through experimental learning methods.

Chapter 3 titled 'Entrepreneurial university practices in Brazil under the lens of qualitative and quantitative research' by Carla Marques, Vitor Braga, João J. Ferreira and Moses Rodrigues discusses entrepreneurship education in an emerging-country context. As most research about entrepreneurial universities focuses on developed countries, it is helpful to take into account emerging economies like Brazil.

Chapter 4 titled 'A systemic approach for universities in the knowledge-based society: a qualitative study' by Ademar Schmitz, Gertrudes A. Dandolini, João A. de Souza, Maribel Guerrero and David Urbano focuses on the role of knowledge for entrepreneurial universities. The chapter discusses the role of universities as organizations in disseminating knowledge. This is crucial in the competitive global landscape that emphasizes the importance of knowledge.

Chapter 5 titled 'Entrepreneurialism in a London university: a case illustration' by Nnamdi O. Madichie, Ayantunji Gbadamosi and Sonny Nwankwo discusses the way in which a university has become entrepreneurial. The chapter provides a case study of a marketing course in terms of its entrepreneurial orientation.

Chapter 6 titled 'The level of competence of young researchers and the knowledge-based economy: the challenges of doctoral education in Poland' by Urszula Wiśniewska and Jacek Lewicki focuses on the importance of educating young people.

Chapter 7 titled 'HEInnovate: facilitating change in higher education' by Andrea-Rosalinde Hofer and Gabi Kaffka discusses the role of education in leading to transformational change. Increasingly, higher education institutions are focusing on entrepreneurship and innovation to deal with market uncertainty. This chapter discusses the role of entrepreneurial universities in society from a policy perspective.

Chapter 8 titled 'Entrepreneurial universities as determinants of technology entrepreneurship' by Guillermo A. Zapata-Huamaní, Sara Fernández-López, Lucía Rey-Ares and David Rodeiro-Pazos discusses the role of new technology-based firms. These types of firms are important in linking entrepreneurship education to economic development.

Chapter 9 titled 'Dynamics of student entrepreneurial teams: understanding individual coping strategies to build efficient teams' by Sandrine Le Pontois and Stéphane Foliard reviews the literature about collective action in entrepreneurship education. This helps to understand how student teams need to embrace a culture of entrepreneurship.

Chapter 10 titled 'The role of entrepreneurship education and its characteristics in influencing the entrepreneurial intention: a study based on India and the UK' by Kavita Panwar Seth, Fintan Clear, Tariq Khan and Sharmaine Sakthi Ananthan discusses the role of entrepreneurship education from a cross-cultural comparative view. This chapter helps to understand whether there are differences in entrepreneurial intention based on cultural and societal conditions.

Chapter 11 titled 'Building technology entrepreneurship capabilities: an engineering education perspective' by Kari Kleine, Ferran Giones, Mauricio Camargo and Silke Tegtmeier focuses on entrepreneurship education from an engineering point of view. As there is more emphasis on the interdisciplinary nature of entrepreneurship education, this chapter provides a useful understanding about science and technology development.

Chapter 12 titled 'Entrepreneurial actions towards the success of exponential technologies' by Sandro Battisti, Eduardo Giugliani, Rafael Prikladnicki and Paolo Traverso discusses the role of information and communications technology in entrepreneurship education. This helps to bring a sense of understanding about the role of innovation ecosystems in education.

Chapter 13 titled 'Conclusion: future suggestions for entrepreneurial universities' by João J. Ferreira, Alain Fayolle, Vanessa Ratten and Mário Raposo concludes the book by providing a summary of the chapters and suggestions for future research.

CONCLUSION

There is still much work required for universities to be seen as entrepreneurial. Some universities do this better than others and can be used as case studies to encourage more entrepreneurship. There is often a time lag occurring between the establishment of entrepreneurship and the actual ecosystem developing at universities. Entrepreneurial ecosystems are important at universities as a way to embrace change, but also to plan for the future. The aim of this book is to focus on entrepreneurial universities in terms of how they are managed and integrated into global society.

In this chapter, the role of entrepreneurial universities in society was examined. This helps to understand the strategic direction universities are taking in the global economy. Much of the change is the result of technological advancements and changes in social trends that affect the lives of individuals. In order to foster more interest in entrepreneurial universities there needs to be increased awareness of their importance. Entrepreneurial universities are higher education institutions that have a clear purpose to embed innovative thinking on their campuses, which the next chapters in the book will discuss in more detail.

REFERENCES

Brown, R. (2016) 'Mission impossible? Entrepreneurial universities and peripheral regional innovation systems', *Industry and Innovation*, **23**(2): 189–205.

Clark, B.R. (1998) 'The entrepreneurial university: Demand and response', *Tertiary Education and Management*, **4**(1): 5–16.

Culkin, N. (2016) 'Entrepreneurial universities in the region: The force awakens?', *International Journal of Entrepreneurial Behaviour and Research*, **22**(1): 4–16.

D'Este, P. and Perkmann, M. (2011) 'Why do academics engage with industry? The entrepreneurial university and individual motivations', *Journal of Technology Transfer*, **36**: 316–339.

Etzkowitz, H. (2010) 'Entrepreneurial universities for the UK: A "Stanford University" at Bamburgh Castle?', *Industry and Higher Education*, **24**(4): 251–256.

Ferreira, J., Fernandes, C. and Ratten, V. (2016) 'A co-citation bibliometric analysis of strategic management research', *Scientometrics*, **109**(1): 1–32.

Formica, P. (2002) 'Entrepreneurial universities: The value of education in encouraging entrepreneurship', *Industry and Higher Education*, June: 167–175.

Gianiodis, P.T., Markman, G.D. and Panagopoulos, A. (2016) 'Entrepreneurial universities and overt opportunism', *Small Business Economics*, **47**(3): 609–631.

Gur, U., Oylumlu, I.S. and Kunday, O. (2017) 'Critical assessments of entrepreneurial and innovative universities index of Turkey: Future directions', *Technology Forecasting and Social Change*, **123**(1): 161–168.

Heinonen, J. and Hytti, V. (2010) 'Back to basics: The role of teaching in developing the entrepreneurial university', *Entrepreneurship and Innovation*, **11**(4): 283–292.

Jessop, B. (2017) 'Varieties of academic capitalism and entrepreneurial universities: On past, research and three thought experiments', *Higher Education*, **73**: 853–870.

Kirby, D.A. (2006) 'Creating entrepreneurial universities in the UK: Applying entrepreneurship theory to practice', *Journal of Technology Transfer*, **31**: 599–603.

Link, A.D., Siegel, D. and Bozeman, B. (2007) 'An empirical analysis of the propensity of academics to engage in informal university technology transfer', *Industrial and Corporate Change*, **16**(4): 641–656.

Martin, C. and Turner, P. (2010) 'Entrepreneurial universities– the key ingredient in the receipt for UK innovation?', *Entrepreneurship and Innovation*, **11**(4): 273–281.

Ratten, V. and Ratten, H. (2007) 'Social cognitive theory in technological innovations', *European Journal of Innovation Management*, **10**(1): 90–108.

Siegel, D.S., Wright, M. and Lockett, A. (2007) 'The rise of entrepreneurial activity at universities: Organizational and societal implications', *Industrial and Corporate Change*, **16**(4): 489–504.

Sporn, B. (2001) 'Building adaptive universities: Emerging organizational forms based on experiences of European and US universities', *Tertiary Education and Management*, **7**(2): 121–134.

Suseno, Y. and Ratten, V. (2007) 'A theoretical framework of alliance performance: The role of trust, social capital and knowledge development', *Journal of Management and Organization*, **13**(1): 4–23.

Zhou, C. and Peng, X. (2008) 'The entrepreneurial university in China: Nonlinear paths', *Science and Public Policy*, **35**(9): 637–646.

2. The role of university–business collaboration in entrepreneurship education programmes*

Ana D. Daniel, Andreia Vitória and Mariana Pita

INTRODUCTION

Entrepreneurship is an important element of Europe's economic prosperity. Currently, its relevance is growing strongly, since Europe faces profound social and economic changes due to the economic downturn. Therefore, it is crucial for the development of entrepreneurial ecosystems that dynamic entrepreneurs are particularly well placed to reap opportunities, for example from globalization and from the acceleration of technological change, and that the innovation potential of small and medium-sized enterprises (SMEs) can be realized (Thomas and Autio, 2014). School-leavers and graduates with entrepreneurial skills and mindset are crucial for making this happen.

As a consequence, in the policy arena, entrepreneurship education (EE) has been attracting considerable interest over recent decades. As mentioned in the 2011 Eurydice survey on 'Entrepreneurship Education at School' (assessing primary education, ISCED level 1, and general secondary education, ISCED levels 2 and 3), the great majority of European countries address entrepreneurship education through national strategies or initiatives. Also, nearly half of the countries have incorporated the objectives linked to the promotion of entrepreneurship education within broader strategies (lifelong learning, education and youth, growth), while several countries, located mainly in Northern Europe, have launched specific entrepreneurship education strategies (Eurydice, 2012). In the case of higher education, countless courses and programmes on entrepreneurship have been developed and implemented all over the world (Katz, 2008), since in most countries higher education institutions have a higher level of autonomy than schools regarding curriculum design.

Although this progress clearly reflects the wide recognition of the importance of entrepreneurship education in Europe, there are still imbalances in Europe regarding the approaches and strategies followed to promote and leverage EE. Also, there is still much discussion about the scope, objectives and methodologies that should be addressed in entrepreneurship education (Fayolle and Gailly, 2015; Hills, 1988; McMullan and Long, 1987; Vesper et al., 1989), as well as its actual impact. In fact, there is a growing debate about the impact of EE which has been fuelled by studies with contradictory conclusions. Recently, Nabi et al. (2017) conducted a systematic review of literature on the impact of EE in higher education, and observed that the most common impact indicators are related to lower-level indicators of subjective or personal change: attitude, skills and knowledge, perceived feasibility, and entrepreneurial intention. Only a minority of studies explore emotion or related approaches to assessing EE impact. More specifically, most articles in the review claim that EE programmes have a positive impact on students' entrepreneurial intentions (Daniel and Castro, 2017; Kuttim et al., 2014; Martin et al., 2013), which has been one of the key variables used as a predictor of entrepreneurial action. However, others have reported the opposite outcome, and say that EE has had no impact at all (Graevenitz et al., 2010; Lorz et al., 2011; Oosterbeek et al., 2010). The variety of methodologies and instruments used to measure impact is one of the main reasons why contradictory conclusions are obtained by different researchers and research teams. Context- and gender-specific differences are also an important reason for contradictory findings (Nabi et al., 2017).

The relationship between the impact of EE and teaching methods is not completely understood, but there is a general agreement that active methods – such as case studies, group discussions, business and computer game simulations, role models, business plan development or guest speakers – are likely to be more appropriate for fostering entrepreneurial behaviour among students (Bennett, 2006; Mwasalwiba, 2010; Nabi et al., 2017). Also, newer tools for business models design (Osterwalder and Pigneur, 2010) and lean start-up movements (Paço et al., 2016; Ries, 2011), as well as the design thinking method, are today being adapted by teachers in entrepreneurship classes (Daniel, 2016).

Despite these new teaching approaches, the role of university–business collaboration in EE has not yet been assessed. Thus, the main aim of this chapter is to discuss the relevance of university–business collaboration in EE, as well as its impact on students' enterprising qualities. The chapter addresses this issue as follows. It first covers a theoretical approach to the most relevant concepts, mainly entrepreneurial university, entrepreneurship education and impact assessment. This is followed by a case study analysis of an innovative teaching approach to entrepreneurship education where companies play a key role. The final section draws conclusions.

ENTREPRENEURIAL EDUCATION: WHAT COMPETENCIES TO DEVELOP?

Competences usually refer to the knowledge, skills, attitudes, values and behaviours that people need to successfully perform a particular activity or task (Brophy and Kiely, 2002). Rooted in the early work of Boyatzis (1982) on managerial competences, several research studies have assessed the link between entrepreneurial competences and venture performance (e.g., Colombo and Grilli, 2005; Rasmussen et al., 2011). Nevertheless, there is still a lack of consensus regarding the relative importance of particular competencies in an entrepreneurial context. For instance, Rezaei-Zadeh et al. (2014) identified 82 entrepreneurial competencies from a review of 63 journal papers published in the area of entrepreneurship, through the constant comparative method in the context of a systematic literature review. More specifically, emphasis has been placed on personality attributes, such as need for achievement, need for autonomy, initiative taking, creativity, performance orientation, problem solving, calculated risk taking, capacity for reflection and communication skills (Athayde, 2009; Draycott and Rae, 2011; Gibb, 2008; Littunen and Hyrsky, 2000; Schelfhout et al., 2016). Also, through the use of the collective intelligence method, Rezaei-Zadeh et al. (2017) explored the interdependencies amongst core entrepreneurial competencies involving three stakeholder groups of students, academics and entrepreneurs. The study identified that productive thinking, interpersonal skills and leadership are core entrepreneurial competences that need to be developed in educational contexts, and they are interdependent across groups and regions. Recently, in 2016, the Joint Research Centre (JRC) of the European Commission has published the Entrepreneurship Competence Framework, also known as EntreComp, which aimed at building consensus around a common understanding of entrepreneurship competences (Bacigalupo et al., 2016). The framework highlights three competence areas: 'Ideas and opportunities', 'Resources' and 'Into action'. Each area includes five competences, which together are the building blocks of entrepreneurship as a competence. Nevertheless, the framework has not yet been adapted to, or tested in, real settings.

Despite the relevance of those studies, an interesting approach is to understand the impact of entrepreneurship education on entrepreneurial competences. Morris et al. (2013) identified a core set of 13 entrepreneurial competences, split into behavioural competences (such as opportunity recognition, opportunity assessment, resource leverage and developing a business model) and attitudinal competences (including resilience, self-efficacy and tenacity). These researchers concluded that those competencies could be enhanced based on exposure to an entrepreneurship programme. Similar conclusions were reached by Schelfhout et al. (2016), who assessed the impact of entrepreneurship education in 11 entrepreneurial competences: performance orientation, creativity, taking initiative, taking calculated risks, perseverance, leadership, communication skills, planning and organizing, decisiveness, collaboration and reflection. From those results it could be argued that EE should aim at improving entrepreneurial competences that would allow students to behave in a more entrepreneurial way.

HOW TO PROMOTE ENTREPRENEURIAL LEARNING

Entrepreneurial learning was defined by Rae and Carswell (2001: 152) as 'the dynamic process which enables entrepreneurial behavior to be enacted'. Therefore, entrepreneurial learning enables individuals to build new meanings and knowledge in the process of identifying new ideas, acting on opportunities and managing ventures. The underlying question is: how do students acquire entrepreneurial learning?

Research on entrepreneurial cognition can provide some clues regarding the answer to that question. Entrepreneurial cognition aims at understanding how entrepreneurs think, and how they develop unique knowledge structures. In this case, cognition is defined as all processes by which sensory input is transformed, reduced, elaborated, stored, recovered and used (Neisser, 1967). According to Mitchell et al. (2007), entrepreneurial cognition concerns not just those processes, but also the socio-economic setting in which it occurs. In entrepreneurship one cannot detach the person from their situation or context, since the first step of the entrepreneurial process is the recognition of an opportunity, which in turn is context-dependent. Thus, entrepreneurial cognition is defined as 'the knowledge structures that people use to make assessments, judgments, or decisions involving opportunity evaluation, venture creation and growth' (Mitchell et al., 2002: 97). In line with this argument, it can be concluded that the development of entrepreneurial cognition seems to be determinant in attaining entrepreneurial learning. Several researchers have highlighted that cognitive systems can be created by deliberate practice (Charness et al., 1996; Mitchell, 2005; Schneider, 1998). In turn, deliberate practice occurs when an individual exerts effort in activities designed to optimize improvement of a performance within a specific domain (Ericsson et al., 1993); thus, the more an individual engages in optimal practice, the better their performance will be. In this case, the chance has to be given to learners to try to apply the skills being taught, make mistakes, learn from the mistakes and repeat their attempts in order to gain mastery (Norzailan et al., 2016).

Additionally, entrepreneurial learning appears to be a co-creation of knowledge constructed in social interaction with peers and lecturers, much in line with entrepreneurial practice outside the boundaries of education (Giones et al., 2012; Secundo et al., 2017). This view highlights the impact of incorporating a social context into the learning process, as in the social-constructivist approach, from which a new paradigm emerges in the teaching of entrepreneurship. Additionally, several scholars have suggested that local context may influence the results of EE, and have recommended that educators strengthen their relationship with local businesses to help students raise awareness of the business environment (Lindh and Thorgren, 2016). Also, through the collaboration with firms, students would have the opportunity to see the entrepreneur in an action context, which would enhance students' social learning through role modelling (Johannisson, 2016). Thus, in order to promote entrepreneurial learning, a learning programme must be designed that allows learners to develop their knowledge through trial and error in a real business context.

HOW TO BE EFFECTIVE IN ENTREPRENEURSHIP EDUCATION

As mentioned by Moore et al. (2010), true learning is the result of students' experience, and the evaluation of and reflection upon their experiences. In order to promote entrepreneurial learning it is necessary to use different teaching methodologies in the classroom that place a greater emphasis on learners and, at the same time, benefit from the classroom's external context. Active or experimental learning has been studied for centuries (Ragains, 1995), and several authors (see Allen, 1995; Silberman, 1996) have highlighted the benefits of this style of teaching, including meeting learners' needs, improving learners' retention of the information presented, increasing learners' interaction with information, and increasing learners' responsibility towards their own learning process.

Active learning is any teaching method that 'involves students in doing things and thinking about what they are doing' (Bonwell and Eison, 1991: 2). In EE, this could mean having students working in groups to promote cooperative learning, problem-solving exercises and speaking activities, as well as class discussion, peer teaching, fieldwork and independent study.

Although there is a growing consensus that the preferred entrepreneurial pedagogy is learner-centred, process-based, experiential and socially situated (Gibb, 1987; Kyrö, 2005; Mwasalwiba, 2010), in practice the analysis of curricula reveals a gap between what is preferable or adequate, and what is being used and implemented. The use of active pedagogies is still limited due to the high cost of active approaches, and their misalignment with the conventional university system of teaching and grading (Daniel et al., 2016; Mwasalwiba, 2010). Consequently, there is a need to identify and share best practices in EE, which can easily be adapted and implemented in different contexts.

Not all students have the same interest in or predisposition towards entrepreneurial learning. This can be atributed to different psychological, emotional, social and contextual causes (e.g., Nabi et al., 2017), such as gender and educational area (business/management or non-business/management) (e.g., Shinnar et al., 2009; Souitaris et al., 2007). The stereotypes applied to women indicate that they have lower aspirations to become an entrepreneur (Steele et al., 2002), and due to the traditional women's role model, there is a normative assumption that the ideal entrepreneur is a male (Henry et al., 2016). The empirical evidence regarding gender differences in terms of entrepreneurial personality and behavioural intentions to start a business is not clear. Some authors find differences between men and women (Wilson et al., 2004), and others do not (Shinnar et al., 2009). Some studies highlight the motivation and interest that students outside management areas have in entrepreneurial education, as well as the positive effects on them obtained through such programmes and courses (e.g., Shinnar et al., 2009; Souitaris et al., 2007). However, it seems that students of management areas continue to be more likely to undertake entrepreneurial education, and also tend to exhibit greater willingness to be an entrepreneur (Shinnar et al., 2009).

'LEARNING TO BE' PROGRAMME[1]

Learning to Be is an innovative teaching programme that aims to foster entrepreneurial learning in non-business students, through an experimental learning methodology inspired by the Design Thinking process (Daniel, 2016). In this programme, students are challenged to develop viable solutions to real-world problems proposed by several companies.

The Learning to Be approach is structured into a three-stage process:

- Phase One: Business Empathy – trying to understand latent customer needs.
- Phase Two: Value Create – building sustainable competitive advantage.
- Phase Three: Strategy Test – validating customer and market acceptance.

The process is designed to improve the fit between the solutions developed and the initial challenge. The first phase aims to enhance students' Business Empathy, or, in other words, the ability to understand latent customer needs. Students are encouraged to undertake field research in order to speak directly with customers, do interviews and make site visits. They look for insights from customers (and other relevant stakeholders in some cases), and use ethnographic-style tools to gather relevant information. In the second phase, of Value Create, students use tools of ideation, brainstorming, and other methods that leverage creativity. They also look for relevant competitive analysis data, and data from substitute products or services. In this phase, activities that involve learning from others are considered very important. As this stage leads into designing prototypes and presenting mock-ups, the main objective is to generate multiple ideas, and to get feedback from peers to help sort out which ideas to take forward and materialize for testing. Students also bounce ideas off the company employees as they develop second iterations, prior to trying to validate these ideas with the company.

The Strategy Test phase is when the students attempt to validate their proposed solutions with the customers. They can return to the field and try to assess whether customers would be interested or willing to pay for the product, and what needs to be improved. In this phase, students evaluate what should be changed, develop new features that are considered necessary, then another round of iteration can begin.

Students are organized into teams of three or four people, who as far as possible should each come from a different disciplinary background. The typical intake is around 60 students, which produces 15 student teams divided between three to five different challenges. The teams work together for an entire semester. In the Learning to Be model, all assessment is done through a process of continuous evaluation. Assessment is a mixture of self-assessment between the members of teams, and dual assessment by professors and students of specific tasks, such as oral presentations, prototypes and product pitches. The Final Pitch is a key element of the evaluation, along with a report that each team must deliver to their company partner. Self-assessment is very effective for evaluating the contribution of each member to each specific assignment. The approach builds responsibility, leadership and teamwork.

METHOD

Procedures and Measuring Instruments

To evaluate the impact of the Learning to Be programme on students, we used two different approaches: (1) a feedback questionnaire in order to assess the students' opinions concerning the programme; and (2) a between-subjects experiment measuring entrepreneurial competences in the students who participated in the programme *ex ante* (at the beginning of the semester, when the programme starts) and *ex post* (at the end of the semester, when the programme ends).

The feedback questionnaire contained 26 statements to which students were asked to respond on a five-point Likert scale (1: strongly disagree; 5: strongly agree). The questionnaire statements were intended to gauge the following: Q1 to Q5 items provided information about the reasons for joining the programme; Q6 to Q10 identified the main expectations of students; Q11 to Q13 evaluated the extent to which such expectations were fulfilled; Q14 to Q19 gathered information about the impacts of the programme from the students' perspective; and Q20 to Q26 assessed the professor's performance, course logistics and training material provided. We also collected some student testimonials to enrich the data analysis.

To evaluate whether the students' entrepreneurial characteristics changed after participation in the Learning to Be programme, we used the General Enterprising Tendency (GET) test, developed by Sally Caird and Cliff Johnson (Caird, 2013). The test appraises five key entrepreneurial characteristics: (1) need for achievement; (2) need for for autonomy; (3) creative tendency; (4) calculated risk taking; and (5) internal locus of control.

The internal consistency (Cronbach's alpha) of the majority of the dimensions was unsatisfactory; for example: need for autonomy: 0.33; creative tendency: 0.27; locus of control: 0.42 (Nunnally, 1978), as well as the GET total: Cronbach's $\alpha = 0.5$. The only dimension whose Cronbach's alpha was satisfactory was 'need for achievement' (Cronbach's $\alpha = 0.73$). In order to validate the GET test results of the Learning to Be students, a control group of students not attending the programme was also used. Those students also responded to the questionnaire, at the beginning and end of the semester.

Data collected were statistically analysed utilizing IBM® SPSS v. 24.0 for Windows (Armonk, New York). Differences between students' opinions (means scores) were analysed using independent t-tests; pre- and post-programme changes were assessed using paired t-tests; and differences between experimental group and control group were tested through independent t-tests. The paired-samples t-test was employed to assess whether the pre- and post-assessment means were statistically different.

The independent t-test is used in experiments in which there are two conditions and different subjects have been used in each condition (Field, 2013). This paired t-test compares two means that come from the same individuals (Field, 2013).

Sample

Among Learning to Be students enrolled on different courses at the University of Aveiro, Portugal, 98 responded to the feedback questionnaire; 66 per cent females and 34 per cent males. Regarding the GET questionnaire, 117 students responded in 'moment 1' (beginning of the programme and the semester) and 166 in 'moment 2' (end of the programme and the semester). Only 83 students responded in both moments; 67 per cent females and 34 per cent males.

Learning to Be students were enrolled in courses from the first cycle of study (management, computer engineering, languages and business relations, medical sciences, chemistry and tourism) and second (management and planning in tourism, chemistry, physics and sustainable energy systems). The first cycle corresponds to bachelor's degree level and the second cycle to master's degree level, according to the Bologna Declaration.

Concerning the control group, students were enrolled in courses from the first cycle of study of courses such as psychology, languages and business relations, and languages, literature and culture. Of the contacted students, 59 responded in moment 1 and 23 in moment 2. Amongst them, only 18 responded at both moments, these being 72 per cent females and 28 per cent males.

RESULTS

Feedback Questionnaire

Analysing the feedback questionnaire and considering the five-point Likert scale (Q.1–Q.4), we can conclude that the majority of students chose to join the Learning to Be programme because they had genuine interest in the entrepreneurship theme and wanted to learn more about the subject, including acquiring entrepreneurial skills (Figure 2.1).

We can also verify that the students joined Learning to Be mainly by themselves, rather than being influenced by friends' opinions or suggestions.

The students' main expectations were related to the improvement of their knowledge about entrepreneurship, as well as their understanding of the abilities needed to become an entrepreneur and to start a new business

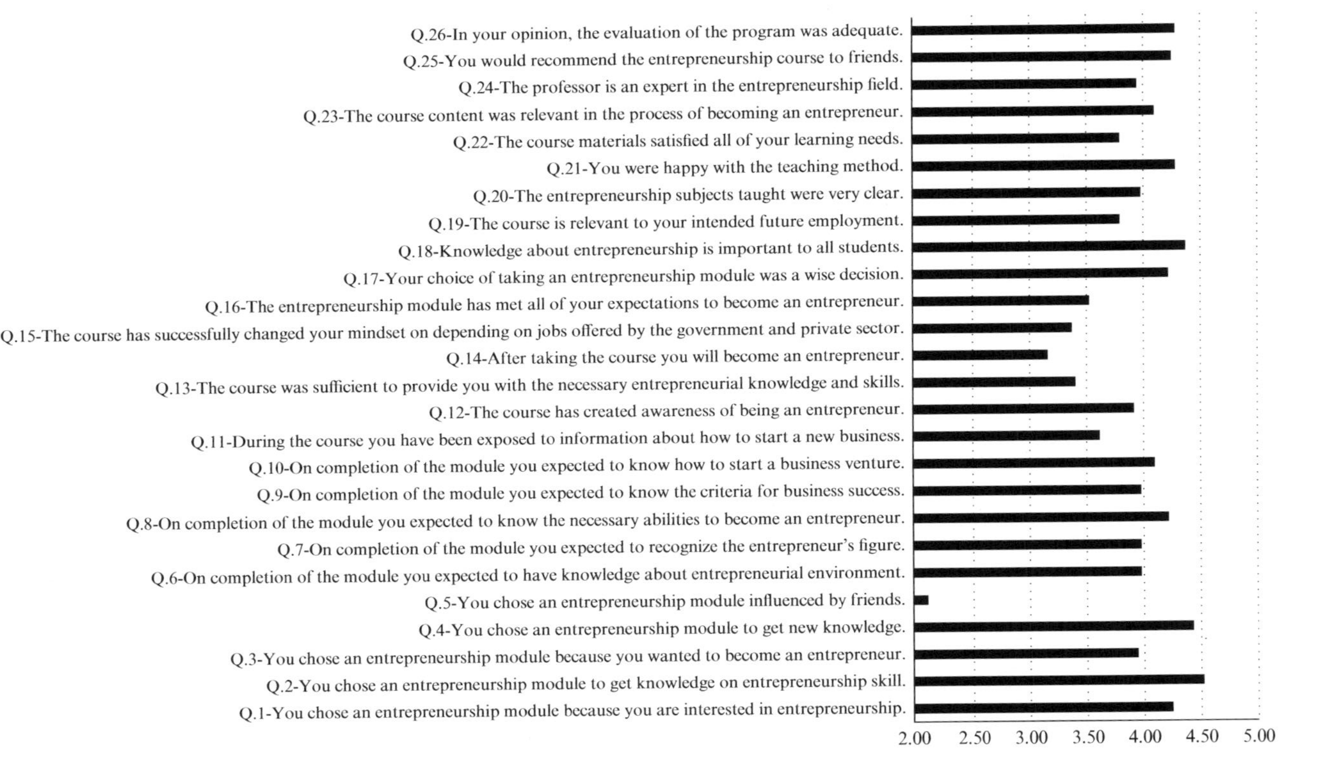

Figure 2.1 Feedback questionnaire results (mean scores)

(Q.6–Q10). Although they recognized that the programme made them more aware of these issues, students felt that the programme could provide a deeper understanding of entrepreneurial knowledge and skills (Q.11–Q.13).

Regarding the programme's impact on students, although they tended, on average, to see benefits of attending the programme, they were more cautious in stating that they would become entrepreneurs after participating in the programme (Q.14–Q.19). The students made a positive assessment of the professor's performance, course logistics and training material provided (Q.20–Q.26).

We carried out an independent t-test to investigate whether the means differed between female and male students and between students of management courses (management, languages and business relations, management and planning in tourism, and tourism) and science courses (chemistry, physics, sustainable energy systems, computer engineering and medical sciences) (Table 2.1).

Although the mean scores of female students are almost all lower than those of male students, only in items Q.1, Q.2, Q.3, Q.5, Q.17, Q.21 and Q.23 are the differences statistically significant. Male students tend to reveal a greater propensity to choose an entrepreneurship module because they are interested in entrepreneurship and want to obtain knowledge and skills on the subject, and because they wish to become entrepreneurs (Q.1, Q.2, Q.3). Even though the influence of friends remains low, regarding the decision to participate in the programme, male students are more likely to be influenced by their friends' opinions or suggestions than female students (Q.5). Male students also tend to be more pleased with the decision to join the Learning to Be programme, and with the teaching method (Q.17, Q.21). Furthermore, they tend to consider that the course content is more relevant in the process of becoming an entrepreneur (Q.23). As a male student stated: 'The Learning to be program is a new, innovative, multidisciplinary and entrepreneurial way of teaching, that fosters a win–win relationship between the university world and the business reality.'

Regarding the differences between students of management and science courses, we can verify that sciences students exhibit higher mean scores in nearly every item; however, there are statistically significant differences in items Q.1, Q.2, Q.3, Q.4, Q.5, Q.12, Q.14, Q.17 Q.22, Q.23 and Q.25. Science students are more likely to choose an entrepreneurship module because they are interested in acquiring knowledge and skills in this subject, and because they are interested in becoming entrepreneurs (Q.1, Q.2, Q.3, Q.4). That intention is also corroborated by their greater tendency to affirm that they will become entrepreneurs after the programme (Q.14). In addition, the science students consider that participation in the programme enabled them to be more aware of what is to be an entrepreneur (Q.12). The science students,

Table 2.1 *Feedback questionnaire results: female versus male students; management versus sciences students*

Female students	Male students		Management courses	Science courses
3.76	4.27*	Q.1	3.65	4.38**
3.92	4.55**	Q.2	3.89	4.53**
3.38	3.97**	Q.3	3.39	3.88*
4.05	4.45	Q.4	3.94	4.49*
1.65	2.12*	Q.5	1.66	2.11*
4.09	4.00	Q.6	4.06	4.03
3.91	4.00	Q.7	3.85	4.06
4.12	4.24	Q.8	4.09	4.26
4.06	4.00	Q.9	3.98	4.09
3.97	4.12	Q.10	3.95	4.14
3.54	3.64	Q.11	3.60	3.51
3.82	3.94	Q.12	3.73	4.09*
3.31	3.42	Q.13	3.20	3.46
2.92	3.18	Q.14	2.82	3.29*
3.22	3.39	Q.15	3.18	3.43
3.23	3.55	Q.16	3.15	3.54
3.64	4.24**	Q.17	3.56	4.23**
4.57	4.39	Q.18	4.56	4.43
4.05	3.82	Q.19	4.06	3.86
3.82	4.00	Q.20	3.76	4.09
3.88	4.30*	Q.21	3.87	4.20
3.62	3.82	Q.22	3.55	3.91*
3.75	4.12*	Q.23	3.71	4.09*
3.78	3.97	Q.24	3.75	3.94
4.23	4.27	Q.25	4.05	4.51**
3.94	4.30	Q.26	3.96	4.11

Note: * $p < 0.05$; ** $p < 0.01$.

compared to the management students, are also more likely to choose to join the programme due to the influence of their friends' opinions or suggestions (Q.5) and to consider themselves satisfied with the decision to participate in the Learning to Be programme (Q.17). Moreover, they tend to reveal higher satisfaction with course materials and teaching methods (Q.22), and to recognize that the course content was relevant in the process of becoming an entrepreneur (Q.23). We can also verify that the science students were more predisposed than the management students to recommend the Learning to Be programme to friends (Q.25). As one science student said:

> The Learning to Be programme has made me see new horizons. I have come out of my comfort zone and I loved every moment. The tools are there, you just have to grab them and build something with them. It is going to be hard! You are going to want to give up . . . But at the end it will have been worth it!

GET Test

We conducted an analysis of the means, standard deviations and correlations of experimental group (Table 2.2).

Gender and the student's courses are not related to any of the dimensions, nor to the total result of GET test. Taking into account that the maximum score for 'need for achievement', 'creative tendency', 'calculated risk taking' and 'locus of control' is 12, we can consider that the mean scores for these dimensions (in moments 1 and 2) are moderate, with 'locus of control' being the highest. Regarding 'need for autonomy', the maximum score is 6, so we can consider that the mean score is relatively low.

'Need for achievement' (moment 1) is positively correlated with 'calculated risk taking' (moment 1) and 'need for achievement' (moment 2). Therefore, we can say that the students who are more driven to achieve success have a greater propensity to assume risk, and after participating in the Learning to Be programme that trait tends to be stronger ('Need for achievement').

'Need for autonomy' (moment 1) is positively correlated with 'need for autonomy' (moment 2), 'need for achievement' (moment 2) and 'creative tendency' (moment 1). Thus, the students who display more autonomy before joining the programme tend to be even more autonomous afterwards, and also tend to improve their creativity and to be more committed to being successful.

'Creative tendency' (moment 1) is positively correlated with 'creative tendency' (moment 2), 'need for achievement' (moment 2) and 'calculated risk taking' (moment 2). Thereby, more creative students tend to increase that characteristic due to their participation in the programme, and are more likely to develop their focus on achieving success and their propensity to assume risks.

'Calculated risk taking' (moment 1) is positively correlated with 'calculated risk taking' (moment 2). 'Locus of control' (moment 1) is positively correlated with 'locus of control' (moment 2). So, students who are more likely to take risks strengthen that characteristic due to participation in the programme, and students who believe they control their own destiny tend to strengthen that trait during the programme.

The five dimensions are positively correlated with 'GET (total)', in moments 1 and 2. 'GET (total)' (moment 1) and 'GET (total)' (moment 2) are also positively correlated. Table 2.3 exhibits the means, standard

Table 2.2 Means (M), standard deviations (SD) and correlations: experimental group

	M	SD	1	2	3	4	5	6	7	8	9	10	11	12
1 Need for achievement (moment 1)	7.87	1.86	–											
2 Need for autonomy (moment 1)	2.40	1.32	0.10	–										
3 Creative tendency (moment 1)	7.28	2.09	0.18	0.13	–									
4 Calculated risk taking (moment 1)	7.63	1.98	0.23*	−0.04	0.27*	–								
5 Locus of control (moment 1)	8.54	1.38	−0.01	0.18	0.01	−0.03	–							
6 GET (total) (moment 1)	33.71	4.72	0.60**	0.41**	0.67**	0.61**	0.33**	–						
7 Need for achievement (moment 2)	8.07	1.84	0.40**	0.24*	0.30**	0.11	0.15	0.44**	–					
8 Need for autonomy (moment 2)	2.76	1.36	0.10	0.53*	0.10	−0.00	0.12	0.24*	0.23*	–				

Table 2.2 (continued)

		M	SD	1	2	3	4	5	6	7	8	9	10	11	12
9	Creative tendency (moment 2)	6.96	2.23	0.01	0.23*	0.62**	0.22	0.06	0.45**	0.40**	0.30**	–			
10	Calculated risk taking (moment 2)	7.36	2.18	0.20	−0.03	0.49**	0.63**	−0.04	0.54**	0.19	0.2	0.39**	–		
11	Locus of control (moment 2)	8.59	1.70	−0.00	0.13	0.17	−0.13	0.51**	0.21	0.11	0.29**	0.15	−0.01	–	
12	GET (total) (moment 2)	33.75	5.70	0.22*	0.32**	0.60**	0.32**	0.23*	0.65**	0.63**	0.52**	0.78**	0.60**	0.46**	–

Note: * $p < 0.05$; ** $p < 0.01$.

deviations and correlations of the control group. The gender and degree field of students are not related to any of the dimensions, nor to the total result of the GET test. Attending to the maximum scores of each factor, we can consider that the mean scores for all dimensions are relatively moderate. 'Need for autonomy' (moment 1) is positively correlated with 'need for autonomy' (moment 2), meaning that during the semester the students who were autonomous became more autonomous.

'Creative tendency' (moment 1) is positively correlated with 'creative tendency' (moment 2) and 'calculated risk taking' (moment 1). Therefore, students who tend to be creative strengthened that characteristic during the semester. Moreover, creative students are also individuals who have a greater propensity for risk taking.

'Locus of control' (moment 1) is positively correlated 'locus of control' (moment 2), thus students tend to develop over time the sense of being responsible for their pathway. 'Calculated risk taking' (moment 1) and 'locus of control' (moment 1) do not correlate with 'GET (total)' (moment 1); and 'need for achievement' (moment 2), 'calculated risk taking' (moment 2) and 'locus of control' (moment 2) do not correlate with 'GET (total)' (moment 2). This may be related to the significantly reduced sample size of the control group.

We carried out an independent-samples t-test to verify whether the means of the experimental group and the control group were statistically different from each other in the dimensions. We can observe (Table 2.4) that means of the experimental group (in moment 1) for all the dimensions (except 'need for autonomy') are higher than those of the control group. However, the difference concerning 'creative tendency' is not statistically significant. Therefore, the students who had participated in the Learning to Be programme were *ab initio* more oriented to success, more predisposed to assume calculated risks and to believe they control their own lives, but were less autonomous. Analysing the moment 2 means of each group and each dimension, we can observe that all of them are higher in the experimental group, although the differences are not statistically significant in the 'creative tendency' and the 'calculated risk taking' dimensions.

We also conducted a paired-sample t-test to evaluate the differences between the means of moments 1 and 2 of each group. The mean of the 'need of autonomy' of the experimental group is the only one whose difference is statistically significant from moment 1 to moment 2. In this sense, and although the means of moment 2 are higher in the experimental group, participation in the Learning to Be programme only had a real impact on the autonomy of the students.

Table 2.3 *Means (M), standard deviations (SD) and correlations: control group*

	M	SD	1	2	3	4	5	6	7	8	9	10	11	12
1 Need for achievement (moment 1)	7.06	1.35	–											
2 Need for autonomy (moment 1)	3.22	1.22	0.32	–										
3 Creative tendency (moment 1)	7.11	1.64	0.29	0.31	–									
4 Calculated risk taking (moment 1)	6.22	1.66	–0.37	0.06	0.68**	–								
5 Locus of control (moment 1)	6.50	1.38	–0.02	–0.11	0.10	–0.03	–							
6 GET (total) (moment 1)	30.11	3.01	0.52*	0.70**	0.47*	0.03	0.45	–						
7 Need for achievement (moment 2)	7.17	1.54	0.19	0.39	–0.26	0.42	0.04	0.35	–					
8 Need for autonomy (moment 2)	2.38	1.31	0.31	0.59*	0.18	–0.00	–0.26	0.35	0.22	–				

9	Creative tendency (moment 2)	6.61	1.88	0.10	0.25	0.70**	–0.42	–0.31	0.13	–0.16	0.27	–			
10	Calculated risk taking (moment 2)	6.72	1.36	0.11	−0.14	0.25	0.44	0.40	0.07	–0.23	–0.14	–0.07	–		
11	Locus of control (moment 2)	5.94	1.35	0.00	0.12	0.40	–0.36	0.49*	0.29	–0.31	0.26	–0.03	0.28	–	
12	GET (total) (2nd moment)	30.18	3.37	0.28	0.53*	0.60**	–0.37	0.10	0.51*	0.24	0.69*	0.55*	0.32	0.46	–

Note: * $p < 0.05$; ** $p < 0.01$.

Table 2.4 Comparing entrepreneurial characteristics (mean scores) between students who participated in the Learning to Be programme and those who did not (differences between moments 1 and 2)

	Experimental group		Control group	
	moment 1	moment 2	moment 1	moment 2
Need for achievement (maximum 12 points)	7.87	8.07	7.06(*)	7.17(*)
Need for autonomy (maximum 6 points)	2.40	2.76*	3.22(*)	2.38(**)
Creative tendency (maximum 12 points)	7.28	6.96	7.11	6.61
Calculated risk taking (maximum 12 points)	7.63	7.36	6.22(**)	6.72
Locus of control (maximum 12 points)	8.54	8.59	6.5(**)	5.94(***)
GET (total) (maximum 54 points)	33.71	33.75	30.11(**)	30.18(*)

Notes:
* $p < 0.05$; ** $p < 0.01$; *** $p < 0.001$.
Differences between moments 1 and 2: paired-samples T-test for equality of means; differences between the experimental group and control group: independent-samples T-test for equality of means – in parenthesis.

DISCUSSION AND CONCLUSIONS

According to several studies, entrepreneurial competences associated with entrepreneurial behaviour are learnable (Kuratko, 2005; Mayhew et al., 2012). The extent to which entrepreneurial competences are acquired by students depends on the development of entrepreneurial cognitions through deliberate learning. Deliberate learning involves active learning methods where students apply the skills being taught, and have the chance of making mistakes, learning from the mistakes, and repeating their attempts in order to gain mastery (Norzailan et al., 2016). Based on those principles, and with the mission of making EE more effective, an innovative approach to EE was designed: the Learning to Be programme. The whole process was entrepreneurial and it aimed at imbuing students with an entrepreneurial mindset, and of a well-thought-through and calibrated approach to taking risks. This approach was much in line with EE best practices where students are involved in the co-creation of knowledge constructed through social interaction with peers and lecturers that simulate the entrepreneurial practice outside the boundaries of education (Giones et al., 2012).

The main goal of this research was to understand the impact of this specific entrepreneurial education programme – Learning to Be – on students' entrepreneurial personality traits. According to the results of the feedback questionnaire we can conclude that students' general opinions about the Learning to Be programme are positive, particularly in the case of male and science students. They believe that the participation in the programme had an impact on them, providing a clear understanding about companies' reality and possibilities to deal with and solve real problems. Such experience enabled students to develop intrapreneurship (that is, acting like an entrepreneur within an existing company), which is not addressed in most entrepreneurship educational programmes and initiatives.

Findings indicate that female students are less likely to join the Learning to Be programme because they want to acquire knowledge and skills on entrepreneurship, corroborating some stereotypes associated to women (Steele et al., 2002). However, gender differences are not reflected in the effectiveness of entrepreneurial education on female students, because males are not more liable to improve their entrepreneurial skills as a result of participation in an entrepreneurial education programme.

Findings also indicate that science students reveal more willingness to join the Learning to Be programme because they want to develop their knowledge and entrepreneurial skills. These results challenge some past findings (e.g., Shinnar et al., 2009) which noted that students from the business and management areas are more predisposed to entrepreneurial education. Despite science students' opinions regarding the Learning to Be programme tending to be more positive in several aspects, in fact this does not correspond to an effective improvement in their entrepreneurial abilities, since there is no correlation between the course that the students attend and the development of students' entrepreneurial skills (from moment 1 to moment 2). Regarding the impact on students' entrepreneurial personality traits, a slight increase in students' GET scores was observed when taking the Learning to Be programme, although students maintained medium enterprising qualities, both at beginning and at the end of the programme.

Considering the individual item analysis, the Learning to Be programme had a significant impact on students' need for autonomy. In this case, students improved their ability to work as an intrapreneur and as a valuable member of an organizational team. Autonomy has huge importance in the ability of students to learn, solve problems and to grow in the organizational environment.

In addition, this kind of entrepreneurial education programme allows students to face and solve real problems, from real companies. Thus, students become more aware of organizational and professional realities, and develop networks which can help them in the future (for example, to get a job). It is interesting to verify that students who look for programmes such as Learning to Be tend to exhibit more entrepreneurial traits (experimental group) than those who do not seek such programmes (control group). Thus, our findings show a positive influence on students' expectations and personal traits of enrolling businesses in EE programmes. The enrolment of companies seems to have reinforced the teaching practices and methodologies used, making the process close to entrepreneurial practice. Also, students feel more motivated in participating in the experience, since they could envisage the benefits for their future professional career (real-world business experience), such as relevant business contacts and vital networking skills in the course of interacting with companies.

However, and taking into account the results from the GET test (that is, the majority of entrepreneurial characteristics improvements were not statistically significant through participation in the programme), perhaps such programmes should be introduced in early childhood education. As mentioned by Cunha and James (2007), personality abilities are both inherited and created, and are formed over time. As this programme involves university students, their non-cognitive skills could be less malleable to change.

Therefore, the results obtained may provide relevant clues on how to design impactful EE policies. On the one hand, there is the need to foster the development in school curricula of active and hands-on teaching approaches that place a greater emphasis on learners and, at the same time, benefit from the external context or ecosystem of academia. In this case, the enrolment of companies could be of paramount importance, since it fosters the development of entrepreneurial cognition through experiencing real-world cases, especially related to spotting business opportunities, and creating and developing businesses. On the other hand, those teaching approaches should be incorporated in early education, since their impact could be higher in the development of students' entrepreneurial mindset.

Limitations

This study has several limitations. First, it is important to note that the GET measuring instrument reveals several weaknesses, since it does not have a clear factorial structure. We carried confirmatory factor analysis (CFA with LISREL; maximum likelihood estimation method) to test the five-factor model and, as other authors had already verified (e.g., Lyons et al., 2015), the model does not fit the data satisfactorily (e.g., GFI 0.73; NNFI 0.46; CFI 0.49; IFI 0.52; Byrne, 1998). The internal consistency indices of the dimensions are also very poor (except 'need for achievement').

Second, the two samples are small (especially the control group sample). Although we had a greater number of answers in both moments 1 and 2, the paired answers (those that allowed us to carry out the analysis we intended to do) were much fewer.

Third, as the students responded to the questionnaire about themselves, the risk of self-reported bias exists, because they may have answered not exactly what they are, but what they would like to be. In addition to that, the questionnaires were not completely anonymous, which may have increased the students' desire to project a certain image of themselves.

Recommendations for Further Research

In order to capture the impact of EE, more methodological work is needed to develop suitable methods to assess changes in attitudes and behaviour, as well as in mindset and emotions, as suggested by Nabi et al. (2017). The development of those methods is of crucial importance to examine the relationship between pedagogical methods and specific learning outcomes. Therefore, as future research lines it is suggested that emotions are included as a proxy to study the dynamic processing of learning in entrepreneurship education. In this case, methods of analysing emotions could be explored, such as the study of body language and facial expressions, and measures of self-reporting as indicators of positive or negative emotions, which are fundamental for studying such process dynamics.

NOTES

* This research work was funded by European Structural Funds and Investments, and COMPETE2020, through FCT – Foundation for Science and Technology, I.P., under the project PTDC/IVO-PEC/5514/2014.

1. Programme description retrieved from https://www.ub-cooperation.eu/index/casestudies.

REFERENCES

Allen, E. (1995). Active learning and teaching: improving postsecondary library instruction. *Reference Librarian*, **51**, 89–103.

Athayde, R. (2009). Measuring enterprise potential in young people. *Entrepreneurship: Theory and Practice*, **33**(2), 481–500. http://doi.org/10.1111/j.1540-6520.2009.00300.x.

Bacigalupo, M., Kampylis, P., Punie, Y., and Van den Brande, G. (2016). *EntreComp: the Entrepreneurship Competence Framework*. Publication Office of the European Union, June. http://doi.org/10.2791/593884.

Bennett, R. (2006). Business lecturers' perception of the nature of entrepreneurship.

International Journal of Entrepreneurial Behaviour and Research, **12**(3), 165–188. http://doi.org/http://dx.doi.org/10.1108/13552550610667440.
Bonwell, C., and Eison, J. (1991). *Active Learning: Creating Excitement in the Classroom*. Washington, DC: George Washington University.
Boyatzis, R.E. (1982). *The Competent Manager: A Model for Effective Performance*. New York: John Wiley and Sons.
Brophy, M., and Kiely, T. (2002). Competencies: a new sector. *Journal of European Industrial Training*, **26**(2), 165–176. http://doi.org/10.1108/03090590210422049.
Byrne, B.M. (1998). *Structural Equation Modelling with Lisrel, Prelis and Simplis: Basic Concept, Application and Programming*. Mahwah, NJ: Lawrence Erlbaum.
Caird, S. (2013). General Measure of Enterprising Tendency test. www.get2test.net.
Charness, N., Krampe, R., and Mayr, U. (1996). The role of practice and coaching in entrepreneurial skill domains: an international comparison of life-span chess skill acquisition. In K.A. Ericsson (ed.), *The Road to Excellence: The Acquisition of Expert Performance in the Arts and Sciences, Sports, and Games* (pp. 51–80). Hillsdale, NJ: Lawrence Erlbaum Associates.
Colombo, M.G., and Grilli, L. (2005). Start-up size: the role of external financing. *Economics Letters*, **88**(2), 243–250. http://doi.org/10.1016/j.econlet.2005.02.018.
Cunha, F., and James, H. (2007). The technology of skill formation. *American Economic Review*, **97**(2), 31–47.
Daniel, A.D. (2016). Fostering an entrepreneurial mind-set by using a Design Thinking approach in entrepreneurship education. *Journal of Industry and Higher Education*, **30**(3), 215–223. http://doi.org/10.1177/0950422221665319.
Daniel, A.D., and Castro, V.R. (2017). Entrepreneurship education: how to measure the impact on nascent entrepreneurs? In A.C. Moreira, J.G. Dantas, and F.M. Valente (eds), *Nascent Entrepreneurship and Successful New Venture Creation* (pp. 85–110). Hershey, PA: IGI Global. http://doi.org/10.4018/978-1-5225-2936-1.ch004.
Daniel, A.D., Colpas, F., and Quaresma, R. (2016). O ensino formal do empreendedorismo ao nível universitário: análise de ferramentas e metodologias pedagógicas. Paper presented at II Jornadas do Ensino do Empreendedorismo em Portugal, Coimbra, Portugal: Instituto Pedro Nunes.
Draycott, M., and Rae, D. (2011). Enterprise education in schools and the role of competency frameworks. *International Journal of Entrepreneurial Behavior and Research*, **17**(2), 127–145. http://doi.org/10.1108/13552551111114905.
Ericsson, K.A., Krampe, R.T., and Tesch-Römer, C. (1993). The role of deliberate practice in the acquisition of expert performance. *Psychological Review*, **100**(3), 363–406. http://doi.org/10.1037//0033-295X.100.3.363.
Eurydice (2012). *Entrepreneurship Education at School in Europe: National Strategies, Curricula and Learning Outcomes*. Brussels: EACEA.
Fayolle, A. and Gailly, B. (2015). The impact of entrepreneurial education on entrepreneurial attitudes and intention: hysteresis and persistence. *Journal of Small Business Management*, **53**(1), 75–93.
Field, A. (2013). *Discovering Statistics using SPSS Statistics*. London: SAGE Publications.
Gibb, A. (1987). Designing effective programmes for encouraging the business start-up process: lessons from the UK experience. *Journal of European Industrial Training*, **11**(4), 24–32.
Gibb, A. (2008). Entrepreneurship and enterprise education in schools and

colleges: insights from UK practice. *International Journal of Entrepreneurship Education*, **6**(2), 101–144.
Giones, F., Zhou, Z., Miralles, F., and Katzy, B. (2012). A constructivist approach for technology-based entrepreneurship. XXIII ISPIM Conference – Action for Innovation: Innovating from Experience. Barcelona, Spain.
Graevenitz, G., Harhoff, D., and Weber, R. (2010). The effects of entrepreneurship education. *Journal of Economic Behavior and Organization*, **76**(1), 90–112.
Henry, C., Foss, L., and Ahl, H. (2016). Gender and entrepreneurship research: a review of methodological approaches. *International Small Business Journal*, **34**(3), 217–241. http://doi.org/10.1177/0266242614549779.
Hills, G.E. (1988). Variations in university entrepreneurship education: an empirical study of an evolving field. *Journal of Business Venturing*, **3**(2), 109–122.
Johannisson, B. (2016). Limits to and prospects of entrepreneurship education in the academic context. *Entrepreneurship and Regional Development*, **28**(5–6), 403–423.
Katz, J.A. (2008). Fully mature but not fully legitimate: a different perspective on the state of entrepreneurship education. *Journal of Small Business Management and Marketing*, **46**(4), 550–566.
Kuratko, D.F. (2005). The emergence of entrepreneurship education: development, trends, and challenges. *Entrepreneurship: Theory and Practice*, **29**, 577–597. http://doi.org/10.1111/j.1540-6520.2005.00099.x.
Kuttim, M., Kallaste, M., Venesaar, U., and Kiis, A. (2014). Entreprenurship education at university level and students' entrepreneurial intentions. *Procedia – Social and Behavioral Sciences*, **110**, 658–668.
Kyrö, P. (2005). Entrepreneurial learning in a cross-cultural context challenges previous learning paradigms. In P. Kyrö and C. Carrier (eds), *The Dynamics of Learning Entrepreneurship in a Cross-Cultural University Context* (pp. 68–103). Tampere: University of Tampere, Research Centre for Vocational and Professional Education.
Lindh, I., and Thorgren, S. (2016). Entreprenership education: the role of local business. *Entrepreneurship and Regional Development*, **28**(5/6), 313–336.
Littunen, H., and Hyrsky, K. (2000). The Early entrepreneurial stage in Finnish family and nonfamily firms. *Family Business Review*, **13**(1), 41–53. http://doi.org/10.1111/j.1741-6248.2000.00041.x.
Lorz, M., Müller, S., and Volery, T. (2011). Entrepreneurship education: a meta-analysis of impact studies and applied methodologies. FGF G-Forum 2011. Zurich.
Lyons, R., Lynn, T., and Ciarán, M.B. (2015). Individual level assessment in entrepreneurship education: an investigation of theories and techniques. *Journal of Entrepreneurship Education*, **18**(1), 136–156.
Martin, B.C., McNally, J.J., and Kay, M.J. (2013). Examining the formation of human capital in entrepreneurship: a meta-analysis of entrepreneurship education outcomes. *Journal of Business Venturing*, **28**, 211–224.
Mayhew, M.J., Simonoff, J.S., Baumol, W.J., Wiesenfeld, B.M., and Klein, M.W. (2012). Exploring innovative entrepreneurship and its ties to higher educational experiences. *Research in Higher Education*, **53**(8), 831–859. http://doi.org/10.1007/s11162-012-9258-3.
McMullan, W.E., and Long, W.A. (1987). Entrepreneurship education in the nineties. *Journal of Business Venturing*, **2**(3), 261–275.
Mitchell, R.K. (2005). Tuning up the global value creation engine: the road

to excellence in international entrepreneurship education. *Advances in Entrepreneurship, Firm Emergence and Growth*, **8**, 185–248. Retrieved from https://www.scopus.com/inward/record.uri?eid=2-s2.0-33645934233&partnerID=40&md5=cc870757a3e64eb5e61657cbf6211fbe.

Mitchell, R.K., Busenitz, L.W., Bird, B.J., et al. (2007). The central question in entrepreneurial cognition research. *Entrepreneurship Theory and Practice*, **31**(1), 1–27.

Mitchell, R.K., Busenitz, L., Lant, T., et al. (2002). Toward a theory of entrepreneurial cognition: rethinking the people side of entrepreneurship research. *Entrepreneurship: Theory and Practice*, **2**(27), 93–104. http://doi.org/10.1111/j.1540-6520.2004.00061.x.

Moore, C., Boyd, B.L., and Dooley, K.E. (2010). The effects of experiential learning with an emphasis on reflective writing on deep-level processing of leadership students. *Journal of Leadership Education*, **9**(1), 36–52. http://doi.org/10.12806/V9/I1/RF3.

Morris, M.H., Webb, J.W., Fu, J., and Singhal, S. (2013). A competency-based perspective on entrepreneurship education: conceptual and empirical insights. *Journal of Small Business Management*, **51**(3), 352–369. Retrieved from https://www.scopus.com/inward/record.uri?eid=2-s2.0-84879176730&partnerID=40&md5=c86e6714fd07817c9acb5ebcc63c58fe.

Mwasalwiba, E.S. (2010). Entrepreneurship education: a review of its objectives, teaching methods, and impact indicators. *Education and Training*, **52**(1), 20–47. http://doi.org/http://dx.doi.org/10.1108/00400911011017663.

Nabi, G., Liñán, F., Fayolle, A., Krueger, N., and Walmsley, A. (2017). The impact of entrepreneurship education in higher education: a systematic review and research agenda. *Academy of Management Learning and Education*, **16**(2), 277–299.

Neisser, U. (1967). *Cognitive Psychology*. New York: Appleton-Century-Crafts.

Norzailan, Z., Othman, R.B., and Ishizaki, H. (2016). Strategic leadership competencies: what is it and how to develop it? *Industrial and Commercial Training*, **48**(8), 394–399. http://doi.org/10.1108/ICT-04-2016-0020.

Nunnaly, J.C. (1978) *Psychometric Theory*, 2nd edn. New York: McGraw-Hill.

Oosterbeek, H., van Praag, M., and Ijsselstein, A. (2010). The impact of entrepreneurship education on entrepreneurship skills and motivation. *European Economic Review*, **54**(3), 442–454.

Osterwalder, A., and Pigneur, Y. (2010). *Business Model Generation: A Handbook for Visionaries, Game Changers, and Challengers*. Hoboken, NJ: John Wiley & Sons.

Paço, A., Ferreira, J., and Raposo, M. (2016). Development of entrepreneurship education programmes for HEI students: the lean start-up approach. *Journal of Entrepreneurship Education*, **19**(2), 39–52.

Rae, D., and Carswell, M. (2001). Towards a conceptual understanding of entrepreneurial learning. *Journal of Small Business and Enterprise Development*, **8**(2), 150–158.

Ragains, P. (1995). Four variations on Drueke's active learning paradigm. *Research Strategies*, **13**, 40–50.

Rasmussen, E., Mosey, S., and Wright, M. (2011). The evolution of entrepreneurial competencies: a longitudinal study of university spin-off venture emergence. *Journal of Management Studies*, **48**(6), 1314–1345. http://doi.org/10.1111/j.1467-6486.2010.00995.x.

Rezaei-Zadeh, M., Hogan, M., O'Reilly, J., Cleary, B., and Murphy, E. (2014). Using interactive management to identify, rank and model entrepreneurial competencies as universities' entrepreneurship curricula. *Journal of Entrepreneurship*, **23**(1), 57–94. Retrieved from https://www.scopus.com/inward/record.uri?eid=2-s2.0-84893511558&partnerID=40&md5=3d9e63075283153e0f74530851e047b3.

Rezaei-Zadeh, M., Hogan, M., O'Reilly, J., Cunningham, J., and Murphy, E. (2017). Core entrepreneurial competencies and their interdependencies: insights from a study of Irish and Iranian entrepreneurs, university students and academics. *International Entrepreneurship and Management Journal*, **13**(1), 35–73. http://doi.org/10.1007/s11365-016-0390-y.

Ries, E. (2011). *The Lean Startup: How Today's Entrepreneurs Use Continuous Innovation to Create Radically Successful Businesses*. New York: Crown Business.

Schelfhout, W., Bruggeman, K., and De Mayer, S. (2016). Evaluation of entrepreneurial competence through scaled behavioural indicators: validation of an instrument. *Studies in Educational Evaluation*, **51**, 29–41. Retrieved from https://www.scopus.com/inward/record.uri?eid=2-s2.0-84989193389&partnerID=40&md5=86df0c8a0ac70d61f7291e5bd0c53d1e.

Schneider, W. (1998). Innate talent or deliberate practice as determinants of exceptional performance: are we asking the right question? *Behavioral and Brain Sciences*, **21**(3), 423–424. http://doi.org/10.1017/s0140525x98411233.

Secundo, G., Del Vecchio, P., Schiuma, G., and Passiante, G. (2017). Activating entrepreneurial learning processes for transforming university students' idea into entrepreneurial practices. *International Journal of Entrepreneurial Behavior and Research*, **23**(3), 465–485. http://doi.org/10.1108/IJEBR-12-2015-0315.

Shinnar, R., Pruett, M., and Toney, B. (2009). Entrepreneurship Education: attitudes across campus. *Journal of Education for Business*, **84**(3), 151–159. http://doi.org/10.3200/JOEB.84.3.151-159.

Silberman, M. (1996). *Active Learning: 101 Strategies to Teach any Subject*. http://books.google.co.uk/books/about/Active_learning.html?id=9x9T2_WEAM8C&pgis=1.

Souitaris, V., Zerbinati, S., and Al-Laham, A. (2007). Do entrepreneurship programmes raise entrepreneurial intention of science and engineering students? The effect of learning, inspiration and resources. *Journal of Business Venturing*, **22**, 566–591. http://doi.org/10.1016/j.jbusvent.2006.05.002.

Steele, C.M., Spencer, S.J., and Aronson, J. (2002). Contending with group image: the psychology of stereotype and social identity threat. *Advances in Experimental Social Psychology*, **34**, 379–440. http://doi.org/http://dx.doi.org/10.1016/S0065-2601(02)80009-0.

Thomas, L.D.W., and Autio, E. (2014). The fifth facet: the ecosystem as an organizational field. Academy of Management Annual Meeting. Philadelphia, PA.

Vesper, K., McMullan, W.E., and Ray, D.M. (1989). Entrepreneurship education: more than just an adjustment to management education. *International Small Business Journal*, **8**(1), 61–65.

Wilson, F., Marlino, D., and Kickul, J. (2004). Our entrepreneurial future: examining the diverse attitudes and motivations of teens across gender and ethnic identity. *Journal of Developmental Entrepreneurship*, **9**(3), 177–197.

3. Entrepreneurial university practices in Brazil under the lens of qualitative and quantitative research

Carla Marques, Vitor Braga, João J. Ferreira and Moses Rodrigues

INTRODUCTION

Universities, as we know them today, are the result of a long evolution. Many consider contemporary universities to be representative of a model of inertia: bureaucratic, inefficient and much less flexible organizations than private sector firms (Lehrer et al., 2009). Nevertheless, the current environment offers universities many challenges: that is, they have to deal with rapidly expanding knowledge frontiers and a growing variety of additional responsibilities beyond teaching and research, including cooperation with industries, technology transfer and start-ups. The contemporary paradox has resulted in an extensive, heterogeneous body of research on the entrepreneurial university (Etzkowitz, 1983; Clark, 1998; Siegel et al., 2003; Culkin and Mallick, 2011).

The idea of the entrepreneurial university sharing the results of research with society is, however, more recent (Mascarenhas et al., 2017). In a context where universities seek to produce adequate research to meet the needs of the society, the question of what is the most appropriate organizational structure and management approach to teaching, research and extension is raised (Rubens et al., 2017).

The organizational structure of universities has evolved over time, largely as a result of internal conflicts such as, for example, dichotomies between traditional disciplines versus the most recent areas of knowledge; natural sciences versus the humanities; general education versus education in specialty areas; teaching versus research; and education at undergraduate versus graduate levels.

Given this context of conflict, universities sought to adapt based on three main areas. The first was related to the process of transformation into a centre of knowledge supply, providing education to the society for centuries. The second was the inclusion of research as one of their main objectives. The third was the adoption of a hybrid approach that combines teaching and research on a new mission of building an entrepreneurial university with the following distinctive features: to stimulate the integration between departments; to gain effectiveness by trying to gradually expand the integration between education, research and extension; and the production and transfer of technology.

Given this context, internal policy in entrepreneurial universities should be focused on: establishing solid links with the societies in which they operate; revealing the results of their research; monitoring scientific, technological and business trends; exploiting the more favourable opportunities; and positioning the higher education institution (HEI) in promising and/or profitable market niches.

In order to adapt to new social and economic demands, the entrepreneurial university evokes a modern core mission, values and behaviours in the emergence of a joint business model (Mets, 2015). Several models have been proposed to explain the role of the entrepreneurial university (Etzkowitz, 2002, 2003; Clark, 2003; Kirby, 2006; Rothaermel and Thursby, 2007; Kirby et al., 2011). Universities attempting to create high levels of added value, in carrying out their mission and realizing their entrepreneurial side, must, in today's competitive landscape, assume the function of generating and transferring knowledge and technology to the society (Sirén et al., 2012; Bozeman et al., 2013; Mascarenhas et al., 2017).

The efficiency of knowledge transfer between universities and industry reflects environmental factors, institutional factors and organizational practices in university management. The organizational factors include, among others: the legal framework involving the political and institutional frameworks; mission; forms of governance; and financial management. Organizational management involves the factors included in the management process of a technological innovation centre and human resources involving the specificities linked to knowledge and technology transfer dynamics (Siegel et al., 2003).

Higher education institutions are increasingly assessed by the extent to which they contribute to the economic and social growth of the environment in which they operate, stimulating the creation of new businesses and innovation in existing businesses. To be or to turn into an entrepreneurial HEI is a response to this challenge. HEInnovate (2014) is an online tool launched in 2013 by the European Commission, in cooperation with the Organisation for Economic Co-operation and Development (OECD), and it was developed as an attempt to assist higher education institutions in responding to this challenge. Freely available, the tool allows an HEI to monitor its levels of entrepreneurship, taking into account seven areas considered critical for the performance and development of entrepreneurial institutions.

HEInnovate works as a learning tool and an inspiration to HEIs which propose to meet the challenges faced in the knowledge society by systematically evaluating the promotion of the entrepreneurship process through the ability to diagnose strengths and weaknesses of their achievement; to develop strategies to encourage the process and observe its evolution over time; to evaluate partnerships with external entities; and to foster the creation of start-ups.

The purpose of this chapter is to analyse, based on a mixed qualitative and qualitative approach and using the HEInnovate tool, how a higher education institution, located in a peripheral area in a developing country (Brazil), promotes and supports entrepreneurship in the region.

This chapter is structured as follows. It first provides a preliminary review of the literature that addresses the topics of the entrepreneurial university and regional development. The following section presents the methodology used. Next, we describe the results, before discussing the implications and study limitations and presenting our conclusions.

CONCEPTUAL FRAMEWORK

Literature Review

The origins of the study of entrepreneurial universities date to Etzkowitz's (1983) paper that focused on how the rising research costs and stagnating state or business support impacted on the academic mindset of both researchers and university administrators. As a consequence of such challenges, universities were forced to develop alternative forms of financing, resulting in more entrepreneurship-oriented research. Consequently, universities were required to evolve into institutions providing training and/or teaching for firms and academics' expert advice, which, in line with the more orthodox approach to economics, can be seen as a production factor, where the input is research and the output is the transfer to firms, allowing economies of scale on the value creation (Svensson et al., 2012; Etzkowitz et al., 2005). This new paradox has not only made universities more engaged with society but has also allowed a diversification of income sources, making them more independent from governments (De Zilwa, 2005).

The change into an entrepreneurial university brings exciting possibilities as universities distinguish from the previous paradigm with a new approach, offering opportunities, practices, cultures and favourable environments that actively encourage and embrace the entrepreneurship of students and graduates. Under these circumstances, entrepreneurship plays a central and very critical role (Barnes et al., 2002).

The changing paradigm of the 'new' entrepreneurial universities, over the last two decades, was triggered by the demand for innovation and knowledge and it has resulted in a reconfiguration of research scenarios in universities. This change produced different entrepreneurial activities, materialized in different forms (in some cases with government initiatives, for example), in different spaces (that is, global, regional or local) and in different organizational contexts (that is, institutional, technological and social) (Guerrero et al., 2016). Entrepreneurial universities, therefore, are able to exploit opportunities and knowledge in order to promote new entrepreneurial phenomena (Sam and van der Sijde, 2014).

The previous idea that universities were isolated 'islands of knowledge' has evolved, with institutions that favour involvement with external partners and where business activities take place (Zhang et al., 2016). Such change results in many opportunities to establish links with industry through university spin-offs, conducting licensing, generating research contracts, providing consultancy services and facilitating the mobility of graduates and researchers between these sectors. The association of universities, and higher education in general, with social and economic development required that university research and development (R&D) activities are no longer considered as purely academic, but rather as part of the triple or quadruple helix of knowledge (Miller et al., 2016; Mok, 2013; Sperrer et al., 2016).

Universities have a role as catalysts for regional economic development and growth (Gianiodis et al., 2016; Urbano and Guerrero, 2013). Nevertheless, the increasing academic attention given to the entrepreneurial university very often reveals contrasting behaviours and attitudes in industries and in academia, which remains as an obstacle to more effective collaboration. Therefore, there is substantial room for improvement in terms of partnerships with the private sector (Abreu et al., 2016).

The entrepreneurial universities can be distinguished as being multifaceted, ensuring the existence of mechanisms aimed at supporting technology transfer to industries (Guenther and Wagner, 2008). They have an important role in regional economic and social development due to their catalyst function, mainly in the generation and exploitation of knowledge (Harrison and Leitch, 2010; Urbano and Guerrero, 2013). Therefore they need to be seen as important drivers for self-development and innovation inasmuch as they provide a response in highly turbulent and unpredictable markets and contexts, and they are seen by many as the next step in the development of higher education (Sperrer et al., 2016).

As a consequence, they serve to channel knowledge through a spillover effect, adding to socio-economic development through their teaching, research and entrepreneurial activities. A production functions approach has recognized in entrepreneurial universities the ability to create human, knowledge, social and entrepreneurship capital (Guerrero et al., 2015; Brown, 2016).

In line with the arguments developed above, the entrepreneurial university needs to be seen as a driver for self-development and innovation, contributing to success in the presence of less favourable conditions, as is the case of turbulent and unpredictable markets (Sperrer et al., 2016). Therefore, it is critical that the university regularly makes an assessment to identify the dimensions that need to be included or strengthened within its strategic plan, so that it can be considered an entrepreneurial university. Aware of the importance of this concept and its practice, the European Commission has proposed a self-assessment tool for higher education institutions: HEInnovate.

Entrepreneurial Universities within the HEInnovate Framework

Higher education institutions are, increasingly, being judged on how they contribute to the economic and social growth of society, stimulating new enterprise start-ups and innovation in existing ones. Being or becoming an entrepreneurial HEI is a response to that challenge. In this section, HEInnovate is presented as a tool for the HEIs' self-evaluation with regard to entrepreneurship.

HEInnovate is an online tool launched in 2013 by the European Commission, jointly with the OECD. It is freely accessible and it allows HEIs to monitor their degree of entrepreneurship by analysing seven domains considered critical for the performance and development of entrepreneurial institutions. HEINnovate works as a learning and inspirational tool for higher education institutions, allowing them to face the challenges of the knowledge society, by systematically evaluating the process of promoting entrepreneurship, through the possibility of monitoring their strengths and weaknesses; to conceive strategies to encourage the process and to validate its evolution over time; to evaluate partnerships with external entities; and to encourage the creation of start-ups.

The tool's self-evaluation framework is based on seven factors (Table 3.1):

1. Leadership and governance. Leadership and governance are expected to foster the definition of guidelines and organizational strategies that promote processes leading the academic community to assume

Table 3.1 Categories, items and theoretical support for the data collection instruments

Category	Items	Theoretical support
Leadership and governance: HEI leadership and governance foster entrepreneurship	• The HEI organizational strategy encourages entrepreneurship • The HEI and the academic community are committed to fostering entrepreneurship • The activities to promote entrepreneurship are integrated into the daily experiences of the HEI • The HEI provides the academic community with the autonomy to foster entrepreneurship • The HEI fosters entrepreneurship at the local and regional level	Clark (1998) Crow (2008) Etzkowitz (2003) Gibb (2012) HEInnovate (2014) OECD (2012) Sirén et al. (2012)
Organizational capacity: HEI organizational structure favours entrepreneurship	• The promotion of entrepreneurship within the HEI is supported by a diversified network of sources of funding, including investment by external agents • The HEI has a sustainable financial strategy to foster entrepreneurship • The HEI promotes joint work and the use of synergies among members of the academic community to foster entrepreneurship • The HEI has a formal policy of fostering entrepreneurship by the academic community • Members of the academic community who actively support entrepreneurship receive incentives and rewards from the HEI • The HEI supports external entrepreneurs who can contribute to the entrepreneurial culture	Crow (2008) HEInnovate (2014) Jacob et al. (2003) Kirby (2006) OECD (2012) Sirén et al. (2012)
Teaching and learning: the supply of education and training, in terms of both formal education and professional training, fosters entrepreneurship	• The organizational structure of the HEI encourages and supports the development of entrepreneurial skills • The promotion of entrepreneurship by the HEI involves the process of teaching and learning of students and the process of professional training of teachers and administrative technical staff • The HEI fosters entrepreneurship across all university experiences, from awareness, encouragement and ideas, to development and implementation • The HEI validates the formal and informal skills resulting from the learning process carried out by the academic community in the context of entrepreneurship promotion	HEInnovate (2014) OECD (2012)

Table 3.1 (continued)

Category	Items	Theoretical support
	• The HEI promotes the involvement of external entities in teaching and learning processes as an incentive for entrepreneurship • The HEI promotes research based on the results of teaching activities developed in the promotion of entrepreneurship, and its results are considered feedback for future actions	
Pathways to entrepreneurship: the HEI offers the academic community the conditions for enjoying entrepreneurship experiences, under supervision	• The HEI promotes awareness among the academic community about the value and importance of the development of entrepreneurial skills • The HEI promotes a culture of entrepreneurship among members of the academic community • The HEI offers opportunities for entrepreneurial action by the academic community • The HEI provides support to the academic community to materialize their ideas in entrepreneurial actions • The HEI provides mentoring to support development by the academic community of entrepreneurship projects • The HEI facilitates access to finance to members of the academic community who are potential entrepreneurs • The HEI offers access to business incubation services for members of the academic community who are potential entrepreneurs	Clark (2003) Crow (2008) Etzkomitz (2003) Gibb (2012) HEInnovate (2014) OECD (2012)
Interplay between the university and the business sector: the HEI provides the interplay of knowledge and technology to entrepreneurial institutions, while promoting entrepreneurship	• The HEI businesses and external relations for the exchange of knowledge and technology aim to foster entrepreneurship. • The HEI has an active participation in partnerships to foster entrepreneurship • The HEI has strong links with incubators, science parks and other external initiatives, creating opportunities to foster entrepreneurship through knowledge exchange • The HEI provides opportunities for employees and students to engage in entrepreneurial activities with the external business environment • The HEI fosters entrepreneurship by offering opportunities for the mobility of teachers, students and administrative staff between the academy and the external environment • The HEI seeks to involve teaching, research and the local community in an ecosystem of knowledge, as a result of partnerships aimed at fostering entrepreneurship	HEInnovate (2014) OECD (2012) Sirén et al. (2012)

Internationalization of the HEI: the HEI promotes internationalization as a tool for fostering entrepreneurship	• The HEI includes internationalization as part of its strategy to promote entrepreneurship • The HEI supports the international mobility of its employees and students to foster entrepreneurship • The HEI fosters entrepreneurship by receiving researchers and students as a result of the internationalization process • The HEI, aimed at fostering entrepreneurship, demonstrates internationalization in its teaching approach • The HEI actively participates in international networks aiming to promote entrepreneurship	HEInnovate (2014) OECD (2012)
Impact measurement: the HEI assesses its impact on entrepreneurship promotion	• The HEI evaluates the impact of its entrepreneurship promotion strategy, and as a result of this evaluation changes the processes • The HEI regularly assesses the impact of the presence of entrepreneurship on teaching and learning in the institution • The HEI regularly assesses the impact of fostering entrepreneurship as regards teaching and learning activities • The HEI conducts a regular assessment of the impact of knowledge transfer and technology activities with external entities • The HEI makes a regular assessment of the impact of the promotion of entrepreneurship	Byrne and Fayolle (2010) Fayolle et al. (2006) HEInnovate (2014) OECD (2012)

the institutional commitment to increase entrepreneurship levels in combination with the routine work of HEIs.

2. Organizational capacity. The constant validation of the organizational structure should seek to foster entrepreneurship, by removing barriers; identify network financing strategies; promote the attraction, development and retention of talent; encourage joint efforts among members of the academic community that stimulate external and internal synergies; and promote schemes for incentives and rewards.
3. Teaching and learning. The teaching and learning of, and the professional training provided to, teachers and administrative staff are expected to stimulate and support the promotion of entrepreneurship, in a process with continuous monitoring of the research process.
4. Pathways to entrepreneurship. Universities must offer the academic community the conditions for the development of entrepreneurship projects, considering the promotion of entrepreneurship, supervised experimentation, and the existence of infrastructures for incubation.
5. Interplay between the university and the business sector. Building networks of strong relationships and active partnerships between higher education institutions and external partners contributes to the HEI's ability to reach its full potential in fostering entrepreneurship.
6. Internationalization of HEIs. Internationalization should be a vehicle for the promotion of entrepreneurship in higher education institutions, involving the exchange of knowledge in teaching, research and outreach activities, as well as taking advantage of the mobility of academic staff and students.
7. Impact measurement. The changes resulting from the promotion of entrepreneurship at HEIs should be measured in terms of their local and global impact.

METHODOLOGY

This study explores how INTA Faculties, located in the state of Ceará, Brazil, promoted entrepreneurship in the region between 2011 and 2014. The case study is considered an appropriate strategy to investigate phenomena in which there are a variety of factors and relationships that are directly observed with basic laws to determine their importance (Stake, 2005). This research can be described as a single case study (integrated), given that, despite being a single organization – Faculties INTA – the analysis is based on its subunits: teachers, coordinators and directors, as well as other community members with relations with the HEI aimed at the promotion of the entrepreneurship process (Stake, 2005).

A hybrid qualitative–quantitative methodology was adopted, combining semi-structured interviews administered to the Chief Executive Officer (CEO); Administrative Pro-Director; Pro-Director of Undergraduate Studies; coordinators of courses and institutions responsible for maintaining educational, institutional and commercial relations with the INTA Faculties, such as the director of Sobral Hospital; the book publishing industry marketer; and the President of the Municipal Assembly of the City of Sobral Municipality. In addition, a questionnaire was aplied to a sample of teachers. The questionnaire was based on HEInnovate (2014) as a self-assessment tool for HEIs on entrepreneurship; an online tool launched in 2013 by the OECD. The tool includes self-assessment based on seven factors: leadership and governance, organizational capacity, teaching and learning, paths to entrepreneurship, interplay between the university sector and the business sector, internationalization of HEIs, and impact measurement. Data were collected during the first half of 2015.

The questionnaire applied in this research is divided into seven parts, corresponding to the seven dimensions of the HEInnovate tool, each with several items (see Table 3.1), with closed questions whose answers follow a five-point Likert scale, ranging between 1: 'completely disagree/never/insignificant' and 5: 'completely agree/always/very significant'.

In addition, content analysis of open questions on the assessment of the semi-structured interviews was conducted using the IBM Many Eyes software, preceded by standardization and uniformity of terms contained in the speech of the respondents. Treatment of qualitative data was done using confirmatory factor analysis and one-way ANOVA tests using the software SPSS 22.0.

RESULTS

Characterization of the Sample: Quantitative Data

Taking into account the objectives of this research, the target population included all pro-directors, coordinators and managers of the courses in the areas of pedagogy, research, internship, complementary activities and outreach working in INTA Faculties, with a total of 57 people. Our sample is female dominated (64.3 per cent of respondents are female) and relatively young, since the majority of respondents (58.7 per cent) are aged between 20 and 39 years old. The sample is characterized by a high level of education, and the majority of respondents receive between R$5000 and R$10 000 per month. Professionally, 57.9 per cent of the sample are

Table 3.2 Analysis of the feasibility of factors that influence entrepreneurship and innovation

Dimensions	Number of items	Cronbach α
Leadership and governance	12	0.943
Organizational capacity	12	0.930
Teaching and learning	15	0.970
Pathways to entrepreneurship	8	0.958
Interplay between the university and the business sector	11	0.974
Internationalization of HEIs	9	0.964
Impact measurement	9	0.975

teachers (45.6 per cent full-time and 12.3 per cent part-time), 21.1 per cent are course leaders and 19.3 per cent are pro-directors.

Analysis of Items Feasibility

The internal reliability analysis of the seven dimensions that influenced entrepreneurship and innovation in the HEI was carried out, and all of them presented very good internal reliability, since all Cronbach's alphas are greater than 0.9, as shown in Table 3.2.

The INTA Faculties' commitment to fostering entrepreneurship was evaluated by respondents, on a scale of 1 to 5, as being at least sufficient (average over 3) in six of the seven dimensions of the HEInnovate scale (Box 3.1).

The highest score was attributed to the 'Leadership and governance' dimension (3.85), which had two items better classified, respectively 'HEI fosters entrepreneurship at local and regional level' (4.17) and 'Activities of entrepreneurship are integrated into the daily life of HEI' (4.09).

The lowest score was given to the 'Internationalization of the institution' dimension, with an average of 2.88, with negative results in three of the five items: 'HEI considers internationalization a part of its strategy to promote entrepreneurship' (2.73), 'HEI fosters entrepreneurship by receiving researchers and students as a result of internationalization' and 'HEI, aiming to foster entrepreneurship, demonstrates internationalization in its approach to teaching'.

Considering the items in all dimensions, the results obtained in the HEI partnerships and networks at local and regional levels, and at internal and external levels, for the promotion of entrepreneurship, it is possible to conclude that:

BOX 3.1 AVERAGE ASSESSMENT OF THE DIMENSIONS

1. Leadership and governance (3.85).
2. Teaching and learning (3.64).
3. Interplay between the university and the business sector (3.64).
4. Organizational capacity (3.58).
5. Pathways to entrepreneurship (3.58).
6. Impact measurement (3.22).
7. Internationalization of HEIs (2.88).

- 'HEI fosters entrepreneurship at a local and regional level' (4.17) stands out within in the 'Leadership and governance' dimension.
- 'The promotion of entrepreneurship in HEI is supported by a diversified network of sources of funding, including investment by external agents' (3.79) is the best-assessed item within the 'Organizational capacity' dimension.
- 'HEI promotes the involvement of external institutions in teaching and learning actions while promoting entrepreneurship' (3.98) is the best-ranked item in the 'Teaching and learning' dimension.
- 'HEI offers access business incubation services to potential entrepreneurs, members of the academic community' (3.82) is the item performing best within the 'Pathways to entrepreneurship' dimension.
- 'HEI has an active participation for partnerships aimed at fostering entrepreneurship' (3.96) is the item performing best within the 'Exchange between the university and the business sector' dimension.
- 'HEI actively participates in international networks aiming to promote entrepreneurship' (3.33) is the best-ranked item in the 'Internationalization of the institution' dimension.
- The impact of the HEI promotion of entrepreneurship, expressed in dimension 6, obtained the best evaluation for the item 'HEI evaluates the impact of its entrepreneurship promotion strategy and as a result of this evaluation changes the processes' (3.3).

The relationship between the dimensions that influence entrepreneurship and innovation in the HEI and the professional activity of the research population was evaluated, in order to verify whether there were any differences between the three groups in the sample (see Table 3.3).

We found that only the first two dimensions present statistically significant differences, that is, 'Leadership and governance' is the dimension that receives the best evaluation by the three groups, but the course leaders assign a significantly lower evaluation than the other two groups. In fact,

Table 3.3 Factors for entrepreneurship according to the professional group

Dimensions	Directors		Course leaders		Teachers		p
	Average	Standard deviation	Average	Standard deviation	Average	Standard deviation	
Leadership and governance	4.15	1.02	3.51	0.67	3.85	0.65	0.008
Organizational capacity	3.79	1.02	3.23	0.65	3.62	0.68	0.044
Teaching and learning	3.86	1.06	3.23	0.77	3.69	0.73	0.065
Pathways to entrepreneurship	3.89	1.13	3.24	1.07	3.57	0.84	0.195
Interplay between the university and the business sector	3.83	1.06	3.30	1.05	3.70	0.89	0.322
Internationalization of HEIs	3.36	1.29	2.53	1.18	2.81	0.90	0.183*
Impact measurement	3.32	0.95	3.04	1.03	3.24	0.83	0.616

Note: * 1-way ANOVA test.

this professional group always shows a less positive evaluation in all the factors when compared to the directors and teachers. In relation to the 'Organizational capacity' dimension there is also a statistically significant difference between the three groups, due to the lower average evaluation assigned by the course leaders.

Qualitative Results

The qualitative part of this research involved eight interviewees: five people working in the HEI and three from the external community. The results presented in this section refer to the qualitative analysis of the interviews, taking into account different aspects of the interview guide.

Considering the data collected in the interviews, it is clear that in light of the growing demand for higher education institutions to take actions to foster entrepreneurship, INTA Faculties is committed to promoting entrepreneurship. This process involves differentiated management practices, focused on innovation and on the exploitation of opportunities, as well as on the training and mobilization of human resources to create a culture of entrepreneurship. The effectiveness of an HEI policy to promote entrepreneurship in the external community involves establishing partnerships aimed at the regional entrepreneurial fabric, promoting information and technology sharing. It also involves students' internships and scientific research, as well as the development of social responsibility actions (for example, provision of free entrepreneurship training). In addition, within the scope of external partnerships, INTA Faculties has benefited from a solid internationalization strategy, including joint development of educational activities with international institutions and international mobility programmes. The work developed by the HEI in the area of entrepreneurship promotion is subject to systematic evaluations.

In the analysis of the interviews, the necessity to reinforce the organizational capacity to foster entrepreneurship, involving corporate responsibility in the recognition of talent, transparency, equity and autonomy of the members of the academic community, is highlighted. It also involves reinforcing the internationalization strategy via the establishment of partnerships with institutions of higher education aiming at, for example, teacher mobility. In the process of fostering entrepreneurship, the need to involve students in a process of teaching and learning aimed at educating for the promotion of entrepreneurship is emphasized. The impact resulting from the changes brought by the promotion of entrepreneurship within the HEI should be guided by a permanent evaluation.

DISCUSSION OF THE RESULTS

The results of both the qualitative and quantitative analyses are coherent in the evaluation of the INTA Faculties' performance, taking into account the growing challenge posed to higher education institutions to take a positive position in fostering entrepreneurship in the region. This approach is rooted in the management of this HEI, which has been focused on the creation of an entrepreneurship culture. Therefore, the HEI has gathered partners in order to establish a network involving the academic community, the local business community and governmental bodies, through which information and technology sharing are promoted. The strategic dynamics of the HEI to foster entrepreneurship also includes the establishment of international partnerships. The development of partnerships has consolidated the promotion of entrepreneurship in teaching and learning dynamics and reinforced its actions of social responsibility. These partnerships also boost the support provided to potential entrepreneurs in terms of incubation and business funding. INTA Faculties is permanently evaluating the impact of implemented actions for fostering entrepreneurship in the region.

An analysis of the factors where INTA Faculties performs poorly also reveals interesting findings, as it reveals where there is room for improvement. These results point to the necessity to reinforce the process of fostering entrepreneurship, involving strengthening the organizational capacity for its development and implementation; the valuation of talents; and the autonomy of the members of the academic community. In order to overcome this weakness, students should be more involved in the process of teaching and learning aimed at educating for the promotion of entrepreneurship. The HEI should also improve its partnerships, aiming at exchanging knowledge and fostering links with incubators, science parks and other national and international external partnerships, and ensuring access to funding for potential entrepreneurs. The interviews also reveal that the HEI must maintain its permanent concern with the evaluation of the results obtained as a consequence of the promotion of entrepreneurship and the introduction of possible adjustments.

CONCLUSIONS

The study found that INTA Faculties contributed to the development of entrepreneurship at the local and regional levels, and the development of entrepreneurial activities involving synergies based on the work of the academic community and, furthermore, the consolidation of relations in strong and active partnerships with external stakeholders including the public sector, regional and local organizations, small and medium-sized organizations, educational institutions and former students. Fostering entrepreneurship also includes making available to the academic community the necessary conditions for its operations as regards processes of entrepreneurship and business incubation, in which funding reinvests the revenue generated by the entrepreneurial activities. The dimension that presents a lower evaluation is internationalization: HEI needs to place a particular emphasis on this process in order to foster international partnerships and international recruitment of employees who can contribute to promote a culture of entrepreneurship. Another detail that deserves attention is the application of the HEI self-assessment tool (HEInnovate). This is a process to encourage the evaluation of the activities for entrepreneurship development and it provides feedback and review of the strategy and mission of the university in this area. In addition, a questionnaire was used that, given the theoretical framework of research, will allow the universities to self-assess their development on fostering the entrepreneurship.

This study empirically explores the potential of the self-evaluation tool, developed by the European Union, for HEIs to consolidate the efforts of strategies for promoting entrepreneurship and connecting to their environments (local, regional and global).

The implications of the study also involve HEI managers: regarding the in-house actions of contemporary university leaders, much still needs to be done in terms of internal policies that support academic entrepreneurship, relevant training, contracted research and outreach to the surrounding community. Today's economy requires constant innovation, so universities must increasingly open their doors to the private sector, public organizations and society. This is how universities can truly assist entrepreneurs, favouring their regions and countries and bringing economic benefits to academia as well. Higher education also faces global competition and international opportunities, forcing HEIs' managers to think globally and not just locally, to answer the question of what are the university's strategies.

This study proposes and applies a self-assessment tool for the promotion of entrepreneurship for a Brazilian HEI that can and should be used as a tool in their management and strategy definitions (Etzkowitz, 2003). Universities should have a self-assessment department for the promotion of entrepreneurship that is sufficiently flexible and able to intervene in the HEI organizational structure in order to motivate permanent updates to the processes (Clark, 1998; Röpke, 1998; Kirby et al., 2011). Furthermore, this study and tool also opens the debate over whether the governmental bodies, within the educational services, can use the self-evaluation tool in the process of fostering the entrepreneurial mission of HEIs.

A study of this nature entails some limitations, which we intend to identify, and briefly present. First, the results were obtained through the adaptation of a questionnaire initially constructed for the evaluation of European HEIs and adapted to the specifics of a Brazilian HEI (case study). The need for a tool that can consider the specific Brazilian reality is one objective of this work. A second limitation concerns the representativeness of the sample, taking into account that, despite the questionnaire being applied to all managers, course leaders and teachers, only 57 people were included, and therefore our conclusions are limited to represent INTA Faculties.

However, despite the limitations present in this research, it allowed us to detect several areas worthy of future research. The application of the HEInnovate tool to other HEIs in Brazil and to different geographic regions would give a clear perception of the adjustment that may be needed for a general tool, taking into account the stage of economic development and the entrepreneurial culture. We suggest the questionnaire is applied to another type of group or sample, considering all the members of the academic community.

In conclusion, we argue that the field of entrepreneurial university studies is a source of potential research of great interest to the academic community, policy makers and civil society. The entrepreneurial university reinforces its orientation towards innovation and the development of an entrepreneurial culture, which involves a new managerial attitude with effects on leadership, planning, academic community, external sources of financing, internal and external partnerships.

REFERENCES

Abreu, M., Demirel, P., Grinevich, V. and Karatas-Özkan, M. (2016), 'Entrepreneurial practices in research-intensive and teaching-led universities', *Small Business Economics*, **47**(3), 695–717.

Barnes, T., Pashby, I. and Gibbons, A. (2002), 'Effective university–industry interaction: a multi-case evaluation of collaborative R&D projects', *European Management Journal*, **20**(3), 272–285.

Bozeman, B., Fay, D. and Slade, C.P. (2013), 'Research collaboration in universities and academic entrepreneurship: the-state-of-the-art', *Journal of Technology Transfer*, **38**(1), 1–67.

Brown, R. (2016), 'Mission impossible? Entrepreneurial universities and peripheral regional innovation systems', *Industry and Innovation*, **23**(2), 189–205.

Byrne, J. and Fayolle, A. (2010), *University Graduate Entrepreneurship Support: Policy Issues, Good Practices and Recommendations*, OECD. Available at: http://www.oecd.org/edu/imhe/46588578.pdf (accessed 20 June 2015).

Clark, B. (1998), 'Creating entrepreneurial universities: organizational pathways of transformation', *Issues in Higher Education*, **12**(3), 373–374.
Clark, B. (2003), *Creating Entrepreneurial Universities*, Oxford: IAU Press Elsevier Science.
Crow, M. (2008), 'Building an entrepreneurial university', Third Annual Kauffman Foundation-Max Plank Institute, Entrepreneurship Research Conference, Munich, Germany.
Culkin, N. and Mallick, S. (2011), 'Producing work-ready graduates: the role of the entrepreneurial university', *International Journal of Market Research*, **53**(3), 347–368
De Zilwa, D. (2005), 'Using entrepreneurial activities as a means of survival: investigating the processes used by Australian universities to diversify their revenue streams', *Higher Education*, **50**(3), 387–411.
Etzkowitz, H. (1983), 'Entrepreneurial scientists and entrepreneurial universities in American academic science', *Minerva*, **21**(2/3), 198–233
Etzkowitz, H. (2002), 'Incubation of incubators: innovation as a triple helix of university–industry–government networks', *Science and Public Policy*, **29**(2), 115–128.
Etzkowitz, H. (2003), 'Research groups as "quasi-firms": the invention of the entrepreneurial university', *Research Policy*, **32**(1), 109–121.
Etzkowitz, H., Mello, C. De and Almeida, M. (2005), 'Towards "meta-innovation" in Brazil: the evolution of the incubator and the emergence of a triple helix', *Research Policy*, **34**(4), 411–424.
Fayolle, A., Gailly, B. and Lassas-Clerc, N. (2006), 'Assessing the impact of entrepreneurship education programmes: a new methodology', *Journal of European Industrial Training*, **30**(9), 701–720.
Gianiodis, P.T., Markman, G.D. and Panagopoulos, A. (2016), 'Entrepreneurial universities and overt opportunism', *Small Business Economics*, **47**(3), 609–631.
Gibb, A. (2012), 'Exploring the synergistic potential in entrepreneurial university development: towards the building of a strategic framework', *Annals of Innovation and Entrepreneurship*. Available at http://www.innovationandentrepreneurship.net/index.php/aie/article/view/16742 (accessed 25 February 2017).
Guenther, J. and Wagner, K. (2008), 'Getting out of the ivory tower – new perspectives on the entrepreneurial university', *European Journal of International Management*, **2**(4), 400–417.
Guerrero, M., Cunningham, J.A. and Urbano, D. (2015), 'Economic impact of entrepreneurial universities' activities: an exploratory study of the United Kingdom', *Research Policy*, **44**(3), 748–764.
Guerrero, M., Urbano, D., Fayolle, A., Klofsten, M. and Mian, S. (2016), 'Entrepreneurial universities: emerging models in the new social and economic landscape', *Small Business Economics*, **47**(3), 551–563.
Harrison, R.T. and Leitch, C. (2010), 'Voodoo institution or entrepreneurial university? Spin-off companies, the entrepreneurial system and regional development in the UK', *Regional Studies*, **44**(9), 1241–1262.
HEInnovate (2014), *What is HEInnovate?* Available at: https://heinnovate.eu/intranet/tef_guide/ (accessed 28 June 2015).
Jacob, M., Lundqvist, M. and Hellsmark, H. (2003), 'Entrepreneurial transformations in the Swedish university system: the case of Chalmers University of Technology', *Research Policy*, **32**(9), 1555–1568.

Kirby, D.A. (2006), 'Creating entrepreneurial university in the UK: applying entrepreneurship theory to practice', *Journal of Technology Transfer*, **31**(5), 599–603.
Kirby, D.A., Urbano, D. and Guerrero, M. (2011), 'Making universities more entrepreneurial: development of a model', *Canadian Journal of Administrative Sciences*, **28**(3), 302–316.
Lehrer, M., Nell, P. and Gaerber, L. (2009), 'A national systems view of university entrepreneurialism: inferences from comparison of the German and US experience', *Research Policy*, **38**(2), 268–280.
Mascarenhas, C., Marques, C.S., Galvão, A. and Santos, G. (2017), 'Entrepreneurial university: towards a better understanding of past trends and future directions', *Journal of Enterprising Communities: People and Places in the Global Economy*, **11**(3), 316–338.
Mets, T. (2015), 'Entrepreneurial business model for classical research university', *Engineering Economics*, **66**(1), 80–89.
Miller, K., Mcadam, R., Moffett, S., Alexander, A. and Puthusserry, P. (2016), 'Knowledge transfer in university quadruple helix ecosystems: an absorptive capacity perspective', *R and D Management*, **46**(2), 383–399.
Mok, K.H. (2013), 'The quest for an entrepreneurial university in East Asia: impact on academics and administrators in higher education', *Asia Pacific Education Review*, **14**(1), 11–22.
OECD (2012), 'European Commission–Organisation for Economic Co-operation and Development: a guiding framework for entrepreneurial universities'. Available at: http://www.oecd.org/site/cfecpr/ECOECD%20Entrepreneurial%20 Universities%2.
Röpke, J. (1998), *The Entrepreneurial University: Innovation, Academic Knowledge Creation and Regional Development in a Globalized Economy*, Marburg: Philipps-Universitat Marburg.
Rothaermel, F. and Thursby, M. (2007), 'University–incubator firm knowledge flows: assessing their impact on incubator firm performance', *Research Policy*, **34**(7), 305–320.
Rubens, A., Spigarelli, F., Cavicchi, A. and Rinaldi, C. (2017), 'Universities' third mission and the entrepreneurial university and the challenges they bring to higher education institutions', *Journal of Enterprising Communities: People and Places in the Global Economy*, **11**(3), 354–372.
Sam, C. and van der Sijde, P. (2014), 'Understanding the concept of the entrepreneurial university from the perspective of higher education models', *Higher Education*, **68**(6), 891–908.
Siegel, D.S., Waldman, D. and Link, A. (2003), 'Assessing the impact of organizational practices on the relative productivity of university technology transfer offices: an exploratory study', *Research Policy*, **32**(1), 27–48.
Sirén, C.A., Kohtamäki, M. and Kuckertz, A. (2012), 'Exploration and exploitation strategies, profit performance, and the mediating role of strategic learning: escaping the exploitation trap', *Strategic Entrepreneurship Journal*, **6**(1), 18–41.
Sperrer, M., Mueller, C. and Soos, J. (2016), 'The concept of the entrepreneurial university applied to universities of technology in Austria: already reality or a vision of the future?', *Technology Innovation Management Review*, **6**(10), 37–44.
Stake, R.E. (2005), 'Qualitative case studies', in N.K. Denzin and Y.S. Lincoln (eds), *The SAGE Handbook of Qualitative Research*, 3rd edn, Thousand Oaks, CA: SAGE Publications, 433–466.
Svensson, P., Klofsten, M. and Etzkowitz, H. (2012), 'An entrepreneurial university

strategy for renewing a declining industrial city: the Norrköping way', *European Planning Studies*, **20**(4), 505–525.

Urbano, D. and Guerrero, M. (2013), 'Entrepreneurial universities: socioeconomic impacts of academic entrepreneurship in a European region', *Economic Development Quarterly*, **27**(1), 40–55.

Zhang, Q., MacKenzie, N.G., Jones-Evans, D. and Huggins, R. (2016), 'Leveraging knowledge as a competitive asset? The intensity, performance and structure of universities' entrepreneurial knowledge exchange activities at a regional level', *Small Business Economics*, **47**(3), 657–675.

4. A systemic approach for universities in the knowledge-based society: a qualitative study*

Ademar Schmitz, Gertrudes A. Dandolini, João A. de Souza, Maribel Guerrero and David Urbano

INTRODUCTION

Knowledge has become an important production and development factor in current society, known as the knowledge-based society (Audretsch, 2014; Etzkowitz, 2013; O'Shea et al., 2005). This means that economic and social development of regions, states and countries are strongly related to their ability to deal with knowledge. Therefore, universities, as organizations that produce, disseminate and with great potential to disseminate and apply knowledge, have started to play a larger role in the economy and in society (Etzkowitz, 2003a, 2003b), becoming a key element in innovation systems (Etzkowitz et al., 2000). The rise of the knowledge-based society has made higher education even more important for individuals and for society (Sam and van der Sijde, 2014).

In the knowledge-based society, universities are increasingly challenged to become more socially and economically relevant organizations (Nelles and Vorley, 2011). To do so, universities have gone through some changes, called academic revolutions. A first revolution added the mission of generating knowledge through research to the traditional mission of preserving and transmitting knowledge (teaching) with which the university was established. Then, a second revolution made economic and social development a third mission of universities in addition to teaching and research (Etzkowitz, 2003a). Originating as a medieval organization for the conservation and transmission of knowledge, the university has evolved over the centuries into an organization in which knowledge is also created and put to use (Etzkowitz, 2013).

In addition, in the knowledge-based society universities need to interact closely with industry and government for the achievement of socio-economic development, known as the triple helix of innovation. The triple helix of innovation refers to the interweaving of university, industry and government with a pattern of linkages to advance economic and social development through the strategy of innovation (Etzkowitz et al., 2000). It implies the breaking down of traditional organizational, cultural and normative barriers that in the past have separated these spheres to the detriment of economic competitiveness and technological progress (Etzkowitz et al., 2000).

The need to fulfil the three missions simultaneously, and the need to closely interact with industry and government for socio-economic development, implies and requires changes in the function and structure of universities (Etzkowitz et al., 2000; Goldstein, 2010). Realignments include new understandings and metrics for the traditional teaching and research missions, internal organizational changes that are more conducive to interdisciplinarity and collaborations with government and industry, new modes of governance and management, and new organizational capacities (Goldstein, 2010), among others.

These changes in universities have gained substantial importance in recent literature and they are usually discussed from the perspective of innovation (Clark, 1996; van Vught, 1999) and entrepreneurship (Clark, 1998; Etzkowitz, 2003a, 2003b; Etzkowitz et al., 2000; Guerrero et al., 2015; Urbano and Guerrero, 2013). Studies claim that the changes taking placed within universities somehow manifest themselves in the form of innovation and entrepreneurship activities. These activities include both traditional activities of innovation and entrepreneurship, more related to economic development, and those related to social development (Abreu and Grinevich, 2013). The literature also claims that these activities, besides contributing to economic and social development, should contribute to the sustainability of the university (Etzkowitz, 1998; Etzkowitz et al., 2000; Philpott et al., 2011).

Despite the increasing scientific literature on innovation and entrepreneurship in the academic setting, the literature is still fragmented and broadly conceptualized (Rothaermel et al., 2007; Mars and Rios-Aguilar, 2010; Nelles and Vorley, 2011; Wood, 2011; Urbano and Guerrero, 2013; Miller et al., 2018), requiring more systematic and holistic studies (Guenther and Wagner, 2008; Wood, 2011; Mazdeh et al., 2013; Ribeiro-Soriano and Urbano, 2009; Urbano and Guerrero, 2013), including both economic and social aspects of innovation and entrepreneurship within universities (Mars and Rios-Aguilar, 2010; Wood, 2011; Abreu and Grinevich, 2013; Mazdeh et al., 2013).

Furthermore, no study has been identified considering systematically innovation and entrepreneurship together at theoretical and empirical levels within universities (Schmitz et al., 2017a). Therefore, and considering universities as complex organizations (Baldridge, 1980; Baldridge et al., 1997; Grigg, 1994; Lockwood, 1985; Mainardes et al., 2011), it seems plausible to study innovation and entrepreneurship in the academic setting from the perspective of complex systems (Axelrod and Cohen, 2000; Bunge, 2003; von Bertalanffy, 1968).

Complex systems, also known as complex systems theory or complexity science, is a scientific field that studies common properties of complex systems that might appear in nature, society and science. One research approach in the realm of complex systems theory is systemism, proposed by Bunge (1997, 2000, 2003, 2004), in which both individual agency and structure are considered within a given context (Bunge, 2003, 2004). Systemism applies to systems in general, but it has found in the social sciences the most relevant discussions and applications (Casti, 1981; Gräbner and Kapeller, 2015; Hofkirchner, 2007; Pickel, 2004, 2007; Reihlen et al., 2007; Schneider, 2013; Wan, 2011, 2012a, 2012b).

To study innovation and entrepreneurship within universities from the perspective of complex systems theory, it is argued that universities are social systems in the context of the knowledge-based society that through knowledge creation, dissemination and application need to contribute to socio-economic development, while preserving their own sustainability. It is further argued that innovation and entrepreneurship are mechanisms that allow universities to do so.

This chapter aims to explore innovation and entrepreneurship in the academic setting from the perspective of complex systems. It tries to understand how innovation and entrepreneurship support universities to contribute to regional socio-economic development and to preserve their own sustainability, considering four universities in two different regions and countries: Catalonia in Spain (Universitat Autònoma de Barcelona, UAB; and University of Barcelona, UB) and Rio Grande do Sul in Brazil (Pontifical Catholic University of Rio Grande do Sul, PUC-RS; and University of Vale do Rio dos Sinos, UNISINOS). More specifically, this study tries to identify the systemic elements of the university in the context of the knowledge-based society, with emphasis on the mechanisms related to innovation and entrepreneurship that enable universities to contribute to regional socio-economic development and to preserve their own sustainability.

This chapter makes theoretical and practical contributions. Theoretical contributions include a unique discussion related to modelling universities as social systems in the context of the knowledge-based society from the perspective of complex systems. This is especially relevant because it gives a systemic view of innovation and entrepreneurship in the academic setting, allowing not only the study of the events, but also the study of the components of the system, its environment, and their inter-relations. Practical contributions include the fact that finding mechanisms allows not only understanding of the system, but also the possibility of controlling it. In this sense, understanding the mechanisms that make the system behave the way is does, allows the creation of more adequate policies to increase the performance of universities.

By considering this broader view of innovation and entrepreneurship within universities, this research considers the three main aspects of this book: collaboration, education and policies. Collaboration is considered both in the sense of collaborative research and in the interaction of the university with industry, government and communities. Education is considered especially when discussing entrepreneurship education, but also through other activities of the university that are crucial to the training of entrepreneurial students and business creation. Finally, policies are considered both from the internal perspective, that is, policies related to innovation and entrepreneurship; and from the external perspective, that is, public policies that affect the university and public policies created from the university's participation in society.

This chapter is organized as follows. After this brief introduction, the conceptual framework is presented. The next section brings the methodological procedures by which the study was conducted. The main results of the multiple cases are then presented, considering within and cross-case analysis. The final section presents the main conclusions, the limitations, and future research lines.

CONCEPTUAL FRAMEWORK

Literature Review

Schmitz et al. (2017a) conducted an extensive and detailed systematic literature review on innovation and entrepreneurship in the academic setting, consisting of bibliometric and content analysis of relevant scientific literature. Bibliometric analysis showed an increasing and multidisciplinary literature on innovation and entrepreneurship in the academic setting: articles have been published for more than 40 years, with a significant increase over the last decade. Journals and research areas showed that innovation and entrepreneurship within universities are being studied by several disciplines and areas, but business and economics prevail: more than half the articles originated from these areas. Keyword analysis showed that innovation and entrepreneurship studies within universities are closely related to management, and the predominance of entrepreneurship (academic entrepreneurship, university entrepreneurship, entrepreneurial university) over innovation (academic innovation, university innovation, innovative university), even though the term 'innovation' by itself appeared more than 'entrepreneurship'. Furthermore, bibliometric analysis showed that studies predominantly originated in the United States of America (USA) and Europe. While the USA figures as the country with the largest number of articles, European universities prevail among those that have the largest number of publications (Schmitz et al., 2017a).

Content analysis consisted of the identification of main terms and their respective definitions, research approaches and units of analysis, theoretical frameworks, and empirical models. Academic innovation, university innovation, innovative university, academic entrepreneurship, university entrepreneurship and entrepreneurial university, with some variations such as university entrepreneurialism and innovation university, were identified as the main terms being used. These terms and their respective definitions' analysis showed that, despite the increasing literature, it is still fragmented and undertheorized. However, regardless of this fragmentation, the term 'entrepreneurial university' best represents a university that embraces the missions of creating, disseminating and applying knowledge for economic and social development, in addition to pursuing improved sustainability for itself. Definitions do not show a clear relation between innovation and entrepreneurism within universities, and there is no clear evidence that the terms 'innovation' and 'entrepreneurism' in the academic setting are used in coherence with the traditional definitions of innovation and entrepreneurism (Schmitz et al., 2017a).

Research approaches analysis showed that among the theoretical studies, nine did not explicitly specify their research design, and four are based on literature reviews. Among the empirical studies, nine used surveys and/or questionnaires, another nine used case studies, in six studies interviews were used, and other five used qualitative or quantitative approaches on secondary data. Some empirical studies used more than one research technique, such as interviews and questionnaires, or study cases and interviews. As for the unit of analysis of the empirical studies, the university level prevailed (with one exception only), being the university from different countries, mainly from Europe and the USA. Only a few studies considered universities from more than one country (European countries only; or European countries, Latin American countries and the USA) (Schmitz et al., 2017a).

Both theoretical frameworks and empirical models are very heterogeneous and originated from different disciplines and research areas. Despite the heterogeneity of both theoretical and empirical studies in their theoretical frameworks, four groups of articles were formed. The first group is composed of those studies, both theoretical and empirical, discussing innovation and entrepreneurship in the academic setting based on changes that occur inside universities and on their relations with government and industry knowledge-based society, based on academic revolutions, the triple helix of innovation, higher education models, substantive academic growth, and innovative organizations, among others (Schmitz et al., 2017a).

The second group is formed by empirical articles studying the factors affecting the creation and development of entrepreneurial universities, and the respective economic and social impacts. This group of studies is based on institutional economics, resource-based theory and endogenous growth theory, and represents a very consistent set of articles. The third group is formed by those articles, both theoretical and empirical, which explain innovation and entrepreneurship in the university based on the definitions of academic entrepreneurship, academic innovation, university entrepreneurship, academic entrepreneurship, academic innovation and the entrepreneurial university. Finally, the fourth group of articles is composed of those studies investigating ways to define and measure the performance of universities related to entrepreneurship, based on entrepreneurship, entrepreneurial intensity and entrepreneurial orientation (Schmitz et al., 2017a).

As for the empirical models, even though they also originated from different disciplines and research areas, analysis showed that different terms (academic entrepreneurship, academic innovation and entrepreneurial university) share the same components and variables. There are no clear boundaries to the different models and components being used. Furthermore, the models are very fragmented and there is no model considering holistically and systematically both innovation and entrepreneurship within universities (Schmitz et al., 2017a).

Schmitz et al. (2017b) present an extensive list of activities related to innovation and entrepreneurship in the academic setting. The activities are related to teaching, research and other functions of the university. By supporting academic entrepreneurship, universities can address several expectations whilst also becoming more entrepreneurial. However, more knowledge is needed on how this support is provided by different levels in the university organization (Bienkowska et al., 2016).

In Ratten (2017), literature about entrepreneurial universities is reviewed with a focus on the role of communities, people and places. She argues that the entrepreneurial universities need to consider the people in society in terms of how they relate to learning, education and teaching about new ideas and business practices. Complementing this, Saiz-Santos et al. (2017) show how educational innovation in entrepreneurship and technology transfer consolidates the third mission and transforms universities into entrepreneurial organizations.

Despite the development of the area, research is fragmented and lacks coherent frameworks and conceptualizations that fully depict its dynamic (Miller et al., 2018). Consequently, a systemic view of this phenomenon is missing in order to understand how innovation and entrepreneurship support universities to contribute to regional socio-economic development, while preserving their own sustainability.

Systemism Approach

According to Bunge (2000, 2003), there are three main worldviews and research approaches in social studies. One is individualism, according to which everything is either an individual or a collection of individuals (Bunge, 2003). Another is holism, according to which the universe is an undifferentiated blob, so that every part of it influences every other part (Bunge, 2003). However, both individualism and holism are deficient. Individualism, by only studying the components of social systems, overlooks their structure (Bunge, 2000), ignoring the emergent properties of the system (Bunge, 1979). Holism, on the other hand, by only studying the structure of social systems, plays down individual action (Bunge, 2000), refusing to explain emergent properties (Bunge, 1979). The alternative to both individualism and holism is systemism, according to which everything is either a system or a component of a system, and every system has peculiar (emergent) properties that its components lack, making room for both individual agency and social structure (Bunge, 2000).

According to systemism, social science research is about social systems research, in which society is not an unstructured collection of independent individuals, but a system of interrelated individuals organized into systems (Bunge, 2000). Therefore, the emergence, maintenance or dismantling of any social system can ultimately be explained in terms of individual preferences, decisions and actions, but these individual events are largely determined by social context (Bunge, 2000). This means that in order to model and understand a social system, it is necessary to take into consideration what it consists of, the environment in which it is located, how its components and environmental items are related to one another, and how it works. This means that a system can be designed in terms of its composition, environment, structure and mechanism (Bunge, 2003), as shown in Table 4.1.

Table 4.1 Elements of a system according to systemism

Symbol	Element	Description
C(s)	Composition	Collection of all the parts of s
E(s)	Environment	Collection of items, other than those in s, that act on or are acted upon by some or all components of s
S(s)	Structure	Collection of relations, in particular bonds, among components of s or among these and items in its environment
M(s)	Mechanism	Collection of processes in s that make it behave the way it does

Source: Bunge (2003).

The system's composition is the collection of all parts of the system (Bunge, 2003). In the case of social systems, composition at a micro level is made up of individuals and artefacts (Bunge, 2003). The system's environment is the collection of items, other than those in the system, that act on or are acted upon by some or all components of the system (Bunge, 2003). In the case of social systems, environment may include aspects of society, economy and politics, among many others. The system's structure is the collection of relations, in particular bonds, among components of the system, and among these and items in its environment (Bunge, 2003). In the case of social systems, structures are real bounds (Bunge, 2004), such as rules and conventions. Finally, the system's mechanism is the collection of processes that make it behave the way it does (Bunge, 2003), that is, the processes that bring or prevent some change in the system (Bunge, 1997, 2003). In the case of social systems, these are social mechanisms, which are processes involving at least two agents engaged in forming, maintaining, transforming or dismantling the system (Bunge, 1996).

Even though systemism ontology is very clear, its methodology, as in any other approach to modelling complex systems, brings some challenges (Pickel, 2007), including the definition of the entities to be considered (von Bertalanffy, 1968) and the identification of the interactions between components (Axelrod and Cohen, 2000). In the case of systemism, only notions of the composition, environment, structure and mechanism at a given level are used (Bunge, 2003). This is because to model complex systems requires the knowledge of all parts of the system and of all their interactions, as well as all their links with the rest of the world, which is unwieldy in practice. Furthermore, even though systemism postulates that social systems are concrete entities, this does not make them self-evident

Table 4.2 Methodological prescription for systemism

No.	Step description
1	Recognize the study object as a social system, placing it into a wider context
2	Conjecture the system's composition, environment and structure
3	Distinguish the various levels of the system and exhibit their relations
4	Hypothesize the mechanism that keep the system running or leads to its decay or growth
5	Test empirically the hypothesized mechanisms considering the conjectured system
6.1	If hypotheses are true, explain the system functioning based on the proposed model
6.2	Otherwise, refine or modify the model and start again

Sources: Bunge (1997, 2000, 2003).

and easily observable (Pickel, 2007). Therefore, they have to be conjectured in order to be modelled (Pickel, 2007).

The overall procedure presented in Table 4.2 might be used as a methodological prescription, allowing studies to be conducted at both the theoretical and the empirical levels. The first step is to recognize the study object as a social system within a wider context. In the second step, the system has to be broken down into its composition, environment and structure. As social systems are real, but partly hidden (Pickel, 2007), their composition, environment and structure can only be conjectured (Bunge, 1997). The third step is to distinguish the various levels of the system and exhibit their relations. In some cases, the relationship between the components of a system, and between the systems and its environment, does not need to be reduced to its individual constituent parts (Bunge, 2003; Schneider, 2013). The fourth step is to hypothesize the mechanism that keeps the system running or leads to its decay or growth. By focusing on social mechanisms, it is possible to offer an intermediary level of explanation that avoids theorizing at a level that is either to abstract or too close to the empirical data (Pickel, 2004; Schneider, 2013). In the fifth step, the hypothesized mechanisms have to be tested. The conjectured system needs to be empirically testable if it is to be regarded as scientific (Bunge, 1997). Finally, in the sixth step, if the hypothesized mechanisms turn out be true, the system's functioning might be explained. Otherwise, the model will need to be refined or modified, and tested again.

Systemic Framework

Universities are social systems formed by individuals and artefacts, inside an economic, political and social context. Dynamic and non-linear interactions between the internal components of a university, and between these and its environment, also make them complex systems. Therefore, universities can be studied from the perspective of complex social systems. Systemism, in particular, allows integrating the three levels of innovation and entrepreneurship in the academic setting: at individual, organization and interaction levels (Ropke, 1998; Guerrero and Urbano, 2012; Urbano and Guerrero, 2013). As argued by Bunge (2000), systemism makes room for both individual agency (individual level) and social structure (organizational level), and emphasizes the role of the environment (interaction level) and the mechanisms that allow it to behave the way it does.

Figure 4.1 depicts a university as a social system, in the context of the knowledge-based society, according to systemism. The university is organized considering micro (individual) and macro (organization) levels, in which individuals contribute to the organization, and the organization affects the individuals. This is represented by bottom-up and top-down bounds and processes.

The university operates in the context of the knowledge-based society, whose main elements are industry, government and communities. The relation of the university with these elements of the environment is also given by bounds and processes. Bounds are formal and informal relations among the components of the university, and among these and those from the knowledge society. Processes, on the other hand, are the mechanisms that allow the university operate the way it does. As argued by Bunge (2003), this conceptual framework allows us to understand the system not only in terms of inputs and outputs, but also in terms of its structure and mechanisms.

Social systems are composed of individuals and artefacts (Bunge, 2003). As such, universities are composed of individuals such as students, faculty, staff and managers, and artefacts such as laboratories, databases and technologies. Individuals and artefacts might be grouped at intermediary levels, according to their roles in academic or administrative structures. Examples of such groupings are classes, research projects, academic departments and administrative departments. Both physical and intellectual technologies, such as computers, networks and systems, might be considered. Even though artefacts do not have agency, they influence the way individuals act and interact in the organization and with the environment.

Social systems' environment includes society, economy and politics (Bunge, 2003). Currently, universities operate in the knowledge-based

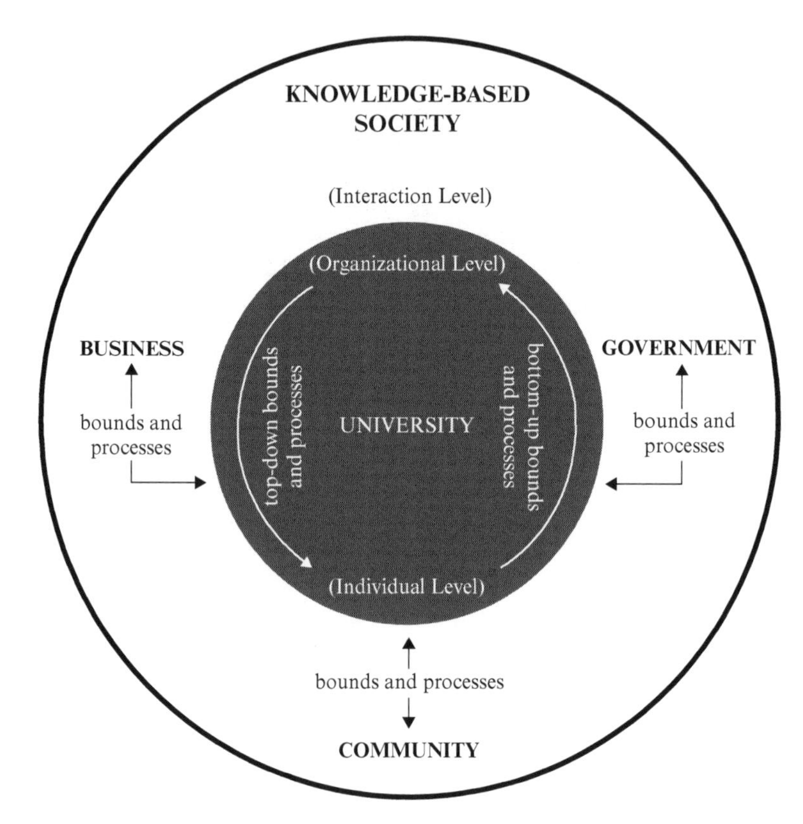

Figure 4.1 A systemic conceptual framework for innovation and entrepreneurship in the academic setting

society, which they affect and are affected by. Therefore, universities' operations are based on not only the individual inputs and outputs, but also the characteristics of their environment. As argued by Etzkowitz et al. (2000), in the knowledge society, universities need to closely interact with industry and government for socio-economic development. However, in order to consider both economic and social aspects of innovation and entrepreneurship, communities also need to be considered. To foster social innovation and entrepreneurship, communities should be considered and involved in the process of knowledge generation (Murray et al., 2010).

The structure of a system is defined by the relations among its components (endostructure), and among its components and those of the environment (exostructure) (Bunge, 2003). Internally, the components of the university are related according to their academic and administrative roles. According to their academic roles, they can be grouped to form classes and project teams, but also act together informally. Concerning the exo-structure, two types of relations can be identified: input and output. Input relations are where elements of the environment affect componemnts of the system. Output relations are where components of the system affect the environment.

A mechanism is a process in a concrete system, such that it is capable of bringing about or preventing some change in the system as a whole or in some of its subsystems (Bunge, 1997). It is hypothesized that innovation and entrepreneurship are mechanisms that allow universities to constantly adapt and respond to challenges imposed by the knowledge society. Innovation and entrepreneurship are considered to be continuous and complementary processes that allow production systems and social standards be replaced by new or better ones (Schmitz et al., 2017a). Mechanisms can take the form of agency–structure relations (bottom-up mechanism or upward causation), or structure–agency relations (top-down mechanisms or downward causation). They can also take the form of input–output relations, linking the components of the system with those of the environment.

METHODOLOGY

This exploratory and descriptive study was conducted using a multiple-case study. Research design and execution is based on Yin (2014) and Eisenhardt (1989). According to Eisenhardt (1989), cases have to be defined theoretically, not randomly. This means that case studies are used for analytic generalization instead of statistical generalization. Universities were chosen in similar environments, allowing the study to concentrate on their systemic elements. This means that cases were selected predicting similar results, for literal replication.

A small number of universities was selected in order to provide information-rich cases. Information-rich cases are those from with one can learn a great deal about issues of central importance to the purpose of the research (Patton, 2002). Four universities were considered, from two different regions and countries: from Barcelona (Catalonia, Spain) the Universitat Autònoma de Barcelona (UAB) and University of Barcelona (UB); and from Porto Alegre (Rio Grande do Sul, Brazil) the Pontifical Catholic University of Rio Grande do Sul (PUC-RS) and the University of Vale do Rio dos Sinos (UNISINOS).

As case studies allow multiple data collecting techniques and procedures (Yin, 2014; Eisenhardt, 1989), interviews, documents and direct observation were used as data sources. According to Yin (2014), multiple sources of evidence allow not only complementing data, but also data triangulation. Direct observation was conducted by visiting each university campus, observing the university management, academic departments, science and research parks, incubator facilities, and so on. Semi-structured interviews were conducted with three or four university managers related to innovation and entrepreneurship for each case. Documents such as university statutes, strategic planning, intellectual property policies and webpage information were collected before and after direct observation and interviews. Documents collected *a priori* allowed for better context knowledge during visiting and interviewing. Documents collected *a posteriori* complemented information on each case.

Interviews were transcribed in their respective languages. Following Yin (2014), the multiple sources of evidence were organized into a text study database, in order to be coded and to maintain a chain of evidence. NVivo® software was used for the study database and to code the data. Data analysis started by coding collected data, following Saldaña (2013). Two coding cycles were executed. In each cycle, a combination of two coding methods was used. Structural codification allowed assigning data to the concepts representing the elements of the systemic approach being used. It met the exploratory objective of the research. On the other hand, descriptive codification allowed assigning labels to the data to provide an inventory of each specific element of the systemic approach, thus meeting the descriptive objective of the research.

Initial codes were generated based on the proposed conceptual framework, and new codes were created as needed throughout the first coding cycle (descriptive coding). At the end of the first descriptive coding cycle, codes were evaluated in order to verify their appropriateness to the systemic view (structural coding). After the structural coding was completed, a new cycle of coding was carried out in order to make sure that coding resulting from the first cycle coding was correct and that all the data had been properly coded. Descriptive and structural coding were used in parallel during second cycle coding.

Following Eisenhardt (1989), who suggests two steps in data analysis – analysis of within-case data, and searching for cross-case patterns in cases – the second part of the data analysis consisted of within-case data analysis and cross-case data analysis, as both within-case and cross-case analyses focus on the system's mechanisms.

RESULTS

Structural coding resulted in the elements shown in Figure 4.2, based on the CESM model of the systemism approach. Related to the system's

- CESM – Composition
  - Macro Level
    - Academic Organization
    - Management Organization
  - Micro Level
    - Artefacts
    - Individuals
- CESM – Environment
  - Community
  - Government
  - Industry
- CESM – Mechanism
  - Dimension 1 – Teaching
  - Dimension 2 – Research
  - Dimension 3 – Extension
  - Dimension 4 – Management
- CESM – Structure
  - Level 1 – People (micro–macro)
  - Level 2 – Organization (micro–macro)
  - Level 3 – Relations (input–output)

Figure 4.2 Final coding structure based on the multiple case studies

composition, at the micro level, evidence was found showing artefacts and individuals as the main components. Artefacts include knowledge, technology, systems, projects, plans, and so on; and individuals include students, staff, faculty, managers and other people from the university community. At the macro level, academic organization and management organization were identified as two main forms of organization.

As for the system's environment, it turned out that industry (funding departments, marketing departments, research departments), government (public policy agencies, grant agencies, public research centres) and communities (neighbourhoods, social organizations, non-governmental organizations) are the main elements of the knowledge society with which the universities interact. Communities can be seen as people living in a given area, people having some common characteristics, and even business associations (communities of businesses).

Related to the system's structure, three levels of innovation and entrepreneurship were identified. The first level is related to people, and it represents the individual agency (micro–macro). The second level is related to the organization itself, and it represents the social structure of the university (macro–micro). Finally, the third level is related to the interaction of the university with its environment (input–output). At this level, there are interactions related to knowledge-push (output), society-pull (input) and social interaction (input–output).

Finally, structural coding revealed the mechanisms related to teaching, research, extension and management, considered in this study as the main functions of the university. Curriculum innovation, pedagogical innovation, entrepreneurship education and technology capacitation were identified as the main mechanisms related to the teaching function.

Entrepreneurship nucleuses were identified as physical structures supporting innovation and entrepreneurship in teaching.

Related to the research function, applied research, collaboration and cooperation, intellectual property preservation, project and contract management, and research publication were identified. Research structures and technological innovation nucleus were identified as the main physical structures supporting innovation and entrepreneurship in research.

Business creation, business hosting, knowledge transfer and specialized services were identified as mechanisms for the extension function, where business incubators, science research and technological parks, technology transfer offices and technological institutes are the main supporting structures.

For the management function, external funding and innovation in processes, in strategy and in structure were identified as the main mechanisms related to innovation and entrepreneurship. It is worth mentioning that the management function comprises both the overall academic and the management organization.

Table 4.3 shows the number of references to each mechanism in the sources of each university studied, which is the result of the descriptive coding. As can be seen, entrepreneurship education, business creation and specialized services are the most referenced mechanisms. On the other hand, research publication and technological capacitation are barely referenced. Mechanisms related to extension are the most referenced, followed by those related to teaching, then research, and finally management.

Table 4.4 gives the evidence found in the sources of each university related to the contribution of each mechanism to regional development (RD) and to the sustainability of the university (SU). Evidence was not found for technological capacitation, nor for research publication. As for pedagogical innovation, only one piece of evidence related to the sustainability of the university was found. In general terms, it can be assumed that mechanisms related to innovation and entrepreneurship in the academic setting do help universities contribute to regional socio-economic development and to maintain their own sustainability.

Within-Case Analysis

Case 1: Universitat Autònoma de Barcelona (UAB)

UAB is located in Cerdanyola del Vallès, Barcelona, Catalonia, Spain. UAB was founded in 1968, fifty years ago, and it has approximately 25 000 students.

Regarding the teaching function, a few references were made to curricular innovation and pedagogical innovation, and technological capacitation

Table 4.3 Coding inventory for the innovation and entrepreneurship mechanisms

Function/mechanism	UAB	UB	PUCRS	UNISINOS	TOTAL
Function Teaching	**23**	**21**	**49**	**30**	**123**
Curriculum Innovation	1	2	3	5	11
Entrepreneurship Education	16	14	32	17	79
Pedagogical Innovation	2	5	3	5	15
Technological Capacitation	0	2	1	2	5
Entrepreneurship Nucleus	*2*	*4*	*8*	*5*	19
Function Research	**17**	**25**	**38**	**34**	**114**
Applied Research	2	6	6	10	24
Collaborative Research	4	4	5	5	18
Intellectual Property Preservation	4	4	4	3	15
Project-Contract Management	4	6	7	8	25
Research Publication	1	0	1	0	2
Research Structures	*5*	*8*	*11*	*3*	27
Technological Innovation Nucleus	*4*	*4*	*4*	*10*	22
Function Extension	**42**	**41**	**68**	**55**	**206**
Business Creation	18	21	13	14	66
Business Incubator	*2*	*2*	*6*	*7*	17
Business Hosting	8	3	11	18	40
Science-Research-Technological Park	*8*	*3*	*11*	*18*	40
Knowledge Transfer	16	15	12	5	48
Technology Transfer Office	*3*	*1*	*4*	*3*	11
Specialized Services	5	18	18	15	56
Technological Institute	*0*	*3*	*3*	*12*	18
Function Management	**17**	**15**	**35**	**23**	**90**
Funding	9	5	9	7	30
Processes	0	0	4	6	10
Strategy	4	3	12	8	27
Structure	0	6	9	10	25

Table 4.4 Evidence related to regional development and university sustainability

Function/ mechanism	UAB		UB		PUCRS		UNISINOS		TOTAL	
	RD	SU	RD	SU	RD	SU	RD	SU	RD	SU
Function Teaching	**2**	**0**	**0**	**0**	**1**	**0**	**0**	**0**	**3**	**0**
Curriculum Innovation	1	1	0	1	1	0	0	0	2	2
Entrepreneurship Education	2	0	0	0	2	2	1	3	5	5
Pedagogical Innovation	0	1	0	0	0	0	0	0	0	1
Technological Capacitation	0	0	0	0	0	0	0	0	0	0
Entrepreneurship Nucleus	*0*	*1*	*0*	*0*	*1*	*1*	*0*	*0*	*1*	*2*
Function Research	**0**	**1**	**0**	**0**	**1**	**0**	**0**	**0**	**1**	**1**
Applied Research	0	1	2	2	3	1	2	1	7	5
Collaboration/ Cooperation	0	0	0	1	0	1	1	0	1	2
Intellectual Property Preservation	0	0	1	1	0	0	0	0	1	1
Project-Contract Management	0	0	1	3	0	2	0	2	1	7
Research Publication	0	0	0	0	0	0	0	0	0	0
Research Structures	*0*	*0*	*0*	*1*	*0*	*0*	*0*	*1*	*0*	*2*
Technological Innovation Nucleus	*0*	*0*	*1*	*0*	*0*	*0*	*0*	*0*	*1*	*0*
Function Extension	**0**	**1**	**1**	**0**	**2**	**1**	**0**	**0**	**3**	**2**
Business Creation	1	4	0	1	2	0	1	1	4	6
Business Incubator	*0*	*0*	*0*	*0*	*0*	*0*	*0*	*0*	*0*	*0*
Business Hosting	3	1	0	0	2	2	6	3	11	6
Science-Research-Technological Park	*0*	*0*	*0*	*0*	*0*	*0*	*0*	*0*	*0*	*0*
Knowledge Transfer	2	2	1	2	1	0	0	0	4	4
Technology Transfer Office	*0*	*0*	*0*	*0*	*0*	*0*	*0*	*0*	*0*	*0*
Specialized Services	0	1	0	0	0	1	1	0	1	2
Technological Institute	*0*	*0*	*0*	*1*	*0*	*0*	*2*	*1*	*2*	*2*
Function Management	**1**	**0**	**0**	**1**	**0**	**0**	**1**	**1**	**2**	**2**
Funding	1	1	0	1	0	4	0	0	1	6
Processes	0	0	0	0	1	0	1	0	2	0
Strategy	1	0	1	0	4	2	2	0	8	2
Structure	0	0	0	0	4	1	0	0	4	1

was not referenced. However, and primarily because of UAB Empren, several references to entrepreneurial education were made. Entrepreneurship education at UAB is supported mainly by UAB Empren, a programme created by UAB to encourage the generation of new ideas and business projects by all members of the university community, but also through activities of the Parc de Recerca UAB (PRUAB), a research park and technological innovation nucleus. In both cases, the need to improve the business skills of students, researchers, and so on is made clear. UAB Empren is UAB's entrepreneurship nucleus.

Concerning the research function, although there are a smaller number of references, there is a better distribution of the references among mechanisms. Applied research, under contracts or in collaboration with companies, was identified and indicated as a way to enhance knowledge transfer. Publication of scientific results, in the perspective of the dissemination of the knowledge generated by the university, was referenced only once. Intellectual property preservation is managed by PRUAB. The roles of research structures and the technological innovation nucleus as support for innovation and entrepreneurship at UAB were also referenced. Research structures are basically laboratories and research centres. UAB's technological innovation nucleus is PRUAB.

The mechanisms related to the extension function are the most referenced in UAB's data, prevailing over those references to businesses creation and knowledge transfer. Business creation is constantly referenced in the UAB Empren programme, which works with students, and in PRUAB, which hosts business incubators that support both UAB researchers (professors, master's/doctoral students) and the companies in the park. Knowledge transfer is prioritized in the scope of PRUAB and is its main mission. Projects and contracts are managed by PRUAB and also directly by the Research Administration of the university. The UAB scientific and technical services are made up of facilities including infrastructure and large-scale equipment dedicated to offering specialized technical services.

Innovation and entrepreneurship in the management function were referred to in UAB's data priority related to external financing and strategy. No references were found to innovation in processes and structures, although they were noticeable during direct observations.

Case 2: Universitat de Barcelona (UB)

UB is located in the city of Barcelona, Catalonia, Spain. It was founded in 1450, with more than 500 years of history. As at 2017, UB had more than 60 000 students.

In the teaching function, references were found to all mechanisms, although curricular innovation and technological capacitation were referenced only twice each. As in the case of UAB, the most referenced mechanism is entrepreneurship education, mainly because of the actions carried out within the Business Department related to innovation and entrepreneurship courses, and by the Barcelona Institute of Entrepreneurship (BIE). The BIE promotes entrepreneurship through various awareness and entrepreneurship training, and it is UB's entrepreneurship nucleus.

Only publication of scientific results was not referenced in UB's data for the research function. Fundació Bosch i Gimpera (FBG) leads the references in these mechanisms with a strong performance in applied research, collaboration and cooperation with companies and the government, and in the projects and contracts management. Intellectual property preservation is also assisted by FBG and by the Patent Centre of UB. Scientific and technological centres support the development of research towards application. FBG is UB's technological innovation nucleus.

FBG is also part of the activities related to the mechanisms of the extension function, primarily acting on technology transfer and in the creation of companies based on the knowledge generated by the university. UB has no formally created business incubator. Support for business creation, especially for students, is also enhanced by BIE. The Parc Científic de Barcelona (PCB) mission is to manage effectively and efficiently the areas that the UB has been assigned to develop its science park. Several references are made to the scientific and technological centres as mechanisms to provide specialized services.

In the management function, no references were found to innovation in processes at UB, but the search for external funding, primarily for research projects and those arising from technology transfer, was referenced. Innovations in strategy and in structure were also referenced, including some leading actions of UB related to innovation and entrepreneurship in the Spanish context.

Case 3: Pontifícia Universidade Católica do Rio Grande do Sul (PUC-RS)

PUC-RS is headquartered in the city of Porto Alegre, Rio Grande do Sul, Brazil. It was founded in 1948, 70 years ago. PUC-RS currently has around 25 000 students, of whom 18 000 are undergraduates and 5000 in graduate studies, and 1000 in other levels of education.

For the teaching function, references were found for all mechanisms, with emphasis on entrepreneurship education. This activity started at the Business School and was recently incorporated into all schools. Originally, entrepreneurship education activities were organized by a Núcleo Empreendedor, and are now organized by IDEAR, an innovation and entrepreneurship laboratory. It involves events and competitions related to entrepreneurship disciplines and programmes focused on the development of innovative and entrepreneurial skills. IDEAR also acts as the entrepreneurship nucleus of PUC-RS, and it produces curriculum and pedagogical innovations.

In the research function, references point to an important role of the Agência de Inovação Tecnológica (AGT), which acts in support of research focused on application, collaboration and cooperation of PUC-RS with companies, government agencies and communities. The AGT also undertakes the project and contracts management. The preservation of intellectual property is carried out by the Escritório de Transferência de Tecnologia (ETT), which acts in this case as the technological innovation nucleus of PUC-RS. Research structures are organized into research nucleus, groups, centres and institutes.

At PUC-RS, mechanisms related to the extension function have the largest number of references. Business creation is supported both RAIAR, a business incubator, and by IDEAR. IDEAR builds the relationship between entrepreneurship education and the business creation. The Parque Tecnológico da PUC-RS (TECNOPUC) was the first structure related to innovation and entrepreneurship of PUC-RS and it represents one of its greatest promoters. The provision of scientific and technological services is carried out through technological centres and institutes, which provide services for research groups of PUC-RS, companies in TECNOPUC, and the external ones with which PUC-RS maintains relationships.

Also in the management function, several references were found to all the mechanisms in PUC-RS's data. PUC-RS's strategy to incorporate innovation and entrepreneurship components into management is the most referenced, followed by the structure that was set up to support these activities and the search for external funding. External funding, which comes from companies and from the government, represents a significant part of PUC-RS's budget.

Case 4: Universidade do Vale do Rio dos Sinos (UNISINOS)

UNISINOS is located in the Porto Alegre area, in São Leopoldo, Rio Grande do Sul, Brazil. Characterized as a community university, it was founded in 1969, nearly 50 years ago. It has approximately 25 000 thousand students, distributed among the various levels of education offered.

In the teaching function, entrepreneurial education was the most referenced, primarily because of the Núcleo de Empreendedorismo e Inovação (NEI), linked to the Business School, but which serves students from all schools. Activities of the NEI lead to curriculum and pedagogical innovations, and to the incubation of business. The interdisciplinarity of students involved in core disciplines is consistently indicated as one of the factors that contributes most to the success of entrepreneurial education at UNISINOS.

The NEI acts as the entrepreneurship nucleus of UNISINOS. Technological capacitation is done by the Technological Institutes of UNISINOS.

In the research function, applied research is organized by the Núcleo de Pesquisa e Pós-Graduação (NPPG) linked to the Academic Pro-Rectory, and by the Parque Tecnológico UNISINOS (TECNOSINOS). These same structures are also responsible for the collaboration and cooperation of UNISINOS with companies and government agencies for the development of joint research. Project and contract management is carried out by the Escritório de Projetos, also linked to the Academic Pro-Rectory. Linked to the NPPG is also the Núcleo de Inovação e Transferência de Tecnologia (NITT) of UNISINOS.

Business creation, related to the extension function, is supported in UNISINOS by the NEI and by UNITEC, a complex for the incubation of new enterprises. TECNOSINOS, in conjunction with the productive sector and government, is responsible for the hosting of companies already constituted. Technological services are offered mainly by the Technological Institutes of UNISINOS.

In the management function, all mechanisms were referenced, with emphasis upon the structures that UNISINOS created to support innovation and entrepreneurship. Also, the pursuit of external support, strategy and processes are often referenced as forms of innovation at UNISINOS.

Cross-Case Analysis

In general terms, and as was expected (cases were selected predicting similar results), the four universities presented similar mechanisms related to innovation and entrepreneurship. Table 4.5 gives the names of the structures related to each mechanism of innovation and entrepreneurship for each of the studied universities.

Technological capacitation is more evident at the Brazilian universities, and UNISINOS gives the most explicit evidence through the Technological Institutes. Spanish universities created their parks and some other structures with different juridical entities. The Brazilian universities, on the other hand, kept all structures under their own National Corporate Registry (NCR). Another difference related to the parks is that UAB and PUC-RS require that companies on campus maintain research relations with the university. On the other hand, UB and UNISINOS do not make such requirements.

Based on these findings, it is possible to better qualify the systemic vision of the university in the knowledge-based society according to systemism, shown in Figure 4.1. Figure 4.3 gives a general overview of the way the mechanisms related to innovation and entrepreneurship in the

Table 4.5 Areas and structures responsible for each mechanism

Function/ mechanism	UAB	UB	PUCRS	UNISINOS
Function Teaching				
Curriculum Innovation				
Entrepreneurship Education	UAB Empren	BIE	IDEAR	NIE
Pedagogical Innovation				
Technological Capacitation				Technological Institutes
Entrepreneurship Nucleus	UAB Empren	*BIE*	*IDEAR*	*NEI*
Function Research				
Applied Research				
Collaboration/ Cooperation	PRUAB	FBG	TECNOPUC, AGT	TECNOSINOS, UNITEC, NITT
Intellectual Property Preservation	PRUAB	FBG	ETT	NITT
Project-Contract Management	PRUAB	FBG	AGT	Project Office
Research Publication				
Research Structures	*Several*	*Several*	*Several*	*Several*
Technological Innovation Nucleus	PRUAB	*FBG*	*ETT*	*NITT*
Function Extension				
Business Creation	PRUAB, UAB Empren	BIE, FBG	RAIAR, IDEAR	UNITEC, NEI
Business Incubator	*At PRUAB*	*Do not have*	*RAIAR*	*UNITEC*
Business Hosting	PRUAB	PCB	TECNOPUC	TECNOSINOS
Science-Research-Technological Park	*PRUAB*	*PCB*	*TECNOPUC*	*TECNOSINOS*
Knowledge Transfer	PRUAB	FBG	ETT	NITT

Table 4.5 (continued)

Function/ mechanism	UAB	UB	PUCRS	UNISINOS
Technology Transfer Office	*PRUAB*	*FGB*	*ETT*	*NITT*
Specialized Services	Research Centers and Institutes	Scientific and Technological Centers	Technological Centers and Institutes	Technological Institutes
Technological Institute	*Several*	*Several*	*Several*	*Several*
Function Management				
Funding	Public and private	Public and private	Public and private	Public and private
Processes				
Strategy	Strategic Planning	Strategic Planning	Strategic Planning	Strategic Planning
Structure				

academic setting help universities to contribute to regional socio-economic development and to maintain their own sustainability.

Mechanisms related to innovation and entrepreneurship manifest themselves in four dimensions (teaching, research, extension and management) at three levels (individual, organization and interaction). There are three forms of interactions: knowledge-push (output), demand-pull (input) and social interaction (input and output).

CONCLUSIONS

The objective of this study was to explore innovation and entrepreneurship in the academic setting from the perspective of complex systems. The research tried to identify the systemic elements of the university in the context of the knowledge-based society, with emphasis on the mechanisms related to innovation and entrepreneurship that make universities contribute to the regional socio-economic development and to preserve their own sustainability.

The systemism approach to model complex systems was adopted, according to which a system might be modelled in terms of its composition, environment, structure and mechanisms. To identify these systemic elements, particularly on the system's mechanisms, an exploratory and

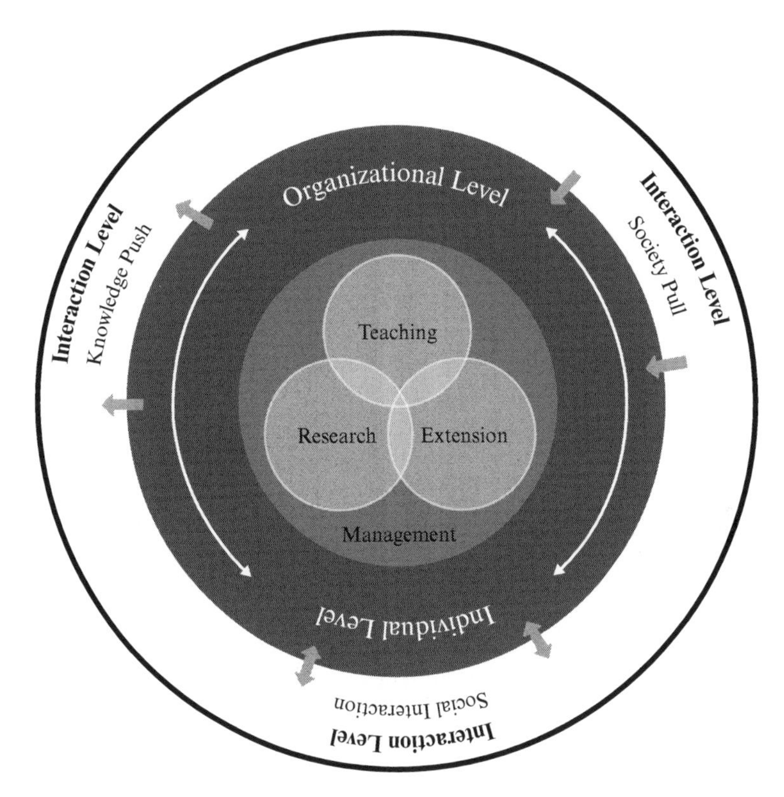

Figure 4.3 Levels and dimensions of innovation and entrepreneurship in the academic setting

descriptive multi-case study was conducted, considering four universities in two different regions and countries: Catalonia, Spain (UAB and UB) and Rio Grande do Sul, Brazil (PUC-RS and UNISINOS). Case study design and execution, including the instruments definition, data collecting and analysis, was done based on the systemism approach of complex systems.

Structural coding revealed that the composition of universities is made of individuals and artefacts at the micro level, and it is organized as academic and management organization at the macro level. As for the system's environment, it turned out that industry, government and communities are the main elements of the knowledge society with which the universities interact. Related to the system's structure, three levels of innovation and entrepreneurship were identified. The first level is related to people, and it represents individual agency. The second level is related to the organization itself, and it represents the social structure of the university. The third level is related to the interaction of the university with its environment. Finally, structural coding revealed the mechanisms related to teaching, research, extension and management, considered in this study as the main functions of the university.

These findings (structural coding) and respective descriptions (descriptive coding) allow us to propose that mechanisms related to innovation and entrepreneurship in the academic setting manifest themselves in four dimensions (teaching, research, extension and management) at three levels (individual, organization and interaction), and that there are three forms of interactions: knowledge-push (output), demand-pull (input) and social interaction (input and output).

Even though the research which originated this chapter had a sound methodological procedure, it presents some limitations, basically related to two aspects: its nature and its scope. Regarding its qualitative nature, the research may have been influenced by the researchers' assumptions on data analysis, given their practical experience with the subject of study. In relation to its scope, the study did not contemplate the perspectives of students, teachers, companies, government and community, and neither did it explore deeply the didactic-pedagogical and organizational dimensions of innovation and entrepreneurship in the studied universities.

The proposed conceptual framework offers many potential paths for future research, including: to empirically test the conjectured model to prove its partial or total functioning; to investigate the specific relationships between hypothesized mechanisms; to investigate how exactly the structure and mechanisms identified impact upon universities' contributions to regional socio-economic development and their own sustainability; to define indicators that allow evaluation of the performance of universities according to the proposed system; and to deepen the studies on the mechanisms related to management.

NOTE

* David Urbano acknowledges the financial support from projects ECO2013-44027-P (Spanish Ministry of Economy and Competitiveness) and 2014-SGR-1626 (Economy and Knowledge Department – Catalan Government). Ademar Schmitz acknowledges the financial support from FAPESC TO 2015TR298 (Fundação de Amparo à Pesquisa e Inovação do Estado de Santa Catarina) and UNIEDU-FUMDES (Programa de Bolsas Universitárias de Santa Catarina).

REFERENCES

Abreu, M. and V. Grinevich (2013), 'The nature of academic entrepreneurship in the UK: Widening the focus on entrepreneurial activities', *Research Policy*, **42**(2), 408–422.

Audretsch, D.B. (2014), 'From the entrepreneurial university to the university for the entrepreneurial society', *Journal of Technology Transfer*, **39**(3), 313–321.

Axelrod, R.M. and M.D. Cohen (2000), *Harnessing Complexity: Organizational Implications of a Scientific Frontier*, New York: Free Press.

Baldridge, J.V. (1980), 'Organizational characteristics of colleges and universities', in Baldridge, J.V. and T. Deal (eds), *The Dynamics of Organizational Change in Education*, Berkeley, CA: McCutchan Publishing, 38–59.

Baldridge, J.V., D.V. Curtis, G.P. Ecker and G.L. Riley (1997), 'Alternative models of governance in higher education', in Riley, G.L. and J.V. Baldridge (eds), *Governing Academic Organisations*, Berkeley, CA: McCutchan Publishing Corporation.

Bienkowska, D., M. Klofsten and E. Rasmussen (2016), 'PhD students in the entrepreneurial university – perceived support for academic entrepreneurship', *European Journal of Education*, **51**(1), 56–72.

Bunge, M. (1979), 'A systems concept of society: Beyond individualism and holism', *Theory and Decision*, **10**, 13–30.

Bunge, M. (1996), *Finding Philosophy in Social Science*, New Haven, CT: Yale University Press.

Bunge, M. (1997), 'Mechanism and explanation', *Philosophy of the Social Sciences*, **27**(4), 410–465.

Bunge, M. (2000), 'Systemism: The alternative to individualism and holism', *Journal of Socio-Economics*, **29**, 147–157.

Bunge, M. (2003), *Emergence and Convergence: Qualitative Novelty and the Unity of Knowledge*, Toronto: University of Toronto Press.

Bunge, M. (2004), 'How does it work? The search for explanatory mechanisms', *Philosophy of the Social Sciences*, **34**(2), 182–210.

Casti, J. (1981), 'Systemism, system theory and social system modeling', *Regional Science and Urban Economics*, **11**, 405–424.

Clark, B.R. (1996), 'Substantive growth and innovative organization: New categories for higher education research', *Higher Education*, **32**(4), 417–430.

Clark, B.R. (1998), *Creating Entrepreneurial Universities: Organizational Pathways of Transformation*, Oxford: Pergamon-Elsevier Science.

Eisenhardt, K. (1989), 'Building theories from case study research', *Academy of Management Review*, **14**(4), 532–550.

Etzkowitz, H. (1998), 'The norms of entrepreneurial science: Cognitive effects of the new university–industry linkages', *Research Policy*, **27**(8), 823–833.

Etzkowitz, H. (2003a), 'Innovation in innovation: The Triple Helix of university–industry–government relations', *Social Science Information*, **42**(3), 293–337.

Etzkowitz, H. (2003b), 'Research groups as "quasi-firms": The invention of the entrepreneurial university', *Research Policy*, **32**(1), 109–121.

Etzkowitz, H. (2013), 'Anatomy of the entrepreneurial university', *Social Science Information*, **52**(3), 486–511.

Etzkowitz, H., A. Webster, C. Gebhardt and B.R.C. Terra (2000), 'The future of the university and the university of the future: Evolution of ivory tower to entrepreneurial paradigm', *Research Policy*, **29**(2), 313–330.

Goldstein, H.A. (2010), 'The "entrepreneurial turn" and regional economic development mission of universities', *Annals of Regional Science*, **44**(1), 83–109.
Gräbner, C. and J. Kapeller (2015), 'New perspectives on institutionalist pattern modeling: Systemism, complexity, and agent-based modeling', *Journal of Economic Issues*, **49**(2), 433–440.
Grigg, T. (1994), 'Adopting an entrepreneurial approach in universities', *Journal of Engineering and Technology Management*, **11**(3–4), 273–298.
Guenther, J. and K. Wagner (2008), 'Getting out of the ivory tower: New perspectives on the entrepreneurial university', *European Journal of International Management*, **2**(4), 400–417.
Guerrero, M. and D. Urbano (2012), 'The development of an entrepreneurial university', *Journal of Technology Transfer*, **37**(1), 43–74.
Guerrero, M., J.A. Cunningham and D. Urbano (2015), 'Economic impact of entrepreneurial universities' activities: An exploratory study of the United Kingdom', *Research Policy*, **44**(3), 748–764.
Hofkirchner, W. (2007), 'A critical social systems view of the Internet', *Philosophy of the Social Sciences*, **37**(4), 471–500.
Lockwood, G. (1985), 'Universities as organizations', in Lockwood, G. and J. Davies (eds), *Universities: The Management Challenge*, Windsor: Society for Research in Higher Education/NFER-Nelson Publishing, 12–23.
Mainardes, E.W., H. Alves and M. Raposo (2011), 'The process of change in university management: From the "ivory tower" to entrepreneurialism', *Transylvanian Review of Administrative Sciences*, **33**, 124–149.
Mars, M.M. and C. Rios-Aguilar (2010), 'Academic entrepreneurship (re)defined: Significance and implications for the scholarship of higher education', *Higher Education*, **59**(4), 441–460.
Mazdeh, M.M., S.M. Razavi, R. Hesamamiri, M.R. Zahedi and B. Elahi (2013), 'An empirical investigation of entrepreneurship intensity in Iranian state universities', *Higher Education*, **65**(2), 207–226.
Miller, K., R. McAdam and M. McAdam (2018), 'A systematic literature review of university technology transfer from a quadruple helix perspective: Toward a research agenda', *R&D Management*, **48**(1), 7–24.
Murray, R., J. Caulier-Grice and G. Mulgan (2010), *The Open Book of Social Innovation*, London: Young Foundation.
Nelles, J. and T. Vorley (2011), 'Entrepreneurial architecture: A blueprint for entrepreneurial universities', *Canadian Journal of Administrative Sciences*, **28**(3), 341–353.
O'Shea, R.P., T.J. Allen, A. Chevalier and F. Roche (2005), 'Entrepreneurial orientation, technology transfer and spinoff performance of US universities', *Research Policy*, **34**(7), 994–1009.
Patton, M.Q. (2002), *Qualitative Research and Evaluation Methods*, 3rd edn, Thousand Oaks, CA: SAGE.
Philpott, K., L. Dooley, C. O'Reilly and G. Lupton (2011), 'The entrepreneurial university: Examining the underlying academic tensions', *Technovation*, **31**(4), 161–170.
Pickel, A. (2004), 'Systems and mechanisms: A symposium on Mario Bunge's philosophy of social science', *Philosophy of Social Sciences*, **34**(2), 169–181.
Pickel, A. (2007), 'Rethinking systems theory: A programmatic introduction', *Philosophy of the Social Sciences*, **37**(4), 391–407.
Ratten, V. (2017), 'Entrepreneurial universities: The role of communities, people

and places', *Journal of Enterprising Communities: People and Places in the Global Economy*, **11**(3), 310–315.
Reihlen, M., T. Klaas-Wissing and T. Ringberg (2007), 'Metatheories in management studies: Reflections upon individualism, holism, and systemism', *Management*, **10**(3), 49–69.
Ribeiro-Soriano, D. and D. Urbano (2009), 'Overview of collaborative entrepreneurship: An integrated approach between business decisions and negotiations', *Group Decision and Negotiation*, **18**(5), 419–430.
Ropke, J. (1998), 'The entrepreneurial university: Innovation, academic knowledge creation and regional development in a globalized economy', Working Paper no. 3, Germany: Department of Economics, Philipps-Universität Marburg.
Rothaermel, F.T., S.D. Agung and L. Jiang (2007), 'University entrepreneurship: a taxonomy of the literature', *Industrial and Corporate Change*, **16**(4), 691–791.
Saiz-Santos, M., A. Araujo-De la Mata and J. Hoyos-Iruarrizaga (2017), 'Entrepreneurial university: Educational innovation and technology transfer', in Peris-Ortis, M., J.A. Gómez, J.M. Merigó-Lindahl and C. Rueda-Armengot (eds), *Entrepreneurial Universities: Exploring the Academic and Innovative Dimensions of Entrepreneurship in Higher Education*, Washington, DC: Springer, 105–122.
Saldaña, J. (2013), *The Coding Manual for Qualitative Researchers*, London: SAGE.
Sam, C. and P. van der Sijde (2014), 'Understanding the concept of the entrepreneurial university from the perspective of higher education models', *Higher Education*, **68**(6), 891–908.
Schmitz, A., D. Urbano, G.A. Dandolini, J.A. de Souza and M. Guerrero (2017a), 'Innovation and entrepreneurship in the academic setting: A systematic literature review', *International Entrepreneurship and Management Journal*, **13**(2), 369–395.
Schmitz, A., D. Urbano, M. Guerrero and G.A. Dandolini (2017b), 'Activities related to innovation and entrepreneurship in the academic setting: A literature review', in Peris-Ortis, M., J.A. Gómez, J.M. Merigó-Lindahl and C. Rueda-Armengot (eds), *Entrepreneurial Universities: Exploring the Academic and Innovative Dimensions of Entrepreneurship in Higher Education*, Washington, DC: Springer, 1–18.
Schneider, C. (2013), 'Researching transnationalisation and higher education in the context of social mechanisms', *Journal of Contemporary European Studies*, **21**(4), 480–495.
Urbano, D. and M. Guerrero (2013), 'Entrepreneurial universities: Socioeconomic impacts of academic entrepreneurship in a European region', *Economic Development Quarterly*, **27**(1), 40–55.
van Vught, F. (1999), 'Innovative universities', *Tertiary Education and Management*, **5**(4), 347–354.
von Bertalanffy, L. (1968), *General System Theory: Foundations, Development, Applications*, New York: George Braziller.
Wan, P.Y.Z. (2011), 'Emergence à la systems theory: epistemological totalausschluss or ontological novelty?', *Philosophy of the Social Sciences*, **41**(2), 178–210.
Wan, P.Y.Z. (2012a), 'Analytical sociology: A Bungean appreciation', *Science and Education*, **21**(10), 1545–1565.
Wan, P.Y.Z. (2012b), 'Dialectics, complexity, and the systemic approach: Toward a critical reconciliation', *Philosophy of the Social Sciences*, **43**(4), 411–452.
Wood, M.S. (2011), 'A process model of academic entrepreneurship', *Business Horizons*, **54**(2), 153–161.
Yin, R.K. (2014), *Case Study Research: Design and Methods*, Thousand Oaks, CA: SAGE.

5. Entrepreneurialism in a London university: a case illustration

Nnamdi O. Madichie, Ayantunji Gbadamosi and Sonny Nwankwo

INTRODUCTION

The growing need for entrepreneurship education in an increasingly competitive and dynamic business environment is well acknowledged in the literature (Leitch and Harrison, 1999; Binsardi and Ekwulugo, 2003; Heinonen, 2007; Redmond and Walker, 2008; Madichie and Gbadamosi, 2017). An increasing number of higher educational institutions (especially universities) have continued to appreciate the need to fine-tune their curricula towards preparing students for the challenges outside the classroom environment (Stern, 2016; Madichie and Gbadamosi, 2017). Indeed, the Stern Report (Stern, 2016), encapsulated within the recent Research Bill in the United Kingdom, highlights the need for impact. It also echoes the underlying pillars of the newly published Teaching Excellence Framework (TEF), which highlights the reporting of the destination of higher education graduates. Both the Research Bill and the TEF provide opportunities for universities to demonstrate some relevance to the workplace. This would certainly entail a repositioning of course offerings to be of relevance to employers in particular, and the wider society at large.

By highlighting the case of a particular module (or course) at a London university, this chapter draws upon a review of literature (Leitch and Harrison, 1999; Binsardi and Ekwulugo, 2003; Heinonen and Poikkijoki, 2006; Tan and Ng, 2006; Solomon, 2007; Bosma and Levie, 2010; Hegarty and Jones, 2008; Fayolle et al., 2016; Madichie and Gbadamosi, 2017; Ratten, 2017) cutting across three sectors (industry, academia and public policy) in order to bolster the argument for entrepreneurship education, and by extension to demonstrate what an entrepreneurial university may look like.

Starting with industry, Tan and Ng (2006) highlighted how students acquire the skills that will provide them the edge to cope with the highly competitive environment where employers require people with entrepreneurial skills to take on the few available jobs. Hence, having gone through an entrepreneurship programme, students should be able to actively demonstrate an entrepreneurial mindset (Hegarty and Jones, 2008) to meet the needs of industry (that is, the workplace)

From an academic viewpoint, Ehiyazaryan and Barraclough (2009), in their study on enhancing employability of the university graduate, found that students were most motivated in subject matter that revolves around engaging in activities that they are likely to encounter in the real business world. Moreover, the belief that entrepreneurship can be learned and taught, at least to some extent (Heinonen and Poikkijoki, 2006), set against the belief that successful entrepreneurs are 'born', is the academic side of the argument in support of entrepreneurship education (Tan and Ng, 2006). Hence, the need for business schools to focus on the everyday realities of the business world by linking theory and practice cannot be ignored (Leitch and Harrison, 1999; Madichie and Gbadamosi, 2017).

This tends to corroborate the view of Heinonen and Poikkijoki (2006), who stress that learning entrepreneurial behaviour gives students the opportunity to experiment with entrepreneurial behaviour in a comfortable learning environment. Reiterating this view further, Solomon (2007) also states that there is a challenge for educators to craft courses and programmes to meet the rigours of academia while retaining a reality-based approach.

From the public policy perspective, the consistent findings of the Global Entrepreneurship Monitor (see, e.g., Tan and Ng, 2006; Bosma and Levie, 2010; Bosma et al., 2009; Fayolle et al., 2016) point to the fact that educational attainment boosts engagement in high-growth-potential entrepreneurial endeavours, and that the relevance of entrepreneurship education in society is contingent upon this. Indeed, Fayolle et al. (2016) talk about the 'institutionalization of entrepreneurship research' in a bid to actualize this possibility.

A clear case for reinvigorating entrepreneurship education in educational institutions toward equipping students with the necessary skills is therefore evident. This chapter thus explores, and highlights, one of the key areas that constitute the interacting curriculum and pedagogical systems of entrepreneurship education – small and medium-sized organization (SME) marketing – at a London-based university by examining the key activities and achievements associated with the delivery of the module since the 2005/06 academic year, when it was first introduced.[1] The chapter draws upon a series of case illustrations of success stories associated with this endeavour, which we tease out to form the platform for the discursive analysis on the impact of the module, and especially on how it has engendered learning at the university (see Madichie and Gbadamosi, 2017).

From a methodological standpoint, the study is based on a longitudinal study of the growth and development of the SME Marketing course at a London university, drawing upon a qualitative analysis (notably a combination of participant observation and action research). These dual qualitative research approaches provide some deep insights into the growth and development of the entrepreneurial marketing course over five academic years – that is, from its launch in the 2005/06 academic year, to the 2011/12 academic year – when it grew from just six pioneering students to more than 200 students, most of whom have either gone on to establish their own firms or opted to undertake further study.

Overall the chapter demonstrates the potential avenues for deploying entrepreneurialism with a business school; something that has been described as being 'a hot topic on the political agenda' (see Fayolle, 2013: 692). The remainder of the chapter has been arranged as follows. The next section presents the literature review on entrepreneurship education, and is followed by a description of the adopted methodology: a mixture of participant observation and action research (primarily from an education perspective; see Fayolle et al., 2016). A discussion of the findings is then undertaken, before the conclusions and implications are reported in the final section.

ENTERPRISE EDUCATION: A REVIEW OF THE LITERATURE

There is growing evidence that consistently indicates the crucial role of entrepreneurship in the global economy. This is evident in the sheer number of SMEs, which now constitute the major proportion of the total existing business establishments. For instance, in the United Kingdom (UK) and United States (US), the percentage of these enterprises among businesses is well over 90 per cent of the total number of firms in these countries. Consequently, nations, governments and educational institutions are confronted with the challenge of promoting entrepreneurship in various integrated forms. As one of the key stakeholders in the society, with huge responsibilities including contributing to the growth of the economy, some academic institutions are making frantic efforts to rebrand by ensuring that entrepreneurship is embedded in their curriculum, so that this leads to the availability of skilled graduates (Jones, 2007).

With reference to Jones et al. (2007) and Jones and Iredale (2010), enterprise education in the UK can be traced back to 1976 when it was first introduced by the Labour Government to ensure that young people leaving school acquire the skills needed to cope with the competitive business world. Nevertheless, in some cases, the enterprise education curriculum package does not contain the right mix of courses or topics required to transform the would-be entrepreneurs who enrol on the course (see Madichie and Gbadamosi, 2017). This is also closely related to the claim of the prevalence of some shortcomings associated with research on entrepreneurship education and training (Matlay, 2005; Heinonen, 2007). Meanwhile, it is important to discuss the elements that constitute the package of the delivery of entrepreneurship education in academic institutions and underpin how it is done. Essentially these are pedagogy and the curriculum for the subject.

According to Moore (2004: 329), pedagogy can be defined as 'the social organization of the process by which members of the situation encounter, engage and participate in this social stock of knowledge'. Taken from a slightly different perspective, Rafste and Saetre (2004) consider it to be the investment to bridge the gaps between the library, professionals in the library, and the librarians. Clearly, these viewpoints both indicate that pedagogy encapsulates the principles and processes of teaching or imparting knowledge or skills in relation to a particular subject.

Meanwhile, in their article titled 'A professional school approach to marketing education', Schibrowsky et al. (2002) explain curriculum not only as the tool used to prepare students for a career in their chosen field, but also as the backbone of professional schools' programmes. These two main elements (pedagogy and curriculum) are described as lenses for examining the socially shaped process of learning (see Moore, 2004). Thus, having a good knowledge of how these two interrelate in entrepreneurship education context is fundamental to providing any logical discussion on how the subject is being taught or should be taught.

One of the challenges associated with entrepreneurship education is that there is no consensus on the exact issues that students will be taught in relation to entrepreneurship (Solomon, 2007). However, drawing from a rich body of literature (see, e.g., Vesper, 1985; Kent, 1990; Gartner and Vesper, 1994), the topics commonly associated with this education are noted to be venture plan writing, case studies, reading and lectures delivered by guest speakers which is becoming increasingly recognized by institutions (Solomon, 2007; Madichie and Gbadamosi, 2017). Going by the view of Jones-Evans et al. (2000), this should include opportunity seeking, initiative taking, making things happen independently, risk taking, problem solving, ability to cope with uncertainty and ambiguity, self-awareness, creativity and persuasiveness.

From a broader perspective and with reference to Bosch and Louw (1998), van der Colff (2004) indicates certain areas of critical skills that must be built into the curriculum to strengthen students to be effective managers and leaders in the twenty-first century. These are highlighted to be strategic insight, leadership skills, decision-making skills, critical analysis, entrepreneurial skills, innovation, problem analysis, planning and organizing, performance management, and team playing. Above all, the common theme among these viewpoints is that there is a need to focus on bridging the gaps between theory and practice, and to fortify the existing efforts towards leading students to the outside world well equipped with relevant skills (see Madichie and Gbadamosi, 2017).

Indeed, this will signal a considerable scale of rebranding in the UK higher education sector. Heinonen and Poikkijoki (2006) suggest the use of an entrepreneurial-directed approach to complement the traditional mode of learning, to facilitate the kind of learning that would support the entrepreneurial process. According to them, three integral parts make the up the suite of processes: the entrepreneurial process, the experiential-learning process, and the entrepreneurial directed approach. As is the case in the mainstream marketing discussion, the significance of people as an element of the system is also noteworthy. This argument leans on the commonly cited view of Booms and Bitner (1981) which pinpoints why businesses, especially service-oriented ones, should embrace the '7Ps' of marketing, to which the people element is pivotal.

Accordingly, Heinonen and Poikkijoki (2006) argue that the teachers also need to act in an entrepreneurial way in discussing opportunities and innovatively exploiting them. Exploring this mode not only promotes entrepreneurship but also has the potential to strengthen employability. This is in tune with the view which suggests that employability enhancement should be handled collaboratively between different parties, such as the staff of the academic institution, the employers' representatives and the students (Zhiwen and van der Heijden, 2008). These dynamics are captured in our approach: a combination of participant observation and action research, which is detailed in the methodology section.

METHODOLOGY

In keeping with the tenet of triangulation, which has been widely acclaimed as very beneficial (Denzin, 1970; Jack and Raturi, 2006), a combination of methods was adopted for teasing out the data reported in this study. The research is based on participant observation, and action research aided by the use of in-depth interviews. The module in question, SME Marketing, was launched in September 2005 under the newly validated BA (Hons) Marketing programme. Amongst its teething problems was the problem of identifying a suitable textbook beyond Carson et al. (1995). Starting with a miniscule number of seven students in the first semester of 2005/06 the course had about 126 students enrolled by 2011/12. This astronomical growth is purely due to the popularity of the subject and renewed students' interest in starting up their own businesses or being able to manage their own existing businesses.

Participant Observation

Participant observation is a qualitative method with roots in traditional ethnographic research, whose objective is to help researchers learn the perspectives held by study populations. As is the case in our present study which uses a London university as the research context, it always takes place in community settings, and locations believed to have some relevance to the research questions. The method is distinctive because the researcher approaches participants in their own environment rather than having the participants come to the researcher. In other words, the researcher who engages in participant observation tries to learn what life is like for an 'insider', while inevitably remaining an 'outsider' (Laurier, n.d.).

In participant observation, the social researcher immerses themself in the social setting under study, getting to know key actors in that location in a role which is either covert or overt (see Table 5.1 for a comparison of these approaches), although in practice the researcher will often move between these two roles. The aim is to experience events in the manner in which the subjects under study also experience these events. In covert observation, on the one hand, the social researcher participates fully without informing members of the social group of the reasons for their presence; thus the research is carried out secretly or covertly. It may also involve contact with a 'gatekeeper', a member of the group under study who will introduce the researcher into the group. On the other hand, overt observation involves the researcher being open about the reason for their presence in the field of study, since the researcher is given permission by the group to conduct research.

Action Research

Kurt Lewin, a German social and experimental psychologist, is generally considered to be the 'father' of action research and one of the founders of the Gestalt school (O'Brien, 2001). He was concerned with social problems, and focused on participative group processes for addressing conflict, crises and, most importantly, change, in the context of organizations (including higher education institutions as in this case). Lewin first coined the term 'action research' in his 1946 paper 'Action research and minority

Table 5.1 Covert and overt participant observation

	Covert	Overt
Advantages	• The researcher may gain access to social groups which would otherwise not consent to being studied. • The avoidance of problems of 'observer effect': the conception that individuals' behaviour may change if they know they are being studied. However, there are problems of recording data.	• The avoidance of problems of ethics, in that the groups are aware of the researcher's role. • The group is being observed in its natural setting. • Data may also be openly recorded. • Problems of 'going native' are avoided.
Disadvantages	• The researcher having to become involved in criminal or dangerous activities, particularly where the research is studying a 'deviant' social group. • Problems of negotiating and having to act out forms of behaviour which the researcher may personally find unethical or distasteful. • The researcher having to employ a level of deceit, since the researcher essentially 'lies' about the nature of their presence within the group. • Close friendships often result from connections with members of the group under study, and the covert nature of the research can put a tremendous strain on the researcher, both in and out of the fieldwork setting. • The problem of 'going native' (that is, the researcher becomes a full-time group participant).	• 'Observer effect', where the behaviour of those under study may alter due to the presence of the researcher.
Classic examples	• Erving Goffman's 1968 study of mental hospitals, published as *Stigma* (Goffman, 2009). The author worked in an asylum for the mentally ill as Assistant Athletic Director, using mainly covert participant observation (with only a couple of staff being privy to the knowledge of his research), in order to uncover the 'unofficial reality' of life in a mental institution.	• William F. Whyte's (1943) study, published as *Street Corner Society* (Whyte, 1947), is a classic in this sense, where the author was protected from potential antagonism by his friendship with 'Doc', his sponsor. However, Whyte, despite employing an overt participant observer role, did increasingly come to view himself as 'one of the gang' during his fieldwork research.

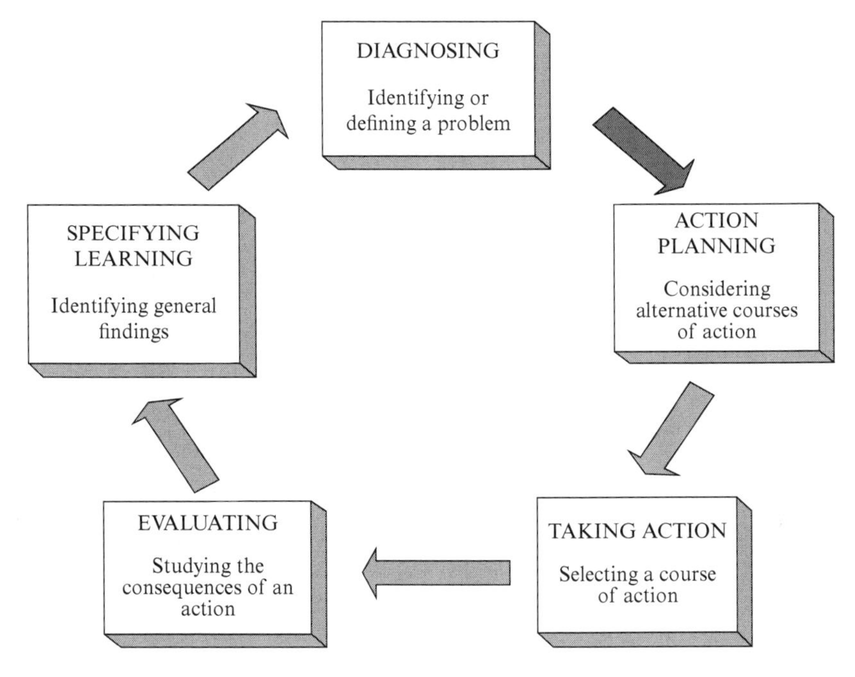

Source: Susman (1983).

Figure 5.1 Action research model

problems' (Lewin, 1946; cf. O'Brien, 2001), characterizing action research as 'a comparative research on the conditions and effects of various forms of social action and research leading to social action', using a process of 'a spiral of steps, each of which is composed of a circle of planning, action, and fact-finding about the result of the action' (see Figure 5.1). Action research is known by many other names, including participatory research, collaborative inquiry, emancipatory research, action learning and contextual action research, but all are variations on a theme.

In other words, action research is 'learning by doing': a group of people identify a problem, do something to resolve it, see how successful their efforts were, and if not satisfied, try again (O'Brien, 2001). A more succinct definition highlighted by Gilmore et al. (1986: 161) puts it this way:

> Action research . . . aims to contribute both to the practical concerns of people in an immediate problematic situation and to further the goals of social science simultaneously. Thus, there is a dual commitment in action research to study a system and concurrently to collaborate with members of the system in changing it in what is together regarded as a desirable direction. Accomplishing this

> twin goal requires the active collaboration of researcher and client, and thus it stresses the importance of co-learning as a primary aspect of the research process.

This is consistent with the focus of this chapter, in which the emphasis is on co-learning. Indeed, O'Brien (2001) highlights four main streams of action research that have been in existence since the mid-1970s: traditional, contextual (action learning), radical and educational action research. Traditional action research stemmed from Lewin's work within organizations and tends toward the conservative, generally maintaining the status quo with regards to organizational power structures. Contextural action research (action learning) is an approach derived from Trist's (1979) work on relations between organizations. It is contextural, insofar as it entails reconstituting the structural relations among actors in a social environment. The radical stream, which has its roots in Marxian dialectical materialism and the praxis orientations of Antonio Gramsci, has a strong focus on emancipation and the overcoming of power imbalances.

Finally, educational action research has its foundations in the writings of John Dewey, the great American educational philosopher of the 1920s and 1930s, who believed that professional educators should become involved in community problem solving. Its practitioners operate mainly out of educational institutions, and focus on development of curriculum, professional development, and applying learning in a social context. It is often the case that university-based action researchers work with primary and secondary school teachers and students on community projects. Consistent with these identified streams, this chapter adopts the educational action research following in the tradition of Dewey (1938), where the authors, in addition to having been instructors on the module, have also been key players in community projects linked to the Centre of Entrepreneurship at the same university (see REF, 2014).

DISCUSSION OF FINDINGS

The considerable increase in the enrolment figures since the course launch in 2005/06 clearly demonstrates the popularity of this module and shows that the university has positioned itself as an entrepreneurial entity in tune with the reality of society. The basic tenet of marketing is that the focus of the organization should be towards creating and delivering value to its target audience. Essentially, this can be achieved by identifying the needs and wants of the market and delivering the offerings that will satisfy it in terms of a profit to the organization, efficiently and effectively better than competitors. Society is now becoming more concerned about employability, creativity and productivity. Accordingly, as this case study illustrates, to be relevant in society, universities need rebranding and repositioning in such a way that will bring employment, employability, opportunity recognition, creativity, and other factors that relate to entrepreneurship, to the forefront of the emerging curriculum and the applicable pedagogy.

As is the case with the participant observation, the findings from the in-depth interviews conducted with the students indicate that they have benefited significantly from the university rebranding and repositioning towards employability and entrepreneurship, as linked to this module in various forms. These verbatim quotes from the respondents support these findings:

> Definitely, the module is brilliant. Every lecture, workshop, and seminar that I have attended has shown me the real principles behind what I have been doing. I have been in business for a long time, and have made a number of mistakes. I can say that with this module, I make far less mistakes as it explains the key principles behind the real things I meet on daily basis. (CEO, DIY Doctor)

> I have been in this new business for 6 months now. There is no family business background at all. The SME Marketing module has reshaped my thoughts about business and I will recommend it to anyone who is presently in business or will like to look at that in the future. It is like an eye-opening thing to me. I presently have 4 employees, and we are into courier services, removal, procurement and logistics and many others. I have tried other businesses before which have failed. That is actually one of the key reasons why I thought I should come and learn about business in the academic world, and with this module I can say that there is no regret. (Owner Manager, Ocean Green)

Those who already have their businesses unanimously emphasize how the module has strengthened their skills in managing these organizations, while others who are planning to enrol on the programme give it very high priority in making their choice. They emphatically claim that that taking this module has ignited their love for entrepreneurship:

> I personally do not want to work for anybody . . . They can never pay you what you value or let me say what you are worth. The ideas I have picked up from this UNI are helping me to run the business well. Some are asking why am I, a man, going into women's hair. But girls spend a lot on their hair. I think that is an example of the opportunity recognition we learn about on this SME marketing module. (Proprietor, Mr Leone)

> It is like the family business but I am the main person managing it. It is called Bomboniere, an events management business . . . We do organize events like birthday, wedding . . . we do decoration, buffet, we can organize everything. To

> be honest, there are many things that I will say make the course very interesting – the lectures give us the theory which is good but the case studies are really helpful. We get to learn from others' experience. Using real life examples and case studies help a lot. Em . . . the name of the business is Italian and means Favour. I believe it works with what the module is all about. Satisfying customers, bringing solutions to their events and making them happy . . . I also love this idea of bringing guest speakers. It is excellent because they share their experience with us so that we can learn from them. (Manager, Bomboniere)

The significant effort of the lecturers in the university has given students a view that the university has become a place where preparatory activities that set them up for the business world are encouraged. These include group interaction and networks:

> I will like to go into training and consulting . . . I will like to give it my name. You know celebrities are brands themselves. Apart from the lecture, seminars and workshops, I also think the group coursework and other group activities encourage us to network. Some of the friendships and connections we have made on the module can last longer and help us in the future in our businesses after this education. (OR, Male Respondent)

> I am from Uganda and had discussed the idea of starting a diary farm, real-estate, and fast food restaurant in the country. My experience since I started this module has convinced me that we can succeed. The principles are there but if one does not know, there may be problem running the business. There is no doubt about whether there is a link between this module and these business ideas. It is not like the other generic marketing module but relates directly to running and managing business. That is the key part which is fantastic. The guest lectures and the group presentations especially the one which we did with those students who came from Belgium to the UK to co-present with us are very good to make the module deliver what the title say. (SD, Male Respondent)

One of the key findings in this chapter is that, because of the development of SME Marketing at the London university, many of the students who have been through the course have developed and/or actualized their entrepreneurial engagements. While some have opted to focus their project or dissertation topics around the subject of small business and entrepreneurship, others have been encouraged to participate and contribute to workshops organized by the Black Business Observatory, which also featured case studies from spin-offs within the Centre for Enterprise Development service, which is an accredited Business Innovation Centre for the European Business network.

By and large, the introduction of the system consisting of the SME Marketing module curriculum and the associated pedagogy has led to an increase in the numbers of entrepreneurs in the society. Having started out on private premises, one of the students in our sample later relocated to the

Enterprise Suite in the 'Hot Hatch'. When asked to highlight any benefit from the module, he opined that:

> The practicality with which the module tends to address issues that confront Entrepreneurs on the day to day management of their business i.e. – Process of decision making; Raising of capital; and Influence of their personal network on the business's success.

Commenting on those areas he thinks needed improving, he identified the need for embedding further practical entrepreneurship activities into the curriculum. According to him: 'there is the need to include direct expressive learning into the curriculum where students could be encouraged as part of the learning and understanding to embark on model business planning and implementation'.

Furthermore, periodic feedback obtained from the students also indicates that they derive significant benefits from taking the module, in various ramifications. Essentially, these revolve around acquisition of relevant skills that would help them in their future entrepreneurial ambitions – opportunity recognition, competitiveness, exploring personal contact networks, and many others – with pedagogical implications (see Figure 5.2).

It is also worth pointing out that our research approach is not considered as 'overt' as it is 'post hoc'. In other words, our study is reflexive in the sense that it happened after the event in a rather unplanned way. This may be a good thing, considering 'observer effect' constraint highlighted in Table 5.1. Moreover, the 'covert' ascription to our participant observation only skims off the merits of that approach: that is, access to the observed

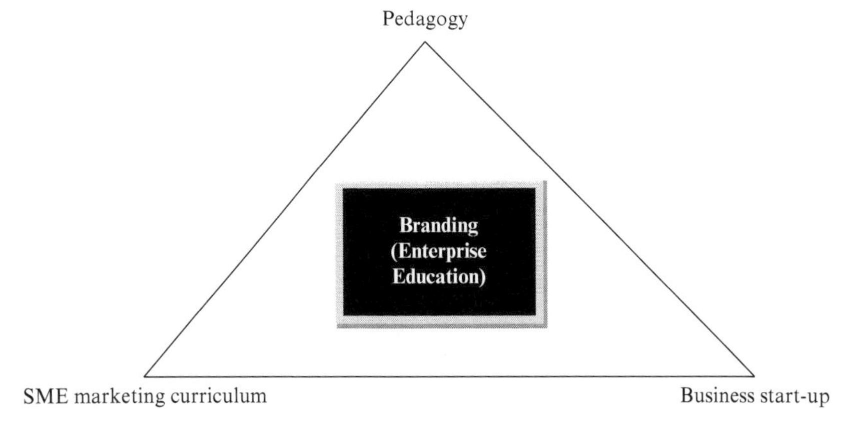

Figure 5.2 The tripartite system of the SME marketing curriculum

Table 5.2 Reinterpreted Susman's (1983) action research model

Susman's variables	Our research application/interpretation
Diagnosing	Identification of the need for SME Marketing and its subsequent launch in 2005/06 academic year
Action planning	Moving the module from an elective to a core module from 2007/08 (see Table 5.1)
Taking action	Developing a custom textbook with Pearson (Madichie, 2007) building on a dated text (Carson et al., 1995) with the same title.
Evaluating	Moving towards an edited text (Nwankwo and Gbadamosi, 2010) five years after the custom text publication, on the back of the success of the custom publication.
Specifying learning	Reflecting on the growth and development of the module and developing a paper for the Institute for Small Business and Entrepreneurship (ISBE) in a bid to implement action – hence the action research grounding for the paper.

group (the six cases outlined in this chapter) as well as avoidance of the 'observer effect' problem (also outlined in Table 5.1). We nonetheless posit that our study is primarily action research oriented, as we seem to have mitigated the constraints of the model advanced by Susman (1983), as illustrated in Figure 5.2 and interpreted in Table 5.2.

CONCLUSIONS AND IMPLICATIONS

This chapter explores the entrepreneurial impact of a module (course) launch, SME Marketing, into the marketing curriculum at a university in London, UK. While noting the remarkable increase in the enrolment figures (an indication of the growing interest in this subject), we also observe the pastoral support epitomized by the former students' business start-ups. We perceive that the pedagogy embedded in the curriculum may have an indirect consequence of business start-ups exhibited by these students. This is evocative of rebranding as evident in the context of this case used for the study. It communicates change to the old university system with operations that constitute a radical departure based on the needs of the society.

It is interesting to note that the pedagogical arrangements for the module, such as organizing group coursework, analysing case studies and inviting guest speakers, all appear to be very interesting to students, and this is strongly supported in the literature (Solomon, 2007). Although the chapter features only a few cases, the narrative feedback received tends to suggest that the respondents have not only benefited from the module, but also found it inspiring and motivating in terms of the skills development embedded in the module's total package. It is therefore not surprising that Rafste and Seatre (2004) argue that pedagogy is an investment that bridges gaps between the elements of the library as a system and the relevant professionals. Hence, it is important to state that ardent commitment to relevant pedagogy in entrepreneurship education could yield considerable outputs, especially in terms of business start-ups.

While interest in entrepreneurship education has witnessed a huge growth in recent years with the proliferation of journals on entrepreneurship and small business development, supported by numerous academic conferences ranging from the annual Institute for Small Business and Entrepreneurship (ISBE) conference and the European Council for Small Business and Entrepreneurship (ECSB) to its amplified version, the International Council for Small Business (ICSB), there remains a paucity of academic papers reporting a similar trend. Indeed, the level of spin-offs resulting from engagement with the course is varied, and enterprise education is well embedded in the course structure and fabric. This is novel and may need to be replicated in other higher education institutions in the UK and beyond.

Although this chapter could be seen as enlightening in some ramifications, its key limitation is in our inability to generalize the findings. As noted by Hamilton (1981), educational research through action research does not produce understanding that has universal truth. It has also been reported as being 'about me in the here and now understanding what I can do to ensure my values and intentions are realised in my teaching situation. If my deliberations produce an understanding which helps me, then I can offer it to others to try.' In this sense, action research can produce generalizations about practice, but such generalizations may only be a part of a wider search for understanding. They are not directly applicable beyond the contingencies of my practice. Indeed, Hamilton (1981) encapsulated this when he reflected that 'to generalise is to render a public account of the past, present or future in a form that can be "tested" through further action and inquiry.'

Overall, however, the chapter should be of benefit to business schools considering modules on enterprise development and entrepreneurship as well as the interface with small business marketing, where the former is indicative of learning how to cultivate it and the latter highlights what to do with it; that is, how to 'flaunt it'. Hence, universities and other education providers alike should not only strive to engage in brand-oriented activities to develop a strong university brand with relevant appeals to their existing and prospective students, but also rebrand as necessary to communicate adaptability and sensitivity to societal demands. It is expected that this study would encourage further research into this important topic.

NOTE

1. The rationale is based on the reignited effort by tutors and interest by publishers in developing: first, a textbook published by Prentice Hall (Madichie, 2007); and second, an edited textbook published by Routledge (Nwankwo and Gbadamosi, 2010). Interest from these two powerhouses in publishing textbooks geared towards deeper learning on the course are clear indications of the exigency of developing entrepreneurial learning within the classroom and beyond. It also draws upon a forthcoming publication that showcases how a course in an English Department resorted to the world of hip-hop for real-world resonance (Madichie and Gbadamosi, 2017).

REFERENCES

Binsardi, A. and Ekwulugo, F. (2003), International marketing of British education: research on the students' perception and the UK market penetration. *Marketing Intelligence and Planning*, **21**(5), 318–327.

Booms, B.H. and Bitner, M.J. (1981), Marketing strategies and organization structures for service firms. *Marketing of Services*, **25**(3), 47–52.

Bosch, J. and Louw, L. (1998), Graduate perceptions on the status and nature of South African MBA Programmes. Centre for Applied Business Management, UPE.

Bosma, N.S., Acs, Z.J., Autio, E., Coduras, A. and Levie, J. (2009), *Global Entrepreneurship Monitor, 2008 Executive Report*. Babson Park, MA, USA and Santiago, Chile: Babson College, Universidad del Desarollo Wellesley.

Bosma, N. and Levie, J. (2010), *Global Entrepreneurship Monitor, 2009 Executive Report*. Babson Park, MA, USA; Santiago, Chile; Iceland; London, UK: Babson College, Universidad del Desarollo and Reykjavík, Háskólinn Reykjavík University, Global Entrepreneurship Research Association.

Carson, D., Cromie, S., McGowan, P. and Hill, J. (1995), *Marketing and Entrepreneurship in SMEs, An Innovative Approach*. Englewood Cliffs, NJ: Prentice-Hall.

Denzin, N. (1970), Strategies of multiple triangulation. In: Denzin, N. (ed.), *The Research Act in Sociology: A Theoretical Introduction to Sociological Method*. New York: McGraw-Hill, pp. 297–313.

Dewey, J. (1938), *Experience and Education*. New York: Collier Books.

Ehiyazaryan, E. and Barraclough, N. (2009), Enhancing employability: integrating real world experience in the curriculum. *Education + Training*, **51**(4), 292–308.

Fayolle, A. (2013), Personal views on the future of entrepreneurship education. *Entrepreneurship and Regional Development*, **25**(7/8), 692–701.

Fayolle, A., Verzat, C. and Wapshott, R. (2016), In quest of legitimacy: the theoretical and methodological foundations of entrepreneurship education research. *International Small Business Journal*, **34**(7), 895–904.

Gartner, W. and Vesper, K. (1994), Executive forum: experiments in entrepreneurship education: successes and failures. *Journal of Business Venturing*, **9**, 179–187.
Gilmore, T., Krantz, J. and Ramirez, R (1986), Action based modes of inquiry and the host–researcher relationship. *Consultation*, **5**(3), 161.
Goffman, E. (2009), *Stigma: Notes on the Management of Spoiled Identity*. New York: Simon & Schuster.
Hamilton, D. (1981), Generalization in the educational sciences: problems and purposes. In: Popkewitz, T.S. and Tabachnik, B.R. (eds), *The Study of Schooling: Field Based Methodologies in Educational Research and Evaluation*. New York: Praeger.
Hegarty, C. and Jones, C. (2008), Graduate entrepreneurship: more than child's play. *Education + Training*, **50**(7), 626–637.
Heinonen, J. (2007), An entrepreneurial-directed approach to teaching corporate entrepreneurship at university level. *Education + Training*, **49**(4), 310–324
Heinonen, J. and Poikkijoki, S. (2006), An entrepreneurial-directed approach to entrepreneurship education: mission impossible? *Journal of Management Development*, **25**(1), 80–94.
Jack, E.P. and Raturi, A.S. (2006), Lessons learned from methodological triangulation in management research. *Management Research News*, **29**(6), 345–357.
Jones, C. (2007), Creating the reasonable adventurer: the co-evolution of student and learning environment. *Journal of Small Business and Enterprise Development*, **14**(2), 228–240
Jones, B. and Iredale, N. (2010), 'Enterprise education as pedagogy. *Education + Training*, **52**(1), 7–19.
Jones, P., Jones, A., Packham, G., Thomas, B. and Miller, C. (2007), It's all in the mix: the evolution of a blended e-learning model for an undergraduate degree. *Journal of Systems and Information Technology*, **9**(2), 124–142.
Jones-Evans, D., Williams, W. and Deacon, J. (2000), Developing entrepreneurial graduates: an action-learning approach. *Education + Training*, **42**(4/5), 282–288.
Kent, C.A. (ed.) (1990), *Entrepreneurship Education*. New York: Quorum Books.
Laurier, E. (n.d.), Participant-observation. Department of Geography and Topographic Science, University of Glasgow. http://www.geos.ed.ac.uk/homes/elaurier/r7/texts/PART-OB.pdf.
Leitch, C. and Harrison, R. (1999), A process model for entrepreneurship education and development. *International Journal of Entrepreneurial Behaviour and Research*, **5**(3), 83–109.
Lewin, K. (1946), Action research and minority problems. *Journal of Social Issues*, **2**, pp. 34–46.
Madichie, N. (2007), *SME Marketing: A Reader*. Harlow: FT/Prentice Hall.
Madichie, N. and Gbadamosi, A. (2017), The entrepreneurial university: an exploration of 'value-creation' in a non-management department. *Journal of Management Development*, **36**(2), 196–216.
Matlay, H. (2005), Researching entrepreneurship and education Part 1: what is entrepreneurship and does it matter? *Education + Training*, **47**(8/9), pp. 665–677.
Moore, D. (2004), Curriculum at work: an educational perspective on the workplace as a learning environment. *Journal of Workplace Learning*, **16**(6), 325–340.
Nwankwo, S. and Gbadamosi, A. (eds) (2010), *Entrepreneurship Marketing: Principles and Practice of SME Marketing*. Abingdon: Routledge.
O'Brien, R. (2001), An overview of the methodological approach of action research. In: Richardson, R. (ed.), *Theory and Practice of Action Research*. João

Pessoa, Brazil: Universidade Federal da Paraíba. (English version). Available at: http://www.web.ca/~robrien/papers/arfinal.htm (accessed 27 July 2010).
Rafste, E.T. and Saetre, T.P. (2004), Bridging gaps – pedagogical investment. *Library Review*, **53**(2), 112–118.
Ratten, V. (2017) Entrepreneurial universities. In Ratten, V. (ed.), *Entrepreneurship, Innovation and Smart Cities*. Abingdon: Routledge, 97–113.
Redmond, J. and Walker, E.A. (2008), A new approach to small business training: community based education, *Education + Training*, **50**(8/9), 697–712.
Research Excellence Framework (REF) (2014), Impact case study for REF 2014 'Black Business Observatory: supporting enterprise development among British Africans in London'. University of East London, Impact Case Study (REF3b). Retrieved from: http://impact.ref.ac.uk/CaseStudies/CaseStudy.aspx?Id=42755.
Schibrowsky, J.A., Peltier, J.W. and Boyt, T.E. (2002), A professional school approach to marketing education. *Journal of Marketing Education*, **24**(1), 43–55.
Solomon, G. (2007), An examination of entrepreneurship education in the United States. *Journal of Small Business and Enterprise Development*, **14**(2), 168–182.
Stern, N. (2016), Building on success and learning from experience: an independent review of the Research Excellence Framework. Retrieved from: https://www.gov.uk/government/uploads/system/uploads/attachment_data/file/541338/ind-16-9-ref-stern-review.pdf.
Susman, G. (1983), Action research: a sociotechnical systems perspective. In: Morgan, G. (ed.), *Beyond Method: Strategies for Social Research*. Beverly Hills, CA: SAGE, pp. 95–113.
Tan, S.S. and Ng, C.K. (2006), A problem-based learning approach to entrepreneurship education. *Education + Training*, **48**(6), 416–428
Trist, E. (1979), New directions of hope: recent innovations interconnecting organizational, industrial, community and personal development. *Regional Studies*, **13**(5), 439–451.
Van der Colff, L. (2004), A new paradigm for business education: the role of the business educator and business school. *Management Decision*, **42**(3/4), 499–507.
Vesper, K.H. (1985), *Entrepreneurship Education*. Wellesley, MA: Babson College.
Whyte, W.F. (1943), Social organization in the slums. *American Sociological Review*, **8**(1), 34–39.
Whyte, W.F. (1947), *Street Corner Society: The Social Structure of an Italian Slum*. Chicago, IL: University of Chicago Press.
Zhiwen, G. and van der Heijden, V. (2008), Employability enhancement of business graduates in China: reacting upon challenges of globalization and labour market demands. *Education + Training*, **50**(4), 289–304.

6. The level of competence of young researchers and the knowledge-based economy: the challenges of doctoral education in Poland

Urszula Wiśniewska and Jacek Lewicki

INTRODUCTION

Analysing the dynamically changing situation in the global economy and the factors that influence it, it is possible to notice the relation between the level and the quality of the education and growth in the economy. Education creates choices and opportunities, reduces poverty, and gives people a stronger voice in society. It is the fundamental enabler of the knowledge-based economy. Well-educated and skilled people are essential for creating, sharing, disseminating and using knowledge effectively in a global environment that is radically changing the types of skills needed for economic success. Basic education provides the foundation for lifelong learning and increases people's capacity to assimilate and use information. Secondary and tertiary education should develop core skills (including technical skills) that encourage the creative and critical thinking inherent in problem solving and innovation. Higher education in engineering and the sciences is needed to monitor technological trends and to use new technologies, while assessing which are relevant for a particular firm or the economy in general.

The production of new knowledge and its adaptation to a particular economic setting is generally associated with higher-level education and research. Indeed, a better and more broadly educated population tends to be more technologically sophisticated, thus generating quality-sensitive demand for advanced goods. This, in turn, tends to stimulate local firms to innovate: to design technologically sophisticated goods and adopt advanced production techniques.

A culture of continuous learning and openness to new ideas is critical for a knowledge-based economy. From early childhood to retirement, a lifelong learning system encompasses learning from all types of sources: formal (schools, training institutions and universities), non-formal (learning on the job and in the household), and informal (family or community members). The basic requirements of a lifelong learning system are comprehensiveness, multiple pathways to learning and problem solving, and multiple education providers. To benefit from such a system, recipients must have the ability to acquire new skills, act autonomously, use tools interactively, and function in socially heterogeneous groups. Basic competencies required by employers in today's labour markets give an indication of the challenges faced by education systems. Like policies related to information and communication technology, efforts to build a knowledge economy through education need to be adapted to each country's economic and social needs as well as to its institutional capabilities (World Bank, 2007).

The impact of the globalization of education is bringing a rapid growth in the field of technology and communication. There are also changes in the education systems worldwide in their ideas, value and knowledge. The area of doctoral studies is the crucial level at which researchers are creating the knowledge-based economy. That is why effective cooperation between these researchers and business is important.

On the other hand, the results achieved by Polish enterprises, in the entire period of the transformation, contributed to forming an economy based on solid foundations and principles of operation. However, there is still a great challenge facing the Polish economy in terms of its development, and increasing its competitiveness in the European and the world markets. This can be done through the increased productivity and innovations of the enterprises.

Nowadays Polish enterprises are competing with low labour costs; they are not using, or are rarely using, the development potentialities of innovations. The enterprises do not implement innovations, nor do they carry out research to modernize the various areas of their activities, or make use of existing innovation projects that would certainly raise their competitiveness on the Polish and international markets.

Poland is ranked one of the lowest amongst members of the Organisation for Economic Co-operation and Development (OECD) and the European Union (EU) in terms of the commercialization of research; it is in the group of so-called 'modest innovators'.

Nowadays the development of innovation is directly associated with the development of the 'knowledge-based economy'. The concept of development of the knowledge-based economy was propagated by the OECD's experts in the 1990s, as the result of observation and analysis of the economic development of the major countries of the world. This concept is quite simple. From the 1940s (1945–85) in economics there was the belief that growth in the economy was the result of the influence of three factors: increase in workloads, increase in investments (dependent upon the relation of investment to gross domestic product), and advances in science and technology. It was assumed that the advances in science and technology were exogenous, that their pace was independent of economic policy. According to this concept, a country with great stores of capital and relatively little investment, in which population growth is slow (for example, the United States of America), should develop more slowly than the rest of the world. At the end of 1980s, however, a competing 'endogenous growth theory' arose. It explained the strange phenomenon that the USA, the richest economy of the world, developed at a very rapid pace.

There were three notable aspects to endogenous growth theory:

- The technical-organizational progress is not given exogenously at all (independent of the economic policy). The policies of the state influence the pace of development of technology (for example, encouraging research and development expenditure), market competition, and the development of the capital market, supporting innovative forms of financing, and new technological solutions;
- One should look at the human capital, instead of the numbers of people working. Human capital accumulates the same as physical capital, so it requires investment. Employees are not all the same: education, experience and ability to accommodate to new technologies determine an employee's productivity.
- Human capital and the production capital can be used in more or less effective ways.

THE AREAS OF THE KNOWLEDGE-BASED ECONOMY

The knowledge-based economy (KBE) is based on the functioning of four areas: human resources, universities and scientific research institutions, financial and credit institutions, and telecommunication infrastructure (European Portal of Integration and the Development, 2016):

1. Human resources. Human resources appropriate for the construction of the new economy are employees with high qualifications based on a reliable education, who are familiar with information technology, know foreign languages, are mobile, and motivated to creative and efficient work for a modern economy.
2. Universities and scientific research institutions. They act as providers of knowledge (ideas, technology) without which a new economy

cannot be built. In science, including in lower-level education, they contribute to creating a climate that is conducive to technical progress and innovation. A necessary condition for the construction of KBE is a strong connection between the scientific and research sector and business. Thanks to this alliance, it is possible to use the knowledge produced by research infrastructures effectively.

3. Financial and credit institutions. They provide capital for high-risk business ventures in the construction of the KBE, in which the innovation is the base (venture capital). The well-developed system of financial and credit institutions that are building the new economy means not only financing of the specific economic and scientific projects, but also the elimination of capital barriers for the entities engaged in building the KBE.
4. Telecommunication infrastructure. This includes information and communication technologies, as well as ways of their assimilation by the public and economic operators. The primary driving force of the KBE is the Internet, through which an unlimited exchange of information is possible. The Internet disseminates knowledge and improves connectivity between scientific institutions and research institutions that forge ideas for the KBE.

Characteristics of the main actors of the knowledge-based economy are presented in Table 6.1.

In this chapter we concentrate on the role of the universities and researchers, because a country's science system takes on increased importance in a knowledge-based economy. Public research laboratories and institutions of higher education are at the core of the science system, which more broadly includes government science ministries and research councils, certain enterprises and other private bodies, and supporting infrastructure. In the knowledge-based economy, the science system contributes to the key functions of:

- knowledge production: developing and providing new knowledge;
- knowledge transmission: educating and developing human resources;
- knowledge transfer: disseminating knowledge and providing inputs to problem solving (OECD, 1996).

All of these entities interact with each other, and depending on their degree of development they contribute to a greater or lesser extent to success in the development of the modern economy. The retardation of the indicated factors is the primary barrier to building a knowledge-based economy. These barriers are different in different countries: they depend

Table 6.1 Characteristics of the main actors of the knowledge-based economy

	The inventor	The university or research institute	Promoter of science to businesses	The businessman	The investor	The state
Resources	The invention (knowledge)	Research infrastructure	Managerial skills	Managerial skills	Money (capital)	Public money
Information	Scientific knowledge (original)	Scientific knowledge (collected)	1. Scientific knowledge (collected) 2. Market knowledge (collected)	1. The needs of the market or production 2. Action of the competition	Alternative investment projects	1. Scientific needs of the state 2. Review of the scientific knowledge
Role in the process	The creation of the invention	Delivery of infrastructure	The association of the demand for knowledge with the supply	The application of the invention	Financing the application of the invention	The incentive to create or use the knowledge
Methods of acting	Scientific work	1. Facilitating the scientific work 2. Motivation for the scientific work	Searching for the demand for knowledge, or the knowledge supply	1. The implementation of the innovation 2. Production activity or market activity	1. Searching for projects 2. Investment activity	1. Regulation 2. Grants 3. Public expenditure or subsidies 4. Other tools of the scientific policy

Table 6.1 (continued)

	The inventor	The university or research institute	Promoter of science to businesses	The businessman	The investor	The state
Desirable motivations	1. Scientific ambitions 2. Financial interest	1. Scientific ambitions 2. Financial interest, direct or indirect	Financial interest	1. Competitive pressure 2. Financial interest (profit)	Financial interest (profit)	Implementation of the science or development policy
Undesirable motivations	1. An unwillingness to commercialize research 2. Excessive desire for profit (at the expense of the university)	1. Jealousy, resentment of the success of the inventor 2. Excessive desire for profit (at the expense of the inventor)	Excessive desire for profit	1. Conservatism (avoiding innovation) 2. Avoiding risks 3. Intellectual piracy	1. Excessive desire for profit 2. Avoidance of risk	1. Bureaucratic ambitions 2. Excessive fiscalism
Source of income	1. Intellectual ownership 2. Remuneration of the university 3. Research grants	1. Intellectual property 2. Reward for using the infrastructure	Bonus for commercialization	Profit from the use (minus investor, broker or salary)	Profit on investment	Long-term tax revenues from GDP growth

Source: Orłowski (2013).

on the degree of economic development of the country, the level of the development of innovation in enterprises, legal and system conditions. In studying the conditions for the development of the concept of a knowledge-based economy in Poland, it is important to study barriers to this development. We can see in Table 6.2 that there are many different barriers, but there is one main point: the lack of interest and action of the market players: business and institutions creating the law and the rules.

THE CONDITIONS OF THE KNOWLEDGE-BASED ECONOMY IN POLAND

Over the past 15 years, Poland has recorded among the highest gross domestic product (GDP) growth rates in the European Union. Also, the product innovation indicators are at a decent level compared to other European countries. On the other hand, the indicators commonly used to measure innovation in the economy are ranked among the lowest among the countries of the EU and the OECD. The annual Innovation Union Scoreboard summary, prepared by the European Commission, includes Poland in the weakest group of 'the humble innovators' in the Union (together with Latvia, Romania and Bulgaria), noting also its slow progress in improving the situation (see Table 6.3).

There are a variety of phenomena that indicate the slow progress of the processes of a knowledge-based economy in the Polish economy. The most commonly used measure of the intensity of R&D in international comparisons is expenditure on R&D. In relation to GDP, it is among the lowest of EU countries and the OECD countries.

The expenditure on research and development (R&D), in relation to the GDP, was in Poland in 2011 at a level of 0.77 per cent of GDP (compared with the OECD average of 2.40 per cent, the EU average of 2.04 per cent, and the Visegrad Group (V4)[1] average of 1.00 per cent). Expenditure regressed in the years 2001–07, reducing from the level of 0.7 per cent of GDP to less than 0.6 per cent of GDP. During this period, the share of expenditure on R&D in developed countries remained stagnant, and participation in developing countries rapidly increased (mostly under the influence of the dynamic growth of expenditure on R&D in the countries of south-east Asia). During the years 2008–11 the share of spending on R&D in Poland gradually increased, but not to an extent that would significantly improve the situation in comparison with the developed countries and those in the forefront of scientific and technical progress. By comparing the expenditure on R&D in Poland and in different groups of

Table 6.2 Barriers to the development of the market research in Poland and proposals for action

Barriers	Proposed actions
Demand side	
Lack of interest in innovation from business	The new industrial policy Supporting international expansion of companies The system of tax incentives Awarding a bonus on cooperation Increase the effectiveness of National Research Programmes as a catalyst for research Educational and promotion activity
Low development of the culture of innovation and little experience in cooperation of business and science	Promotion and dissemination of the examples of success Supporting programme for the development of start-up business Consulting for small and medium-sized enterprises (SMEs) Tax incentives for innovation in SMEs
Foreign decision-making centres in most large companies	The new industrial policy in the field of the direct investment
Weak development of the financial markets in the sphere of innovation financing	Financial incentives for innovation financing by banks Considering the creation of a 'Bank of an Innovative Economy'
Low attractiveness of the supply side, the weakness of the transmission mechanism; the lack of an effective market regulation policy	Actions to improve the attractiveness of the supply side Actions to improve efficiency of the transmission mechanism Actions to improve the effectiveness of the regulatory policy of the market
Supply side	
Little material interest in commercialization from inventors	A clear decision in the field of intellectual property (law transfer for the inventors) Encouragement and assistance in opening own businesses by employees of the scientific institutions
Lack of experience and ability to cooperate with business	Consulting for researchers interested in working with business Education in the academic entrepreneurship
Lack of clear rules of the cost and revenues accounting from the commercialization of the scientific institutions	Clear rules for cost research accounting Programme of refraining voluntarily from burdening the inventor with costs

Table 6.2 (continued)

Barriers	Proposed actions
Internal locking mechanisms in the scientific institutions	Promotion of the long-term benefits from commercialization
	Ban on deterring commercialization through financial burdens and legal-organizational obstacles
Availability of soft financing, and lack of compulsion to seek long-term income from commercialization	Increasing the scale of economic compulsion
	Strengthening the role of the competitive system of competing for grants for research
	Greater use of National Research Programmes as a catalyst for research of a commercial nature
	Contracts between the government and the science institutions
Decline in the quality of human capital in the scientific institutions	Granting funds for research for young researchers
	Support for linking scientific activities with business
Lack of market demand for brokerage services	Financial support for the creation of the companies promoting science
Lack of effective support from the market regulation policy	Support of the circulation of information between science and business
	Education and promotion

Source: Orłowski (2013).

countries it is easy to believe that in Poland it is below the level that would be expected, and that would be consistent with the trends of development of the KBE (Figure 6.1).

The OECD has produced a composite indicator of 'investment in knowledge' made up of investment in R&D, investment in higher education, and investment in information technology (IT) software. By this input measure, we can identify three groups of economies (Brinkley, 2006: 7):

- the high knowledge investment economies of North America, OECD Asia and Japan, investing around 6 per cent of GDP;
- the middle knowledge investment economies of Northern Europe and Australia, investing between 3 and 4 per cent of GDP;
- the low investment economies of Southern Europe, investing between 2 and 3 per cent of GDP.

Table 6.3 Poland's place in the international rankings of innovation

A comparison	Countries covered by the study	Poland's place	Remarks
Innovation Union Scoreboard 2013	27 countries of the European Union	24	24 indicators (human resources, R&D system, the financing of R&D, business activity, economic effects of R&D)
OECD Science, Technology and Industry Scoreboard 2011	34 OECD countries	29–30	12 selected key indicators (education and human resources, financing of R&D, business activity, economic effects of R&D)
Global Competitiveness Report 2012–2013	144 countries of the world	54	The main point in the pillar 'the ability to innovate'

Source: Orłowski (2013).

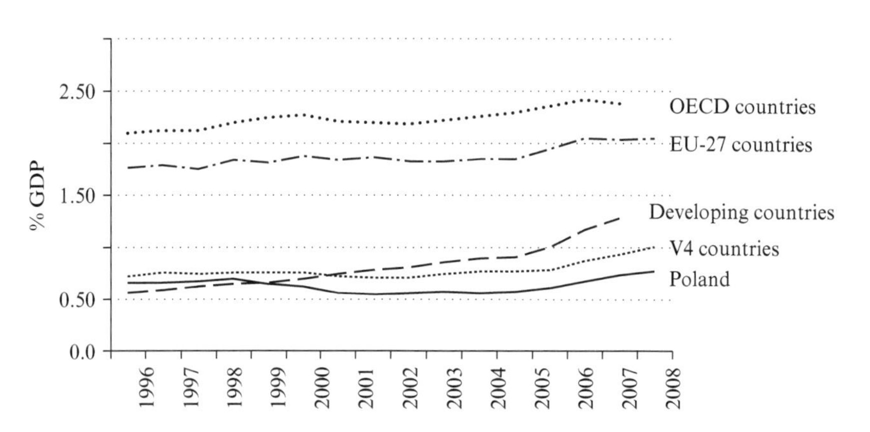

Source: Orłowski (2013).

Figure 6.1 R&D expenditure in relation to GDP in Poland and groups of countries, 1996–2011

In reality, however, the scale of expenditure on R&D incurred by the private sector (the economy), which is usually strictly linked to commercialization and the use of scientific inventions in practice, shows the weakness of the absorption processes of the results of R&D in the Polish economy more than the total scale of expenditure on R&D in relation to GDP. It should be noted that studies funded by the state usually have only an indirect impact on the innovation economy.

In this respect, the situation of Poland looks significantly worse than in the assessment of the total expenditure on R&D. The relationship of the expenditure on R&D to GDP, equal to 0.23 per cent, is many times lower than in developed countries (seven times lower than the average in the OECD, six times lower than in the EU, two times lower than in the V4 countries). The level of business enterprise research and development (BERD) in Poland is one of the lowest reported by the OECD, where it ranges from 0.17 per cent for Mexico to 3.50 per cent for Israel. Among the developing countries observed by the OECD, many levels of BERD are much higher than Poland's (Russia, 0.67 per cent of GDP; China, 1.40 per cent of GDP). The decrease of BERD in the years 2000–2002 was catastrophic (0.29 per cent of GDP to 0.11 per cent of GDP), and the partial reconstruction in the years 2003–11 was very slow.

Low interest in R&D activities in the Polish economy has led to very low-level processes of the knowledge-based economy in the economic development of the country. Until recently the Polish economy was focused almost exclusively on the purchase of ready-made solutions, mostly from abroad. This phenomenon was in itself understandable, given a relatively large-scale technological gap in relation to the countries in the forefront of scientific and technical progress (allowing for easy and affordable acquisition of the necessary technologies), relatively low-cost work, and given the high profitability of capital investment in gradually reducing the technological gap. The situation is slowly beginning to change. On the market, there are more and more Polish solutions: innovative solutions that are implemented in Polish companies, and increasingly also supported and used abroad.

Studies show the reasons for this state of affairs. It was found that cooperation between science and business is hampered by different priorities of researchers and entrepreneurs, a different approach to time and cost, lack of trust, and the excess paperwork and poorly developed environment of the technology transfer intermediaries. More and more scientists understand that the needs of business enable their inventions to see the light of day. Also, more and more entrepreneurs understand that the only way to be competitive on the market is to be equipped with the innovations discovered by scientific research. However, one cannot forget that scientists and entrepreneurs operate on different planes. For the entrepreneurs, the priority is profit; for the researcher it is the answer, the solution of the problem. For the researcher, time is not the most important factor; for the businessman, time is money.

The key barriers to cooperation between the scientific and business spheres are – according to the experts – a different approach to time and cost, different priorities, but also the mutual lack of trust and the deficit of knowledge about each other, and, unfortunately, the still poorly developed environment of the technology transfer intermediaries. In the science and innovation ecosystem, there is a dramatic lack of professional managers who have experience at all levels of company management.

The potential of Polish science is much larger than industry's demand for it. Science is ready to render services for industry, but technological and industrial parks do not have such needs because of the price competition between them, rather than technology and innovation competition. The scale is also important: there are no large industrial companies with large production volumes and high competence in Poland. The economy must be ready to absorb the potential of Polish science (Górski et al., 2016).

As described above, the level of commitment and implementation of strategy that affects the economic development of the country persists in Poland at an 'intermediate' level. There is a gap between the level of functioning of these entities in the highly developed countries and in Poland. Effective actions will reduce this gap. This is the challenge in increasing the efficient use of knowledge and innovation as the main driving force. To do so requires the following measures (Kasperkiewicz and Rogalski, 2016):

- Forward thinking about the economy and setting long-term development goals.
- Ensuring a stable macroeconomic environment that provides a background for the implementation of the modernization programmes, with transparent rules of fiscal policy and monetary affairs, and low and predictable inflation, that make up the framework for the activities of the business.
- Development of innovation requires a well-functioning institutional system. The availability of qualified human capital and high investment in R&D are important factors stimulating innovative processes, but they do not automatically guarantee effective commercialization of the new technologies, or the acceleration of GDP growth. An appropriate institutional order is needed that affects the degree of use of the technological potential of the economy and the diffusion of innovation. A key element of the institutional environment is a wide range of conditions for doing business.

- Increasing and adequate allocation of the financial resources for R&D and implementation coming from the state budget and the enterprises' funds. Changes in this area should rely not only on a significant increase in budgetary outlays, but above all on increasing the investment of the companies on R&D by facilitating access to capital. Important for the financing of innovative projects of the enterprises is the development of high-risk capital market (private equity, venture capital and 'business angels'). The existing commitment of these funds to financing innovation is highly inadequate.
- Education on the permanent connections and the methods of knowledge transfer between the R&D sphere and the sphere of business. Poland lacks an effective system of cooperation between these areas.
- Improving the quality of business management and enhancing microeconomic competitiveness. The lack of these skills cannot be remedied with good fiscal and monetary policies. The policy in these areas can only help, but it is the ability of the enterprises to manage knowledge effectively, and to implement the innovations, that will determine the level of innovation of the Polish economy.
- An important pillar of the strategy for the development of a knowledge-based economy is an education system that places emphasis on creativity and collaboration skills, developing a widely available offer of lifelong learning, knowledge refreshment, or even change of profession, and has increased flexibility in shaping study programmes and their internationalization.

The sector of Polish companies investing in research and development in 2011 included 795 firms. In comparison with the previous period, the number of companies increased by 18.48 per cent (671 firms in 2010). In the four-year period of 2008–11 this sector grew on average by 10.36 per cent.

The most innovative production companies in Poland are the pharmaceutical companies producing coke, refining oil, and producing chemicals and chemical products. In the services sector, the most innovative are insurance and reinsurance companies, financial services firms, and companies operating in the field of information services. Innovative enterprises accounted for 16.1 per cent of industrial companies and 11.6 per cent of service companies (Polish Investment and Trade Agency, 2017).

A major barrier to the development of innovation in Polish companies is the divergence between the business and scientific communities in terms of the directions of research and the resulting effects. Most important for the entrepreneurs are the economic effects achieved in a shorter period than is apparent from the perspective of the research institutions. That is why activities that help to accelerate the commercialization of the innovative solutions and bring the worlds of science and business together are important. The pharmaceutical sector is an example of activities in this type of cooperation.

The impact of the pharmaceutical sector on the Polish economy is steadily growing thanks to its unique ability in effective commercialization of innovation. The PwC (2011) report 'Impact of the innovative pharma industry on the Polish economy' shows the combined impact of pharmaceutical companies in creating added value in the Polish economy to be at 0.8 per cent of GDP. Close to two-thirds of this effect was created by companies considered to be innovative. These companies not only positively affect the development of the economy and the development of medicine by funding clinical trials, but also on the labour market provide an additional source of remuneration for researchers, physicians and research centres.

In 2010 innovative pharmaceutical companies provided on the Polish market products with a value of 9.4 billion PLN, which represents 58 per cent of the value of the prescription drugs market and medicines. They produce more than 70 per cent of drugs used in hospitals, and, in the case of the pharmacy market, this share is 55 per cent. The value of exports in 2010 was about 3.6 billion PLN, which represents 34 per cent of the total sales of the innovative pharmaceutical industry in Poland. These companies invest in the development and modernization of their production, run clinical trials, and form centres providing services to more than 100 international markets in the areas of outsourcing, such as IT, clinical, finance and accounting and distribution and logistics. These data show that the pharmaceutical market has grown much faster than the Polish economy, and it is beginning to play an increasingly important role, with a year-on-year increasing contribution to the creation of added value in Poland (*Harvard Business Review*, 2017).

The same applies to other industries, as shown in studies carried out among businesses. Companies that want to cooperate with scientists are able to reach out to universities. However, this also means that businesses much more often initiate contact than do employees in scientific research, this is in turn evidenced by the low level of the initiative of the representatives of the scientific world. That cooperation is clearly more frequently initiated by business proves the existence of an apparent demand for services from the national research institutes, and the possibility of obtaining competitive advantage associated with the implementation of research results. It seems that one of the primary causes of weak cooperation between businesses and universities may be ignorance of the offer of the sphere of research and development. Businesses also indicated what kind of deals they expect from the world of science: of greatest importance for them is advice on the use of techniques and technologies, and finding inspiration in terms of directions for the development of new technologies (Bąk and Kulawczuk, 2009)

Universities and research institutes may show a low level of interest in maximizing the sales research results for several reasons (Orłowski, 2013):

- the science institutions may not have the resources (especially human) necessary to provide the necessary research for the economy;
- the lack of skills and experience in the commercialization of research and a reluctance to learn them;
- the science institutions may not be forced into the commercialization of research, because of having readily available 'soft' funding sources (that is, sources that ensure they can function without making an effort for the commercialization of research);
- there can be mechanisms clearly blocking commercialization of research in the science institutions, for example the reluctance on the part of the majority of workers to actively seek such capabilities (such mechanisms can be easily hidden under seemingly necessary administrative activities, or masked by arguments concerning the alleged attention to quality basic research);
- in the area of the science institutions, the inventor is encumbered by the costs of implementation.

In the case of the universities and research institutes (the institutions of science), the main reasons for carrying out market research are (Orłowski, 2013):

- to ensure a high degree of intellectual and organizational freedom;
- the existence of strong incentives in terms of the financial interest in commercialization;
- the existence of strong incentives to actively seek long-term benefits from the commercialization of research;
- creating the regulations that will enable and facilitate market research activity.

There is a kind of golden mean needed: the universities must show the directions of the development of science, but also work with entrepreneurs and respond to their specific needs. What is more, the university should be able to indicate potential areas of research that could be useful. Cooperation between universities and business should rely on the bilateral presentation of their expectations and opportunities, and they should learn from each other – only under these conditions can a truly innovative environment be created.

According to experts, it is necessary to search for a modern form of education, adequate for the rapidly changing world, and to build such education programmes at the universities. This should be the background of creating the innovative and creative attitude of the students (Górski et al., 2016).

DEVELOPMENT OF DOCTORAL EDUCATION IN POLAND: AN OUTLINE

The roots of doctoral studies in Poland date back to the early postwar period. Since the early 1950s, doctoral studies were complementary to the assistantship,[2] the way of teaching research and didactic staff (Lewicki, 2011). In Poland under the Soviet-backed communist regime (1945–1989), higher education was centralized and heavily subordinated to the state authorities. The structure of higher education institutions and institutes of the Polish Academy of Sciences (Soviet model) was to implement state plans in the area of science and education. And while higher education had become available to people from all social classes, study programmes and the number of students depended on the general needs of the centrally planned economy (Antonowicz, 2015: 153–159). The situation with the training of future doctors was similar.

The most frequently cited characteristic characterizing the transformation of higher education in Poland after 1989 is the unprecedented increase in the number of students, from 0.4 million in 1990/91 to 1.95 million in 2005/06. Recently, there has been a decrease in the number of students because of the demographic decline, to 1.4 million in 2015/16. The obvious consequence of the increase in the number of students was the increasing number of graduates, from 56 000 in 1991 to 440 000 in 2009. Taking into account the development of the two-cycle study model after 2005, the rise in the number of people holding a master's degree is significant. Massification also affected doctoral studies; while the number of first and second cycle students after 2006 began to decline, the number of doctoral candidates continued to increase. In the academic year 1990/91 at both universities and research institutions (mainly the Polish Academy of Sciences, Polska Akademia Nauk, PAN), doctoral candidates totalled 2695 people, which is less than in 2016 at the Warsaw University alone, or the Jagiellonian University in Krakow alone. In subsequent academic years the number of doctoral candidates was as follows:

- 1995/96: 10482
- 2000/01: 25622
- 2005/06: 32725
- 2010/11: 37492
- 2015/16: 43177.

Among the 43000 the most numerous subjects of study were doctoral studies in the humanities (≈8400), technical sciences (≈6900), social sciences (≈4500), law (≈3700), economics (≈3600), medicine (≈3000), biological sciences (≈2000), chemistry (≈1800), agriculture (≈1700), theology (≈1700) (GUS, 2016). Therefore, the PhD candidates of the social sciences and humanities disciplines dominate, due for example to the lower cost of running such doctoral programmes. Please note that (according to ISCED'97 classification) in Poland the proportions of PhD candidates of different disciplines are different from the EU average. For instance (NKN, 2017a: 31):

- Humanities and arts: Poland, 24.2 per cent; EU, 15.2 per cent.
- Social sciences, business, administration, law: Poland, 28.9 per cent; EU 20.6 per cent.
- Physics, biological, mathematics, ICT: Poland, 15.0 per cent; EU, 24.6 per cent.
- Engineering and technology: Poland, 16.6 per cent; EU, 19.1 per cent.

Despite the significant increase in the number of PhD candidates in last 20 years, the increase in doctoral degrees was much lower (including doctoral degrees awarded without doctoral studies) (NKN, 2017a: 19–20):

- 1996: 2546
- 2001: 4667
- 2006: 5626
- 2011: 4856
- 2015: 6012.

In 2015, 97.8 per cent of PhD degrees were given by higher education institutions (HEIs).

The highest number of doctoral degrees is given in the areas of the humanities and social sciences, and their number is growing. On the other hand, the number of doctoral degrees in natural sciences, engineering, agriculture and veterinary science is decreasing. Rodzik, analysing changes in the number of doctoral candidates and the number of doctoral degrees, indicates that in the years 1999–2005 the effectiveness of PhD studies was higher than in the following ten years (Rodzik, 2016: 145–146). Since 2008, the number of women earning PhDs has been growing.

The next – after 1989 – crucial shift for Poland's higher education system was its involvement in the Bologna Process:

> In Poland, the signing of the Bologna Declaration (1999) coincided with a period of growing criticism of the higher education system. It was pointed out that the university's offer to the labor market was not adjusted . . . Poland, a country that was aspiring to membership of the European Union, could not afford to be marginalized in the area of higher education, especially since the Lisbon Strategy (2000) recognized it [higher education] as one of the priority areas for the development of the European economy. (Antonowicz, 2015: 277)

Some researchers, however, do not overestimate the role of the Bologna Process, which is simply part of a number of reforms of higher education in the post-communist countries (including PHARE programme activities) (Dakowska, 2017: 9–10).

Finally, in 2005, a new Act, the Law on Higher Education, was adopted. The law, referring to the Bologna Process, has again regulated the issue of doctoral studies. PhD candidates were recognized as a separate academic group from (first and second cycle) students and academic staff. Granting doctoral degrees remained independent of doctoral studies and regulated by a separate Act on academic degrees and academic title, and degrees and titles in the field of art (Law HE, 2005; Degrees Act, 2003). It is worth noting that the Communiqué of the Conference of Ministers responsible for Higher Education in Berlin (2003) stressed the importance of research and research training and doctoral education which was introduced into the Bologna Process as one of the links between the European Higher Education Area (EHEA) and the European Research Area (ERA) (Communiqué, 2003).

In 2011 another reform was launched. The amendments to the Law on Higher Education were focused on, for example, qualification frameworks, quality assurance, changes in academic career, and creating the new grants system. For doctoral education a description of the curriculum using learning effects was introduced as well as a new dimension of ECTS (European Credit Transfer System) credits for doctoral studies. The legal link between PhD studies and the procedure for obtaining a PhD degree was strengthened. The list of legal forms of PhD dissertation became wider; before reform, the form of PhD thesis was limited to that of an unpublished book (Law HE, 2005: amendment 2011). Although the reform of 2011 covered doctoral studies at the Polish Academy of Sciences and research institutes, some rights were restricted to PhD candidates at HEIs. PhD candidates became neither students nor faculty (Lewicki, 2011). Some of the regulations for PhD candidates were adopted on the basis of the rights of first and second cycle students (for example, social assistance), others form part of the model for researchers (for example, some grant programmes). One of the main objections to the 2011 reform was the significant increase in bureaucracy. The regulations were therefore revised in 2014 and 2016,[3] but those two amendments have not changed the system. The crucial stakeholders (in particular policy makers and rectors), as well as HE experts, agreed the necessity for complete reform of the system of higher education that was established in 2005.

PHD STUDIES AND PHD DEGREES

Currently, doctoral studies in Poland can be run by institutions (university units, institutes of the Polish Academy of Sciences, research institutes) which have the right to confer the degree of habilitated doctor in at least one discipline, or the right to confer a doctoral degree (PhD) in two disciplines. PhD studies are completed with the 'third-level qualification', which is obtained through the doctoral dissertation. This means that doctoral studies lead to a PhD degree. The procedure for granting the doctorate itself is independent of doctoral studies and, what is more, can be conducted by a person who has never enrolled in a doctoral programme.

Doctoral studies should last from two to four years. A programme should consist partly of organized classes (lectures, seminars and so on, and 30–45 ECTS credits), including training for research or research and development activities (for example, research methodology), and also in preparing for teaching in HEIs. Doctoral candidates at universities have compulsory apprenticeships as academic teachers (10–90 hours per year): they have classes with students, or support faculty members. The second part of doctoral studies is research and preparation of the dissertation under the guidance of a scientific supervisor, which is individually organized. Since the academic year 2016/17, learning outcomes at doctoral studies must be compatible with descriptors of the 8th level of the National Qualification Framework (NQF). Figure 6.2 shows the main elements of PhD studies in Poland and their outcomes.

The procedure for granting a doctoral degree is conducted by a scientific council of an institution (for example, faculty or institute council). The candidate must hold a master's degree (or equivalent, such as an MD),[4] be the author of at least one scientific publication, and pass two or three doctoral exams in a basic discipline (related to the topic), an additional discipline (for example, philosophy) and foreign language (if there is no

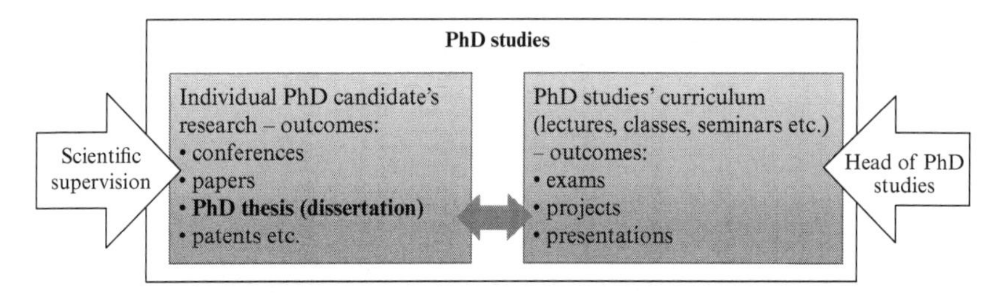

Figure 6.2 Main elements of PhD studies in Poland and their outcomes

language certificate). The candidate submits a doctoral dissertation with the supervisor's opinion to the scientific council, and the council appoints at least two reviewers (from outside the institution). Then the public defence of the doctoral dissertation before the commission (or council) takes place. The reviewers participate in the defence, and after the presentation review, they can ask the candidate questions. After considering the reviews and defence, the council gives the doctor's degree. At this point, it is worth paying attention to the requirements of the doctoral dissertation. The rules do not define the doctoral thesis in terms of learning outcomes, but, generally, requirements for the doctoral thesis are compatible with NQF level 8 knowledge and skills descriptors. There are no social competence issues defined, as for doctoral studies (see above).

The requirements for the doctoral thesis are laid down by law:

> The doctoral dissertation, elaborated under the supervision of a scientific supervisor or under the supervision of a scientific supervisor and an auxiliary scientific supervisor, should be the original solution to the scientific problem or the original solution to the problem based on design, construction, technology or original artistic performance, and demonstrate general theoretical knowledge of the candidate in the scientific discipline or artistic discipline and the ability to independently conduct scientific research or artistic work. (Degrees Act, 2003: Article 13.1)[5]

After 2011, a catalogue of doctoral dissertation forms was further refined and expanded. Alternatives to a traditional typescript of a book (unpublished), a book (published), or a collection of scientific articles, and so on, could be a technical project, construction, technology, or artistic work or artistic performance. Regardless of the form, it must meet the requirements cited above. Table 6.4 refers to the requirements for awarding a PhD degree with learning outcomes for doctoral studies (Ministry Ordinance compatible with NQF level 8). The learning outcomes for the doctoral level are quite universal and can be used for differentiated

Table 6.4 PhD studies learning outcomes and requirements for PhD degree

PhD studies (programme)		Element in the process of obtaining PhD degree that validates learning outcomes
Learning outcomes – level 8 NQF typical for higher education		
Knowledge A graduate knows and understands:	Main development trends in scientific or artistic disciplines relevant to the curriculum	PhD thesis (dissertation) Exam – basic discipline Public defence
	Research methodology	PhD thesis
	Fundamental dilemmas of modern civilization	Exam – additional discipline Thesis (partially)
	Economic, legal and other important determinants of research activity	PhD thesis Public defence (partially)
Skills A graduate can:	Use knowledge from various fields of science or art to create creative identification, formulation and innovative solving of complex problems or to perform research tasks, in particular: – define the purpose and object of the research, formulate a research hypothesis – discover methods, techniques and tools for research and use them creatively based on the research results	PhD thesis Exam – basic discipline Public defence
	Transfer research results to the economic and social sphere	(Depends on the topic)
	Disseminate research results, also in popular forms	Public defence
	Initiate a debate	Public defence PhD thesis (partially)
	Participate in scientific discourse	PhD thesis (partially)
	Use a foreign language to participate in an international academic and professional environment	Foreign language exam or certificate PhD thesis – if it is in foreign language
	Plan and implement an individual or team research or creative venture, also in the international environment	PhD thesis (partially)
	Plan and act independently for their own development, and inspire and organize the development of others	–

Table 6.4 (continued)

PhD studies (programme)		Element in the process of obtaining PhD degree that validates learning outcomes
Learning outcomes – level 8 NQF typical for higher education		
Social competences A graduate is ready to:	Develop education or training programmes and implement them using modern methods and tools	–
	Critical evaluation of the achievements of the represented scientific or artistic discipline	PhD thesis (partially)
	Critical evaluation of their own contribution to the development of this discipline	Public defence
	Recognize the importance of knowledge in solving cognitive and practical problems	–
	Uphold and develop the ethos of research and creative environments, including: – conduct research in an independent way – respect the principle of public ownership of research results, taking into account the principles of intellectual property protection	PhD thesis (partially)

Source: Based on Degrees Act 2003; Rozporządzenie Ministra Nauki i Szkolnictwa Wyższego z dnia 26 września 2016 r. w sprawie charakterystyk drugiego stopnia Polskiej Ramy Kwalifikacji typowych dla kwalifikacji uzyskiwanych w ramach szkolnictwa wyższego po uzyskaniu kwalifikacji pełnej na poziomie 4–poziomy 6–8; Dz. U. 2016, poz. 1594 (Ordinance Ministry of Science and HE of 26 September 2016 On the characteristics of the second degree of the Polish Qualifications Framework typical for qualifications obtained within the higher education after full qualification on level 4–levels 6–8, *Journal of Laws* 2016 item 1694). Own translation.

curricula in all fields of science and arts, as well as for academic and practice-oriented PhD programmes.

As can be seen, the PhD studies should develop additional skills and attitudes other than just providing knowledge and research skills through research, as is the case with obtaining a PhD degree. In other words, the crucial result of PhD studies should be the person who has graduated with a doctorate, not the PhD thesis (dissertation), scientific book, patent, and so on.

PHD AND KNOWLEDGE-BASED ECONOMY

A collaboration between science units and the socio-economic environment is most often found in two processes – commercialization and knowledge transfer – which, although often treated as identical, actually emphasize slightly different stages in the implementation of innovation. Commercialization is understood as transforming knowledge into new products, technologies and organizational solutions; and transfer is the provision of information necessary for one entity to be able to duplicate another. This information comes in two forms: (1) technical in nature: engineering knowledge, science, and so on; and (2) legal, confidentiality agreements, patents, licences, and so on (Matusiak, 2006).

The increase in the number of PhD students is a global trend:

> The number of science doctorates earned each year grew by nearly 40% between 1998 and 2008, to some 34 000, in countries that are members of the Organisation for Economic Co-operation and Development (OECD). The growth shows no sign of slowing: most countries are building up their higher-education systems because they see educated workers as a key to economic growth . . . But in much of the world, science PhD graduates may never get a chance to take full advantage of their qualifications. (Cyranoski et al., 2011: 276)

It is therefore important to prepare future researchers to work outside the academy. In many scientific policy papers and reports three grades of university cooperation with the socio-economic environment in the area of doctoral training are indicated (see Borell-Damian, 2009; Borell-Damian et al., 2015):

- Doctoral studies without cooperation with industry.
- Doctoral studies with limited industry involvement: these are often classic PhD programmes with indirect involvement in the financing of part of the research, delivery, data for a doctoral dissertation, or to enable an internship, but without supervision in the process of creating a dissertation.
- Collaborative doctoral education: these programmes include a close interaction between the company, a doctoral candidate and a university. The key element is the participation of representatives of the company in conducting the PhD programme, and in the research for a dissertation, as well as the writing of doctoral dissertations by people employed in enterprises.

In this context, no less important is the interdisciplinary approach to doctoral education. The idea of interdisciplinary doctoral training was strongly emphasized in the Communiqué of the Conference of Ministers (Communiqué, 2005) as well as by the European Commission in 'Principles for Innovative Doctoral Training' (EC, 2011).

The Polish authorities are also seeking solutions to differentiate pathways of doctoral education. An expert team was set up to meet the needs of one of the ministry projects. The experts pointed out possible hazards and barriers in the Polish socio-economic system (Dokowicz et al., 2017: 28–29), as outlined below.

Lack of Interest of the Socio-Economic Environment of the University in Cooperating in Doctoral Studies

The key motivations for partnerships with universities are: improving the qualifications of workers, discovering and developing new and innovative products, and supporting institutions in long-term development (shaping strategies). Polish innovative enterprises decreased from 28.1 per cent to 23 per cent of all Polish enterprises between 2010 and 2012 (with an EU-wide average of 48 per cent). Dokowicz et al. (2017) stressed that:

> It is essential to promote the idea of engaging companies in the process of generating and implementing innovation in the academic community through information actions, demonstrating good practice in this area, introducing system solutions such as fiscal incentives or additional funding for new technologies.
>
> It is also worthwhile that the universities themselves implement appropriate strategies for soliciting potential partners from the socio-economic environment. It is important to prepare an attractive offer that will show the material and human resources of the individual. This will allow external parties to learn the specifics of the organization and confront it with the developed development plans.

The Problem of Intellectual Property and Access to Information that is a Business Secret

> The intellectual property rights are one of the most important areas that should be included in the formal provisions of the cooperation agreements. This involves, on the one hand, the requirement to make a dissertation available to the scientific community (to review and debate it) and, on the other, to the protection of business secrets. Case studies have shown that when research results have no prospect of direct implementation in the industry, there are no impediments to the name of the business partner. On the other hand, when the results of the research have the potential for commercial applications, there has been a tendency to retain them either by the university (most of the cases studied) or by the business partner. There were also co-ownership solutions.

Dokowicz et al. (2017) find difficulty in recommending specific legal solutions, since each case should be considered individually and negotiated to optimize the interests of all partners involved in the cooperation. Undoubtedly, this issue should be unequivocally described in a tripartite agreement between the company, university and doctoral candidate.

Lack of Interest of the University in Cooperation with the Outside World

Dokowicz et al. (2017) note that:

> many universities perceive doctoral studies only as a process, the core of which is the supervisor–[PhD] student relationship, leading to the preparation and defence of a good doctorate. In this approach, the need to engage with outside actors is reinforced, believing that the relationship with the promoter is sufficient to equip the PhD student with the necessary competences, knowledge and skills.

In their report, Dokowicz et al. recommend various solutions that could be introduced in the current legal status. They point to the need to define the specific competences desired by business, industry, and so on when designing a curriculum for the application path of doctoral programmes.

TOWARDS 'PRO-INNOVATIVE' DOCTORAL EDUCATION IN POLAND

Since the end of 2016, various discussions on the future shape of the system of science and higher education have been taking place in Poland. The possibility of amending laws has been exhausted, and most stakeholders agree that the current solutions require major changes. That is why many of the activities carried out by the Ministry of Science and Higher Education in 2016 and 2017 are ad hoc or are pilot projects of some kind. At this point, it is worth mentioning the Ministry's 'implementation doctorate' programme. Units running PhD studies and having a high research category may apply for extra funds for research and pay for PhD candidates. The condition is that they work with the business environment: the PhD candidate must be (or become) an employee of the company where they will conduct part of the research, while the company appoints an auxiliary supervisor (Ministry of Science and Higher Education, 2017). Collective academic supervision supported by representatives of entrepreneurs was a proposal by, among others, Dokowicz et al. The Ministry's offer for companies is a change in the regulations on innovation. Tax reliefs and procedural easements are the basic solutions for companies looking to invest in research and development. The tax solution could potentially enhance cooperation in the field of doctoral education. Evaluation of these solutions will only be possible over time. Most important for the development of innovative PhD studies, or even HEIs effectively supporting the knowledge-based economy, will be the so-called 'Act 2.0' project (Ustawa 2.0).

As part of the work on the project of the future system of science and higher education (NKN, 2017b; KRD, 2017; CRASP, 2017):

- The Ministry commissioned three teams of experts to develop the new law. These three projects were the start of a broader discussion of the reform, and some of these proposals were used in Act 2.0.
- There have been ten thematic conferences of the National Congress of Science (Narodowy Kongres Nauki).
- The Conference of Rectors of Academic Schools in Poland (CRASP) has developed its own system proposals.
- The students' and researchers' organizations have submitted their proposals.
- The National Representation of PhD Candidates in Poland (Krajowa Reprezntacja Doktorantów, KRD) has submitted postulates for doctoral studies.
- The Ministry presented the first proposal of Act 2.0 in September 2017 at the National Congress of Science in Krakow. After consultations, the next version of the project was officially submitted to Parliament in March 2018.

Although the final form of the law will be known in mid-2018 at the earliest, it is possible to predict the direction of change for PhD studies on the basis of the proposed proposals.

First of all, the right to conduct PhD studies will be provided by the university as a whole, and not its faculties, which will allow for the creation of doctoral schools. Funds (scholarships) for all PhD candidates are to be provided in the first years of study; this may result in a decrease in the number of doctoral candidates. Flexible law for doctoral studies should facilitate the development of interdisciplinary and industry-wide PhD programmes. Probably, more emphasis will be placed on the development of soft skills and building ethical and innovative attitudes.

It will certainly be a good step in the development of resources for the KBE, but without the efforts of entrepreneurs even the best PhDs will not be able to effectively implement their solutions to real business and industry problems and challenges. The cost of change remains a challenge, but is inevitable. In contrast, demographic changes resulting in a decreasing number of students are a good opportunity for Polish HEIs to focus on the quality and innovation of both education and research.

CONCLUSIONS

To summarize the chapter it is worth mentioning three messages from the World Bank that show the exact challenges of education generally, and doctoral education (World Bank, 2007):

1. Knowledge and innovation have played a crucial role in development from the beginnings of human history. But with globalization and the technological revolution of the last few decades, knowledge has clearly become the key driver of competitiveness and is now profoundly reshaping the patterns of the world's economic growth and activity. Both developed and developing countries should therefore think, with some urgency, about their future under a KBE heading.
2. To become successful knowledge economies, countries have to rethink and act simultaneously on their education base, their innovation systems, and their information and communication technology infrastructure, while also building a high-quality economic and institutional regime. Policies for these four pillars have to reflect the country's level of development and will often have to be gradual. However, experience shows that some successful champions of the knowledge-based economy have been able to achieve spectacular leaps forward within a decade.
3. Many if not most of the countries that have made rapid progress have staged nationwide KE-inspired programmes of change.

In this context, the modernization of doctoral education should also take into account the necessity to prepare research staff to also work outside academia. The Polish economy in terms of innovation still has a lot of catching up to do, so multidisciplinary changes in Polish doctoral education all the more are needed.

Legal changes after 2011 (and announcements of further reforms) create a framework at the formal level for developing PhD studies also for R&D needs. First of all, excellence in research should be guiding all PhD studies. Effective implementation of the development of the competencies of future doctors will require changes in the universities themselves, and the strengthening of HEIs' relations with the business, industrial and social environments. In this regard, apart from the mutual understanding of academia and its environment, state-sponsored activities supporting innovation are required (as well as increased expenditures on science and higher education). Only given the right conditions, the right environment, can young scientists become leaders in innovation R&D activities.

NOTES

1. V4, the Visegrad Group, comprises the Czech Republic, Poland, Hungary and Slovakia.
2. *Asystent* (research and teaching assistant) in Poland is the lowest rank at the university for academic staff with a master's degree (or a PhD). An *asystent* is an employee with teaching and research (or only research) duties. The higher rank of *adiunkt* (assistant professor; adjunct) requires a PhD.
3. In October 2015, parliamentary elections took place in Poland, as a result of which the previous opposition took over power.
4. From 2011, there is an exception for the 'Diamond Grant' Minister's Contest winners – BA or BSc degree holders (maximum 100 persons per year).
5. Own translation.

REFERENCES

Antonowicz, D. (2015), *Między siłą globalnych procesów a lokalną tradycją. Polskie szkolnictwo wyższe w dobie przemian* (Between the strength of global processes and the local tradition. Polish higher education in the age of change). Toruń: Wydawnictwo Uniwersytetu Mikołaja Kopernika.

Bąk, M. and Kulawczuk, P. (eds) (2009), The conditions for effective cooperation between science and business. Research Institute on Democracy and a Private Company (IBnDiPP), Warsaw.

Borell-Damian, L. (2009), Collaborative doctoral education. University–Industry Partnership for Enhancing Knowledge Exchange, DOC-CAREERS II Project. European University Association.

Borrell-Damian, L., Morais, R., and Smith, J.H. (2015), Collaborative doctoral education in Europe: research partnership and employability for researchers. Report on DOC-CAREERS II Project, European University Association.

Brinkley, I. (2006), Defining the knowledge economy: knowledge economy programme report. Work Foundation.

Communiqué (2003), Realizing the European Higher Education Area – Communiqué of the Conference of Ministers responsible for Higher Education in Berlin on 19 September 2003. http://www.enqa.eu/wp-content/uploads/2013/03/BerlinCommunique1.pdf (accessed 15 June 2017).

Communiqué (2005), The European Higher Education Area: Achieving the Goals – Communiqué of the Conference of European Ministers responsible for Higher Education, Bergen, 19–20 May 2005. http://media.ehea.info/file/2005_Bergen/52/0/2005_Bergen_Communique_english_580520.pdf (accessed 17 June 2017).

Cyranoski, D., Gilbert, N., Ledford, H., Nayar, A. and Yahia, M. (2011), The PhD factory: the world is producing more PhDs than ever before. Is it time to stop? *Nature*, **472**, 21 April, 276–279.

Dakowska, D. (2017), Competitive universities? The impact of international and European trends on academic institutions in the 'New Europe'. *European Educational Research Journal*, **16**(5), 588–604.

Dokowicz, M., Dyląg, E., Knopik, T., et al. (2017), Opracowanie programów studiów doktoranckich o zróżnicowanych profilach (Development of doctoral programmes with diversified profiles). Ministry of Science and Higher Education, Warsaw.

https://repozytorium.amu.edu.pl/bitstream/10593/17522/1/Opracowanie_programow_studiow_doktoranckich.pdf (accessed 15 June 2017).
European Portal of Integration and the Development (2016), Knowledge based economy. Blog. http://europejskiportal.eu/gospodarka-oparta-na-wiedzy (accessed 16 July 2017).
Górski, J., Mikołajczyk, A., and Tataj, M. (eds) (2016), Raport: Społeczne oblicze innowacji. Jak wspierać postawy innowacyjne i promować etos innowatora? (Report: The social face of innovation. How to foster innovation and promote the ethos of the innovator?). Warsaw. http://docplayer.pl/16096733-Spoleczne-oblicze-innowacji-jak-wspierac-postawy-innowacyjne-i-promowac-etos-innowatora-redakcja-dr-jaroslaw-gorski-adam-mikolajczyk-marzena-tataj.html (accessed 6 April 2017).
GUS (2016), Szkoły wyższe i ich finanse w 2015 r. (Higher education institutions and their finances in 2015). Warsaw: Główny Urząd Statystyczny (Central Statistical Office).
Harvard Business Review (2017), The pharmaceutical sector: the marriage of business and science. https://www.hbrp.pl/a/sektor-farmaceutyczny-mariaz-biznesu-i-nauki/X3J5Onlc (accessed 12 June 2017).
Kasperkiewicz, W. and Rogalski, W.J. (2016), Polish economy in the face of challenges posed by innovativeness development. *Acta Scientifica Academiae Ostroviensis* No. A.7 (1)/2016, ISSN 2300-1739, 50–59. http://zn.wsbip.edu.pl/sectioa/zeszyt_1_2016.pdf.
Lewicki, J. (2011), Studia doktoranckie, doktoranci a reforma szkolnictwa wyższego (Doctoral studies, PhD candidates and the reform of higher education). In: J. Kostkiewicz, M. Szymański, A. Domagała-Kręcioch (eds), *Szkoła wyższa w toku zmian. Debata wokół ustawy z dnia 18 marca 2011 roku* (University in the course of change. Debate around the Act of March 18, 2011). Kraków.
Matusiak, K. (ed.) (2006), *Innowacje i Transfer Technologii – Słownik Pojęć* (Innovation and technology transfer – glossary of terms). Warszawa: Polska Agencja Rozwoju Przedsiębiorczości.
Ministry of Science and Higher Education (2017), *Ogłoszenie konkursu w ramach I edycji programu 'Doktorat wdrożeniowy* (Announcement of the competition within the first edition of the 'Implementation Doctorate' programme), 8 May. http://www.nauka.gov.pl/komunikaty/ogloszenie-konkursu-w-ramach-i-edycji-programu-doktorat-wdrozeniowy.html (accessed 26 July 2017).
NKN (2017a), Ścieżki kariery akademickiej i rozwój młodej kadry naukowej (Paths of academic career and development of young academic staff). Konferencja programowa Narodowego Kongresu Nauki,. (Programme Conference of the National Congress of Science), 26–27 January, Katowice.
OECD (1996), The knowledge-based economy. OCDE/GD(96)102. Paris: OECD.
Orłowski, W.M. (2013), Komercjalizacja badań naukowych w Polsce: bariery i możliwości ich przełamania (Commercialization of scientific research in Poland: barriers and the possibilities of breaking them). Warsaw: PwC. (In Polish.) http://www.biznes.edu.pl/upload/files/komercjalizacja-badan-naukowych-w-polsce---prof.-w.-orlowski.pdf.
Polish Investment and Trade Agency (2017), Research and development. Business support. http://www.paih.gov.pl/sectors/research_and_development# (accessed 26 July 2017).
PricewaterhouseCoopers (PwC) (2011), Impact of the innovative pharma industry

on the Polish economy. Report, September. https://www.pwc.pl/pl/publikacje/pwc_impact_of_the_innovative_pharma_industry_on_the_polish_economy.pdf.
Rodzik, P. (2016), Nadane stopnie i tytuły naukowe – czy coś się zmieniło? (Academic degrees and titles: Has anything changed?). *Nauka i Szkolnictwo Wyższe*, **2**(48). DOI: 10.14746/nisw.2016.2.7.
World Bank (2007), *Building Knowledge Economies: Advanced Strategies for Development*. WBI Development Studies. Washington, DC: World Bank.

Legal Acts

Degrees Act (2003), Ustawa z dnia 14 marca 2003 r. o stopniach naukowych i tytule naukowym oraz stopniach i tytule w zakresie sztuki, t.j. Dz. U. z 2016 r. poz. 882, 1311, z 2017 r. poz. 859. (Act of 14 March 2003 on academic degrees and academic title and degrees and titles in the field of art, Uniform text: *Journal of Laws* 2016 items 882, 1311, z 2017 item 859).
Law HE (2005), Ustawa z dnia 27 lipca 2005 r. Prawo o szkolnictwie wyższym, t.j. Dz. U. z 2012 r. poz. 572, 742, 1544, z 2013 r. poz. 675, 829, 1005, 1588, 1650, z 2014 r. poz. 7, 768, 821, 1004, 1146, 1198, z 2015 r. poz. 357, 860, 1187, 1240, 1268, 1923, z 2016 r. poz. 64, 90 (Act of 27 July 2005 Law on Higher Education, Uniform text: *Journal of Laws* 2012 items 572, 742, 1544, 2013 items 675, 829, 1005, 1588, 1650, 2014 items 7, 768, 821, 1004, 1146, 1198, 2015 items 357, 860, 1187, 1240, 1268, 1923, 2016 r. items 64, 90).
Rozporządzenie Ministra Nauki i Szkolnictwa Wyższego z dnia 26 września 2016 r. w sprawie charakterystyk drugiego stopnia Polskiej Ramy Kwalifikacji typowych dla kwalifikacji uzyskiwanych w ramach szkolnictwa wyższego po uzyskaniu kwalifikacji pełnej na poziomie 4 – poziomy 6–8; Dz. U. 2016, poz. 1594 (Ordinance Ministry of Science and HE of 26 September 2016 On the characteristics of the second degree of the Polish Qualifications Framework typical for qualifications obtained within the higher education after full qualification on level 4 – levels 6–8, *Journal of Laws* 2016 item 1694).

Websites

CRASP (2017), Konferencja Rektorów Akademickich Szkoł Polskich (Conference of Rectors of Academic Schools in Poland). http://www.krasp.org.pl/pl (accessed 26 July 2017).
KRD (2017), Krajowa Reprezntacja Doktorantów (National Representation of PhD Candidates in Poland). http://krd.edu.pl/ (accessed 26 July 2017).
NKN (2017b), Narodowy Kongres Nauki (National Congress of Science). https://nkn.gov.pl/ (accessed 26 July 2017).

7. HEInnovate: facilitating change in higher education*

Andrea-Rosalinde Hofer and Gabi Kaffka

INTRODUCTION

The complexity of our world is constantly adding new challenges for higher education institutions (HEIs). Not all of them require direct responses or can be solved by higher education institutions. Yet, in their totality, these challenges raise questions about the current shape and constitution of the higher education sector. Some scholars call for a 'deep, radical and urgent transformation' (Barber et al., 2013), questioning in particular the relevance of traditional conceptual and organisational models of higher education institutions.

Being, or becoming, an entrepreneurial and innovative higher education institution is a response to this. There is no unique approach, but a variety of ways in which higher education institutions behave entrepreneurially, for example, in how they manage resources and build organisational capacity, involve external stakeholders in their leadership and governance, create and nurture synergies between teaching, research and their societal engagement, and how they promote entrepreneurship through education and business start-up support as well as knowledge exchange to enhance the innovation capacity of existing firms. The rapid advance of new products and services, for example, in the fields of robotics, biochemistry and food processing, have profound implications on research and education and call for more dynamic collaboration of academic disciplines.

Entrepreneurship and innovation in higher education are no longer only associated with start-ups and technology transfer, but are increasingly understood as core elements of a procedural framework for how organisations and individuals behave (OECD and EU, 2017a, 2017b, 2017c). Interest in, and approaches to, the development of entrepreneurship and innovation in, and through, higher education are not confined to Europe. Over the past decade, examples of such approaches can be observed throughout the United States, Canada, Australia, Asia, Latin America, Africa and Eastern Europe (Fayolle and Redford, 2014).

Transforming (traditional) HEIs is neither an easy nor a straightforward endeavour. It requires commitment of resources into areas of change and high impact which, in turn, needs to build on a strategic collaboration between policy makers, HEI leaders, staff, students and partners in the local economy. Governments can support HEIs by adapting incentives and support structures and through specific programmes at national and sub-national levels that favour new approaches in teaching and learning, knowledge exchange and start-up support (OECD and EU, 2017a).

Supporting governments and HEIs in this endeavour is the aim of HEInnovate, a joint initiative by the European Commission (EC) and the Organisation for Economic Co-operation and Development (OECD). HEInnovate defines the entrepreneurial and innovative HEI as an organisation that is 'designed to empower students and staff to demonstrate enterprise, innovation and creativity in teaching, research and engagement/third-mission. Its activities are directed to enhance learning, knowledge production and exchange in a highly complex and changing societal environment, and are dedicated to create public value via processes of open engagement' (HEInnovate, 2014). By grounding HEInnovate in an interwoven and beyond-business concept of entrepreneurship, innovation and institutional change, we seek to counter the view that higher education institutions that behave entrepreneurially are becoming more commercially oriented and lose academic depth.[1]

HEInnovate is a guiding framework that describes the entrepreneurial and innovative higher education institution through seven dimensions, covering strategy, resources, practices and impact, and 37 statements that describe good and proven practice.[2] The guiding framework provides a comprehensive approach and was developed with inputs from a group of experts from academia and industry.

This chapter first presents the guiding framework and its conceptual foundations. It then summarises findings from several country reviews, undertaken by the OECD and the EC as part of the HEInnovate initiative, highlighting common approaches in HEI activities and policy support frameworks to support entrepreneurship and innovation. From the presentation of review findings it becomes clear that higher education institutions are recognising their innovative and entrepreneurial potential and are undertaking specific measures towards its enhancement. These commonalities confirm the usefulness of a common framework, such as HEInnovate, whose aim is to stimulate new practices, and the establishment of entrepreneurship support structures with a HEI-wide reach and allow students and staff to become part of the entrepreneurial agenda.

ORGANISING FOR INNOVATION AND ENTREPRENEURSHIP IN HIGHER EDUCATION INSTITUTIONS

Why does a guiding framework help to enhance innovation and entrepreneurship in higher education? A common tendency is to develop responses to challenges and opportunities within silo structures confined to faculties and departments or specialised professional services (such as technology transfer centres) inside higher education institutions.[3] Whereas this has helped to established often well-functioning islands of novel approaches to teaching and learning, research and engagement, wider spillovers across the HEI remain limited or absent (OECD and EU, 2017b). This raises the potential for a holistic approach for exploring the innovative and entrepreneurial potential of the HEI as the basis for change and future development, in line with the findings of current studies on how dominant organisational patterns in governance have changed from the classical notion of a higher education institution as a republic of scholars, towards the idea of a stakeholder organisation (Kohler and Huber, 2006; Kogan and Blieklie, 2007). For this to happen, a certain degree of autonomy is needed both at the level of individual staff as well as that of the organisation itself. Autonomy at faculty and individual levels needs to be grounded on shared academic values and a common vision in order for the organsation as a whole to become 'biased towards adaptive change' (Clark, 1998).

A note can be made here on the wide range of different organisations currently operating under the higher education banner. Legal frameworks vary between and even within countries, despite growing efforts to harmonise and recognise academic credentials and to facilitate student mobility. In some countries public higher education prevails, whilst in others private institutions are quickly expanding their influence. Hierarchies exist in almost every country, often based upon age and academic rights, but increasingly also upon demand and resources. Differentiation also exists with regard to the disciplinary focus, with specialist institutions for industry sectors, vocational subjects and different links into secondary and further education. The older, venerable, often well-resourced, culturally and sometimes locally embedded institutions will perhaps be able to maintain their current position and ways of practice for some time longer, whereas others will increasingly find themselves confronted by the short-term need for reforms (HEInnovate, 2014).

Despite diversity, there are key common characteristics that an entrepreneurial and innovative HEI embodies. This is reflected in the guiding framework and presented in seven dimensions as follows:

- Leadership and governance are two critical and challenging factors in developing entrepreneurial HEIs. Positive and responsive leadership is what maintains a dynamic and successful organisation, particularly in times of uncertainty, unpredictability and complexity. Leadership and governance can stimulate innovation of all kinds in an organisation that is held together by a shared vision and culture, not overloaded with managerial systems, constantly striving for its autonomy via the entrepreneurial management of its various interdependencies with stakeholders, taking responsibility and being accountable.
- Organisational capacity, people, incentives. Innovative and entrepreneurial HEIs continuously aim at developing their organisational capacity. To this end, incentives and rewards are in place for 'champions', staff, students and stakeholders, removing barriers and constraints within the organisation. The aim is to empower individuals throughout the organisation to run their own initiatives, build personal trust-based stakeholder relationships across external and internal boundaries in search of synergy, and introduce effective mechanisms to ensure institutional spillover and impact of individual activities.
- Entrepreneurial teaching and learning requires something other than standard textbooks and ordinary classroom settings. An entrepreneurial pedagogy seeks to enhance competencies for entrepreneurship amongst students by giving them more autonomy and responsibility in the learning process through experimental, collaborative and reflexive learning. It is not limited to learning about entrepreneurship, but is much more about being exposed to entrepreneurial experiences and acquiring the skills and competences for developing entrepreneurial mindsets.
- Preparing and supporting entrepreneurs entails teaching strategies and learning environments which offer targeted support for students and staff who aim at setting up a business. HEIs can provide this support directly themselves or refer potential entrepreneurs to specialised start-up support services within the (local) entrepreneurship ecosystem.
- Knowledge exchange is determined by the perceptions of the respective other. A negative attitude towards entrepreneurship, entrepreneurs and businesses within a higher education institution can limit and hinder network formation and collaboration with business partners and other stakeholders. Communication that ensures that both sides of a knowledge exchange network have a clear understanding of respective expectations, limitations and

requirements is a major building block of the entrepreneurial higher education institution.
- Internationalisation, an important indicator for quality in higher education, is not an end in itself, but a vehicle for continuous change and advancement. Higher education institutions can internationalise through their activities in teaching, research and knowledge exchange, and through their staff and students. Becoming a truly internationalised institution will build on both.
- Measuring the impact of certain practices on the entrepreneurial higher education institution is neither easy nor straightforward. To measure the impact of the entrepreneurial agenda, it is important to start by monitoring and reviewing entrepreneurship within the leadership of the higher education institution. This will help to establish an understanding of how important entrepreneurship is to the governing and executive boards, compared to other strategic objectives such as, for example, sustainability, excellence in research and attraction of international students. Excellence is judged through the eyes of all of its stakeholders in pursuit of the creation of public value.

Self-Assessment Tool for HEIs

Engaging HEI staff and students in the entrepreneurial agenda requires commitment and continued support from leadership as well as an agenda that does not solely rest on a top-down approach. In every HEI there will be those who resist change – particularly the entrepreneurial notion of it – and those who find it challenging and exciting once the fears have been overcome. Different departments will have different views, dependent upon the degree to which they are threatened by, or see opportunity in, their existing exposure to a wider stakeholder environment. Inspiring initiative and giving the academic community ownership of the entrepreneurial agenda are essential for success. Much will depend upon the presence of champions, who promote entrepreneurship and innovation and integrate these into higher education practice.

To facilitate dialogue and strategic discussions, a free online self-assessment tool – HEInnovate – was developed for HEIs to organise participatory stock-taking exercises to review achievements and identify areas for improvement related to innovation and entrepreneurship. A wide range of stakeholders (leadership, staff, academic and administrative staff, students, key partner organisations, and so on) can be easily involved, and the exercise can be repeated over time. The tool has been used by more than 800 HEIs around the world.[4]

The starting point in effectively supporting innovation and entrepreneurship in an HEI is building a common and shared understanding of what these mean for a specific institution within a given socio-economic context and policy framework. This is a progressive and reflective process relating to the particular focus of the HEI in question. Views will be considerably influenced by culture and the ways of doing things. Also, there are widely different governance and organisation structures which impact on the capacity to change (HEInnovate, 2014).

Knowing, for example, how deans, administrative staff, young researchers, students, and industry partners see the status quo of 'The HEI has the capacity and culture to build new relationships and synergies across the institution' (a statement in the HEInnovate dimension 'Organizational capacity') provides highly valuable information on key stakeholder perceptions where more action or communication is needed. Easy-to-read graphs (radar charts and bar charts) show where stakeholders agree or disagree and provide a basis for strategic discussions in board meetings, the senate or public events.

Users can work with all seven dimensions or choose dimensions that are most relevant for a specific purpose. For example, users are likely to select 'Organisational capacity' and 'Knowledge exchange' if the purpose is to (re-)organise collaboration with external stakeholders. An instant reporting function generates an easy-to-read snapshot of the status quo and potential areas of change in the chosen dimensions, comparing the rating of the user or user group to the global or HEI mean. The report points users to guidance material and case study examples with information on concrete actions that HEIs can undertake to enhance their performance in the respective dimension(s). Results are stored and can be compared over time. Data are accessible only to users, and users can choose to remain anonymous. Explanations of the statements (available in all European Union member state languages), a growing number of case studies, multimedia material and various facilitation tools to organise workshops on the guiding framework, how to use the self-assessment tool and how to use the survey results for strategic discussions make the guiding framework inspirational and very user-friendly.

There are various examples of how HEIs have been using the HEInnovate self-assessment tool. For example, to organise a creative consultation process around their institutional strategy (for example, Manchester Metropolitan University in the United Kingdom), to design new cross-faculty education programmes (for example, the University of Aveiro in Portugal) or for the reorganisation of entrepreneurship support infrastructure (for example, Dundalk Institute of Technology in Ireland).

COMMON TRENDS AND COUNTRY-SPECIFIC FEATURES: EMERGING FINDINGS FROM FOUR EUROPEAN COUNTRIES

The HEInnovate guiding framework is also used for policy and system reviews at the regional and country levels, undertaken by the OECD and the EC. Following a peer-review approach, involving policy makers, HEI leaders, academic and administrative staff members, and researchers from other countries, key areas of strength and areas for improvement are identified and analysed.

The aim of these reviews is to provide a roadmap for strengthening the innovative and entrepreneurial potential of higher education institutions. They help to identify and examine examples of good practice, which provide valuable learning for the higher education system in the country and beyond. This chapter focuses on four of these country reviews, namely Bulgaria (2014), Ireland (2015–16), Hungary (2015–16), and the Netherlands (2016–17) (OECD and EU, 2017a, 2017b, 2018).

The Entrepreneurial Agenda

The anchor concept of the HEInnovate guiding framework is the HEI's 'entrepreneurial agenda'. This is a context-specific concept, which may have different manifestations depending on the HEI's characteristics, such as size, age, coverage of academic disciplines and study programmes, as well as on the surrounding socio-economic situation, the higher education system and the policy framework for innovation and entrepreneurship.

Part of the HEInnovate country reviews is an online survey which is administered to HEI senior management (the HEI Leader Survey). Data presented in this chapter are from a sample of 84 HEIs in Ireland, Bulgaria, Hungary and the Netherlands, with an average response rate of 60 per cent (see the Appendix for an overview of the sample). The HEI Leader Survey seeks to capture the entrepreneurial agenda through eight objectives, which are typically associated with the entrepreneurial university concept in the literature. Respondents from senior management are asked to rate the importance of these objectives on a scale from 1 (not important at all) to 5 (very important). The following order was observed from the survey sample:

1. Cooperation between HEI and local firms ($M = 4.43$, $SD = 0.859$).
2. Developing entrepreneurial competencies and skills in students ($M = 4.37$, $SD = 0.886$).

3. Assuming a leading role in the local development agenda (M = 4.11, SD = 0.968).
4. Supporting business start-ups by students (M = 3.88, SD = 1.047).
5. Promoting self-employment and business start-up as a viable career option to students (M = 3.86, SD = 0.991).
6. Commercialising research results through technology transfer (M = 3.80, SD = 1.142).
7. Generating revenues for the HEI (M = 3.75, SD = 1.272).
8. Supporting business start-ups by staff (M = 3.19, SD = 1.221).

It appears that three types of objectives rank high on the entrepreneurial agenda of the surveyed HEIs across the four countries, namely: (1) the outward orientation of the HEI towards the surrounding local economy, with the objectives of cooperation with local firms, and assuming a leading role in the local development agenda; (2) promoting the entrepreneurial mindset with the objective of helping students to develop entrepreneurial competences and skills, and promoting business creation and self-employment as viable career options; and (3) supporting the application of research results through start-ups by students and standard forms of technology transfer. The lowest-ranked objective was supporting business start-ups by staff.

A Role for Public Policy

Public policy has an important role in promoting the entrepreneurial agenda of HEIs. In the reviewed countries, agreements between HEIs and national ministries or their agencies exist. These agreements were more common in Hungary (77 per cent) and Bulgaria (73 per cent) than in the Netherlands (55 per cent) and Ireland (30 per cent). Across the four countries the focus of these agreements was more on entrepreneurship education (63 per cent) than on the delivery of start-up support measures (56 per cent). In Ireland and the Netherlands, the engagement agenda and valorisation of knowledge are part of the performance and quality agreements that HEIs agree with the central-level government ministry or agency. Even though the set of indicators used to assess and guide performance is not centrally defined, but set by the HEIs themselves, there is a clear tendency to move towards a unique set of assessment indicators.

Reaching Out: Orientation Towards the Surrounding Local Economy

Knowledge exchange through collaboration and partnerships is an important component of any entrepreneurial and innovative HEI. It provides the opportunity to advance organisational innovation, teaching and research while creating value for society. The involvement of HEIs in the development and implementation of the local, regional or national strategies with relevance for entrepreneurship and innovation can be considered an indicator for the HEI's engagement in local development. The most common platforms for the surveyed HEIs were local strategic partnerships (88 per cent), followed by industry clusters (71 per cent) and development fora created by regional or local governments (69 per cent), chambers of commerce and industry (53 per cent), and national government fora on local development issues (49 per cent).

Developing the Entrepreneurial Mindset

Developing the 'entrepreneurial mindset', which combines creativity, a sense of initiative, problem solving, ambiguity tolerance, the capability to marshal resources, and financial and technological knowledge, is a key priority on the entrepreneurial agenda of HEIs. Related education activities are spreading across campus. In more than 90 per cent of the surveyed HEIs, entrepreneurship education activities were integrated in study programmes, and HEIs in the Netherlands were leading on this (this was slightly less common for the surveyed HEIs in Hungary, at 86 per cent). Overall, entrepreneurship education activities have moved beyond economics faculties and business schools, as more than two-thirds of the surveyed HEIs reported that entrepreneurship courses are organised (also) in other faculties. This practice was less common for the surveyed HEIs in Bulgaria and Hungary.

The main target group for entrepreneurship education activities are students in bachelor degree programmes (92 per cent); slightly less HEIs offer these activities for master's students (87 per cent). Only 61 per cent offer entrepreneurship education for doctoral students; however, this is very common in Ireland, with 94 per cent of the HEIs reporting that their doctoral students can undertake entrepreneurship education activities (Figure 7.1).

Consider this chilling statistic from the United States: 96 per cent of university officials surveyed believed that their students were well prepared for life after college; only 11 per cent of businesses agreed (Gallup, 2014). In a changing economy, a key question that HEIs face is how to train professionals with an entrepreneurial mindset. This combination of creativity, initiative, problem solving, marshalling resources, and mastering technological and financial knowledge is what is needed for success, in any field.

Developing the entrepreneurial mindset requires both new skills to be taught, and new ways of teaching them. These approaches have in

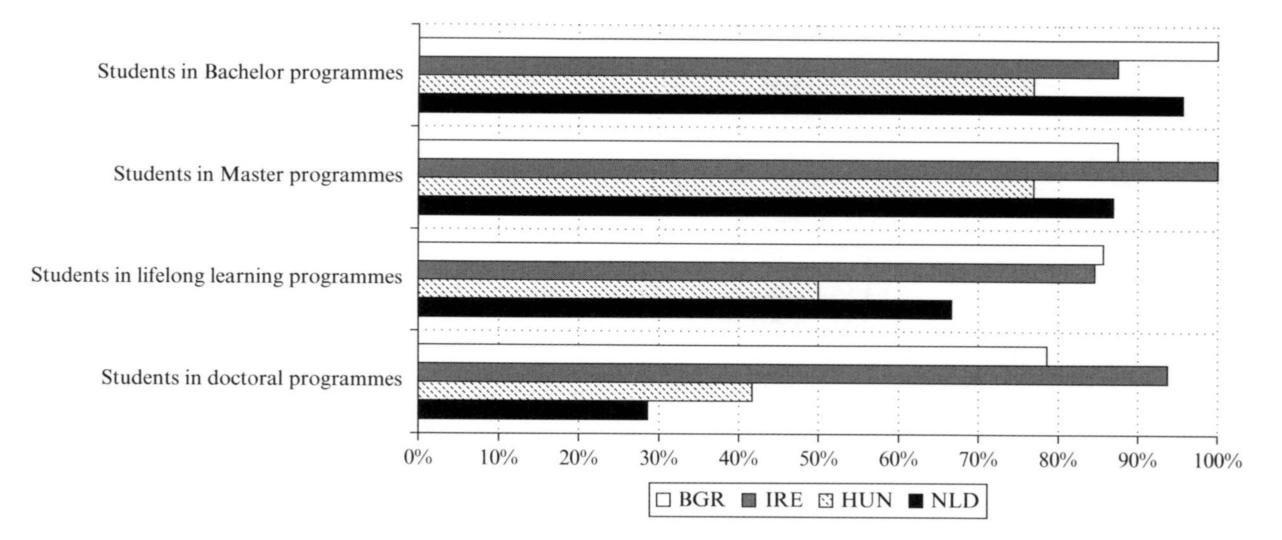

Notes: Higher education institutions (HEIs) currently offering entrepreneurship education activities were asked: 'Which are target groups of the entrepreneurship education activities?' The total number of responses was 93, of which 23 were from HEIs in the Netherlands, 14 from Hungary, 17 from Ireland, and 17 from Bulgaria. The overall survey response rates per country are: the Netherlands, 48%, 25 responses; Hungary, 60%, 21; Ireland, 86%, 21; Bulgaria, 48%, 20.

Sources: Based on OECD (2014) and OECD and EU (2017a, 2017b, 2018).

Figure 7.1 Student targets of entrepreneurship education activities across different programme levels

common the move away from a teacher-centric approach to student-led learning in which students can pose the question, 'What do I need (to learn)?', thus encouraging students to 'learn how to learn', to be resilient, action-oriented and comfortable with significant uncertainty (Kaffka, 2017).

Commitment to Implementing the Entrepreneurial Agenda

An effective and sustainable implementation of the entrepreneurial agenda requires a high level of commitment. The starting point is building a shared understanding of what the entrepreneurial agenda means for the different stakeholders in the HEI, that is, leadership, academic staff, administrative staff and students; and for external partners (for example, government, businesses, civil society organisations, donors). Central to this are communication and consultation about what the entrepreneurial agenda entails in terms of objectives, activities, priorities and resources.

Whole higher education institutions or their departments may be organised in ways that are breaking down traditional disciplinary silos. Responsibilities for graduate employability, alumni relationships, revenue generation, research and entrepreneurship may be placed with departments and faculties in recognition of the fact that each of them faces distinctly different stakeholders, employment and research pathways for their students and staff (Gibb et al., 2012). Faculty and departmental heads have to take on greater responsibility for performance in this respect and be prepared to defend risk taking behaviour and, at times, associated failure as Todorovic et al. (2005) concluded in their analysis of how to make university departments more entrepreneurial from within. Reward and promotion systems will also need to be geared to this scenario so that 'routes to innovation' of all kinds can lead to recognition and rewards (OECD and EU, 2017a).

An effective way to support a shared understanding of what the entrepreneurial agenda is is to nominate a dedicated person at senior management level who is responsible for the implementation of the entrepreneurial vision and strategy. More than 40 per cent of the surveyed HEIs reported to have created top-level management positons related to either entrepreneurship education activities or start-up support. Overall, these positions were slightly more common for entrepreneurship education activities than for start-up support. Top-level management positions in entrepreneurship are common in at least half of the surveyed HEIs in all countries, except for Hungary.

Another aspect of raising organisational capacity through staff development is the creation of positions related to the entrepreneurial agenda. The

HEI Leader Survey investigated at which levels HEIs created positions in relation to entrepreneurship education or start-up support. A tendency can be noted that for entrepreneurship education activities, positions are created at department and faculty level, as reported by 73 per cent of the surveyed HEIs across the four countries, and that start-up support is carried out by administrative staff (24 per cent). Notable is that 46 per cent of the surveyed HEIs reported that entrepreneurship education matters are dealt with at top HEI management level, and 42 per cent of the HEIs reported this for start-up support. Figure 7.2 shows differences by country.

The existence of a permanent contact point (for example, an entrepreneurship centre) where individuals or teams who would like to start up a business or venture can go for support, varies amongst the surveyed countries. Entrepreneurship centres or similar were present in about 80 per cent of the surveyed HEIs in Ireland and the Netherlands, and in less than one-third of the surveyed HEIs in Hungary and Bulgaria. In most cases, the permanent contact point was an integral part of the HEI; in the Dutch sample about one-third of the HEIs reported that the contact point was a legally separated organisation.

Encouraging, Rewarding and Supporting Staff

Encouraging, rewarding and supporting all staff to contribute to the HEI's entrepreneurial agenda are effective ways to ensure and sustain commitment. An HEI could, for example: (1) adjust staff teaching and research workloads for those who take on new responsibilities that support the institution's entrepreneurial agenda; (2) provide institutional funds to staff to stimulate innovation and change; (3) provide development sabbaticals for staff who seek to enhance their entrepreneurial capacity; (4) make office and laboratory space available for staff to pursue entrepreneurial activities; or (5) provide opportunities for professors to work part-time in their own companies (where permissible).

The HEI Leader Survey investigates to what extent the surveyed HEIs in the four reviewed countries have instigated systems for rewards beyond traditional research, publications and teaching criteria. More than 70 per cent of the surveyed HEIs reported the existence of formalised processes to identify and reward excellent performance in teaching; this was slightly less common for research performance (63 per cent) and achievements in areas other than education and research (55 per cent), and 45 per cent reported providing incentives for staff who actively support the commercialisation of research, for example by making research results available or acting as mentors.

An area for which close to 20 per cent of the surveyed HEIs reported

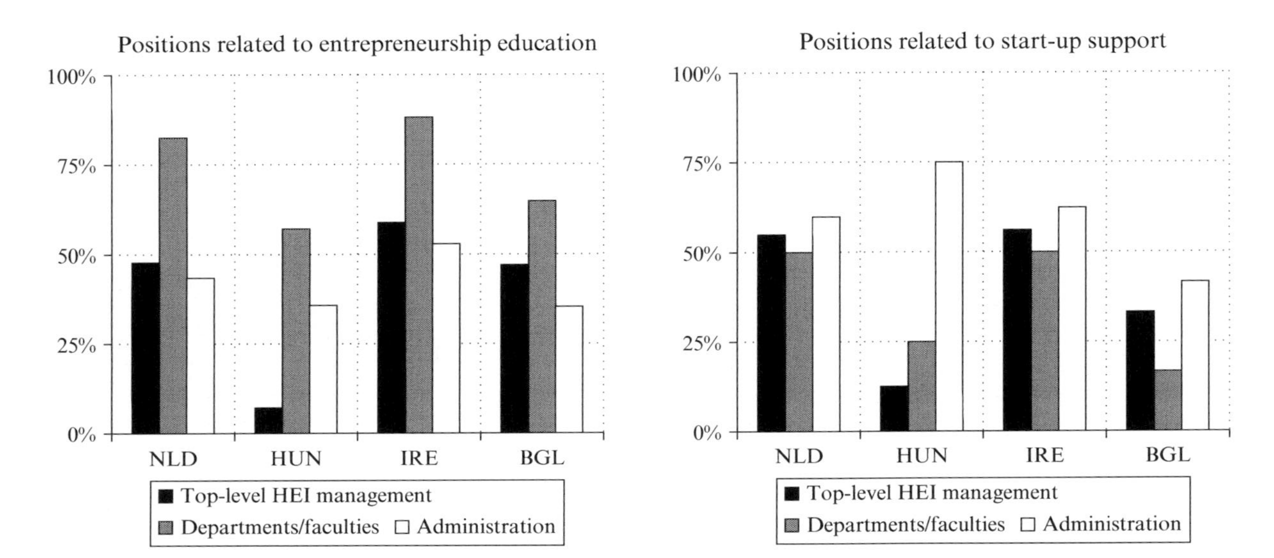

Notes: Higher education institutions (HEIs) currently offering entrepreneurship education activities were asked: 'Do you have positions related to this activity in [. . .]?' This question was answered by 93 HEIs, of which 23 were from the Netherlands, 14 from Hungary, 17 from Ireland, and 17 from Bulgaria. HEIs that currently provide start-up support were asked: 'Do you have positions related to this activity in [. . .]?' The total number of responses was 69, of which 20 were from HEIs in the Netherlands, 8 from Hungary, 16 from Ireland, 10 from Bulgaria. The overall survey response rates per countries are: the Netherlands, 48%, 25 responses; Hungary, 60%, 21; Ireland, 86%, 21; Bulgaria, 48%, 20.

Sources: Based on OECD (2014) and OECD and EU (2017a, 2017b, 2018).

Figure 7.2 Positions in entrepreneurship support

ongoing discussions in their governing boards to introduce new practices is rewarding outstanding achievements in areas other than research and teaching; for example, mentoring would-be entrepreneurs, or other third mission activities such as communication of research results with the help of public events.

Entrepreneurship education and start-up support in HEIs are activities that often involve a highly diverse group of people from different disciplines and professional backgrounds. Particularly in entrepreneurship education, pedagogies and learning outcomes assessment are often different from traditional teaching and learning styles and would therefore benefit from continuous professional development. In the sample of surveyed HEIs from the four reviewed countries, Irish HEIs seem to be most active in training staff members who are involved in entrepreneurship support; 88 per cent of the respondent HEIs who currently offer entrepreneurship support reported offering training for staff involved in entrepreneurship education and start-up support. HEIs in the Netherlands are also very active in this area, with 78 per cent offering training for entrepreneurship education and 60 per cent for start-up support. In Bulgaria, 47 per cent of the HEIs reported providing training in entrepreneurship education and 30 per cent in start-up support.

CONCLUSIONS

Entrepreneurship and innovation are two crucial enablers of change, economic growth, inclusion and sustainability. Higher education has an essential role in building their foundations. To succeed in this, HEIs will have to stimulate and reward leadership at all levels, and create proper support structures and incentives for staff and students to take action for impact. Innovative approaches to teaching and learning, and greater synergies between the core functions – that is, education, research and engagement – are fundamental.

Progress is uneven, both across and within countries. From the presentation of the HEInnovate review findings from these four countries it becomes clear that HEIs are recognising their innovative and entrepreneurial potential and are undertaking specific measures towards their enhancement. There is a clear role for public policy to support higher education institutions in this. Central are targeted resources for initiatives that deliver entrepreneurship education, start-up support, knowledge exchange and societal engagement. The incentives and support frameworks in the national higher education system are also fundamental. Much can be gained from an analysis of what works and why, and an international exchange within a common conceptual framework, such as HEInnovate, whose aim is to stimulate new practices, the establishment of entrepreneurship support structures with an HEI-wide reach, and to allow students and staff to become part of the entrepreneurial agenda.

NOTES

* The authors gratefully acknowledge the contributions of the review panel members – Alain Fayolle, Norris Krueger, Ruaidhri Neavyn, Helena Maria Nazare, Philip Phan, Andrew Gibson, Matthias Geissler, Istvan Kovacs, Lazslo Horvath, Jakob Stolt, Mikkel Trym – and representatives of the European Commission – Heike Fischbach, Juliet Edwards and Peter Baur – for the implementation of the HEInnovate country reviews.

1. The definition of the entrepreneurial and innovative higher education institution used in the HEInnovate guiding framework is based on an input paper prepared by Alain A. Gibb for HEInnovate.
2. The statements were translated into 23 languages.
3. See Kohler and Huber (2006) and Kogan and Blieklie (2007) for an analysis of how dominant organisational patterns in governance have changed, from the classical notion of a higher education institution as a republic of scholars towards the idea of a stakeholder organisation.
4. Access the tool at www.heinnovate.eu.

REFERENCES

Barber, M., K. Donnelly and S. Rizvi (2013), *An Avalanche is Coming: Higher Education and the Revolution Ahead*, London: Institute of Public Policy Research.

Clark, B.R. (1998), *Creating Entrepreneurial Universities: Organizational Pathways of Transformation*, Oxford: Pergamon Press.

Fayolle, A. and D.T. Redford (eds) (2014), *Handbook on the Entrepreneurial University*, Cheltenham, UK and Northampton, MA, USA: Edward Elgar Publishing.

Gibb, A., G. Haskins and I. Robertson (2012), 'Leading the entrepreneurial university: Meeting the entrepreneurial development needs of higher education institutions', in A. Altmann and B. Ebersberger (eds), *Universities in Change*, New York: Springer, pp. 9–45.

Gallup (2014), 'Higher education's work preparation paradox', accessed on 28 November 2017 at http://news.gallup.com/opinion/gallup/173249/higher-education-work-preparation-paradox.aspx.

HEInnovate (2014), 'The entrepreneurial higher education institution – a review of the concept and its relevance today', accessed on 28 November 2017 at https://heinnovate.eu/sites/default/files/heinnovate_concept_note_june_2014.pdf.

Kaffka, G.A. (2017), 'The co-construction of entrepreneurial sensemaking: An empirical examination of socially situated cognitive mechanisms in entrepreneurial cognitive development', doctoral thesis, Twente University, https://ris.utwente.nl/ws/portalfiles/portal/13034237 (accessed 17 August 2017).

Kogan, M. and I. Blieklie (2007), 'Organisation and governance of universities', *Higher Education Policy*, **20**, 477–493.

Kohler, J. and J. Huber (eds) (2006), *Higher Education Governance between*

Democratic Culture, Academic Aspirations and Market Forces, Strasbourg: Council of Europe Publishing.
OECD (2014), 'HEInnovate Reviews. Universities, Entrepreneurship, and Local Development, Bulgaria', accessed on 28 November 2017 at https://www.oecd.org/cfe/leed/OECD-LEED-2015-Bulgaria-report.pdf.
OECD and EU (2017a), *Supporting Entrepreneurship and Innovation in Higher Education in Ireland*, Paris: OECD Publishing, http://dx.doi.org/10.1787/9789264270893-en.
OECD and EU (2017b), *Supporting Entrepreneurship and Innovation in Higher Education in Hungary*, Paris: OECD Publishing, http://dx.doi.org/10.1787/9789264273344-en.
OECD and EU (2018), *Supporting Entrepreneurship and Innovation in Higher Education in the Netherlands*, OECD Skills Studies, Paris: OECD Publishing, http://dx.doi.org/10.1787/9789264292048-en.
Todorovic, W.Z., R.B. McNaughton and P.D. Guild (2005), 'Making university departments more entrepreneurial: The perspective from within', *International Journal of Entrepreneurship and Innovation*, **6**(2), 115–122.

APPENDIX: SURVEY SAMPLE

The questionnaire used for the HEI Leader Survey is based on HEInnovate and contains seven sections with questions about current and planned practices in: (1) the strategic directions of the HEI; (2) management of human and financial resources; (3) the teaching and learning environment; (4) knowledge exchange activities; (5) internationalisation; (6) entrepreneurship education; and (7) business start-up support.

In Bulgaria the invitation to participate in the HEI Leader Survey was sent to the Rector's office of 42 universities (36 public, 6 private). In total, 20 universities fully completed the questionnaire, of which 15 were public and 5 private. The overall survey response rate was 48 per cent. The survey response rates per HEI type are as follows: public universities, 42 per cent; private universities, 83 per cent. Responses were collected between 9 May 2014 and 1 September 2014. The questionnaire was available in Bulgarian and English.

In Ireland the invitation was sent to the President's offices of the 7 universities and the 14 institutes of technology. From the 21 HEIs included in the survey, a total of 18 HEIs, including all universities and 11 institutes of technology, completed the questionnaire with an overall response rate of 86 per cent. The survey response rates per HEI type are as follows: universities, 100 per cent; institutes of technology, 79 per cent. Responses were

Table 7A.1 Overview of country survey samples

Country	Number of HEIs included in the survey population	Number of HEIs that completed the questionnaire	Survey response rate (%)	% of overall sample	Time period
Bulgaria	42	20	48	24	9/5/2014 to 1/9/2014
Ireland	21	18	86	21	15/6/2015 to 29/9/2015
Hungary	35	21	60	25	13/11/2015 to 8/3/2016
The Netherlands	51	25	48	30	14/10/2016 to 13/4/2017
Total sample	149	84	56	100	9/5/2014 to 13/4/2017

Sources: Based on OECD (2014) and OECD and EU (2017a, 2017b, 2018).

collected between 15 June 2015 and 29 September 2015. The questionnaire was available in English.

In Hungary the invitation was sent to the Rector's office of 35 higher education institutions, of which 28 are universities (21 state-owned) and 7 are universities of applied sciences (5 state-owned). A total of 21 HEIs completed the questionnaire – 15 universities and 6 universities of applied sciences – with an overall response rate of 60 per cent. The survey response rates per HEI type are as follows: universities, 54 per cent; universities of applied sciences, 86 per cent. Responses were collected between 29 June 2016 and 3 November 2016. The questionnaire was available in Hungarian and English.

In the Netherlands the invitation was sent by the HEI representatives' organisations to the executive boards of all publicly funded HEIs, including 14 research universities and the University for Humanities (excluded were the University of the Reformed Church, the Catholic Apeldoorn University and the Protestant Universities, and specialist universities providing teacher training), and 37 universities of applied sciences. From the 51 HEIs included in the survey, a total of 25 completed the questionnaire, of which 9 were research universities and 16 were universities of applied sciences. The overall survey response rate was 48 per cent. The survey response rates per HEI type are the following: research universities, 60 per cent; universities of applied sciences, 43 per cent. Responses were collected between 14 October 2016 and 13 April 2017. The questionnaire was available in English.

8. Entrepreneurial universities as determinants of technology entrepreneurship

Guillermo A. Zapata-Huamaní, Sara Fernández-López, Lucía Rey-Ares and David Rodeiro-Pazos

INTRODUCTION

It is generally accepted that new technology-based firms (NTBFs) are an important source of new jobs and play a crucial role in the efficiency of the economic system (Audretsch, 1995; Bertoni et al., 2011). Moreover, NTBFs are frequently seen as a panacea for lack of growth in modern economies (Coad and Reid, 2012). As technology entrepreneurship (TE) gains importance in political agendas as a catalyst for economic development (Mosey et al., 2017), the factors that drive the NTBFs' creation have increasingly attracted the attention of scholars, practitioners and policy makers (Colombo and Grilli, 2010). In fact, promoting entrepreneurs to start NTBFs is one of the key cornerstones of innovation and technology entrepreneurship policies of the European Union (Kuratko and Menter, 2017).

Entrepreneurial universities contribute substantially to the creation of the NTBFs by carrying out their 'third mission' of fostering links with knowledge users and facilitating technology transfer, as the 'second mission', by itself, it is not enough; that is, 'just generating knowledge did not ensure that knowledge would spill over for commercialization driving innovative activity and economic growth' (Audretsch, 2014: 314). Hence, universities have been an important source of NTBFs through the creation of spin-off firms (Wakkee and Van der Sijde, 2002). Nevertheless, universities' entrepreneurial activity can take various forms, from acting as the sole creators of NTBFs to developing closer links with industry and the private sector, which might take place through different channels – licensing contracts, joint research, academic consulting – as highlighted by Goel et al. (2017). It is precisely in this interaction with industry that universities act as driving forces of TE. In such interactions, the knowledge produced by university research is shared with potential entrepreneurs who may exploit it through commercial engagement. As the knowledge spillover theory of entrepreneurship highlights, new business opportunities arise in the process of knowledge creation (Acs et al., 2009; Audretsch et al., 2010). In this chapter, we argue that entrepreneurial universities positively influence the creation of NTBFs by acting as knowledge producers as well as platforms for sharing knowledge with industry, since universities are the only affordable external source of knowledge for a wide range of firms. Thus, Levy et al. (2007) showed that firms in the information technology or pharmacy sectors were more likely than those in other sectors to be the privileged partners of prestigious universities. Similarly, Cohen et al. (2002) highlighted that universities and public research centres play a key role in the high-tech sector as external sources of open science and collaborative research and development (R&D) activities.

In spite of this evidence, there are very few studies that have properly analysed entrepreneurial universities as drivers of TE. Previous evidence motivated us to analyse whether the presence of entrepreneurial universities in a region influences the creation of NTBFs. Drawing on the knowledge spillover theory of entrepreneurship, we argue that the presence of entrepreneurial universities has a positive effect on the emergence of NTBFs. We tested this hypothesis using a sample drawn from 65 countries during the period 2006–13.

We consider this hypothesis especially relevant as there has been debate about policies geared towards promoting entrepreneurial universities, especially in relation to the potential for undesirable 'collateral effects' such as 'academic capitalism' (Slaughter and Leslie, 1997) or 'McUniversities' (Hayes and Wynyard, 2002). However, knowing the role played by entrepreneurial universities could help decision makers to judge how entrepreneurial a university should be, and inform the design of supportive policies. To the best of the authors' knowledge no other study has focused on this issue.

The rest of the chapter is organized as follows. The second section describes the conceptual framework of the analysis and reviews the relevant literature. The third section introduces the methodology used. The fourth section contains the description and discussion of the empirical results. Finally, the fifth section presents the conclusions, recommendations and future lines of research.

THEORETICAL BACKGROUND

It is generally accepted that education systems influence the entrepreneurship rates (Acs, 2006). Given that companies are created by entrepreneurs who exhibit certain attitudes, skills and knowledge that can be acquired, practiced and developed (Timmons, 1990), the education system plays an important role in the education and training of potential entrepreneurs. In so doing, education systems incorporate general questions and programmes related to entrepreneurship into curricula from the first stages of education to higher education (Verheul et al., 2006).

Thus, empirical evidence shows that countries and regions with good levels of education have a greater propensity for entrepreneurship (Audretsch et al., 2010; Alvarez and Urbano, 2011; Colovic and Lamotte, 2015), providing a climate encouraging the creation of NTBFs. Nevertheless, a certain level of innovation is required to generate this climate. In fact, the effect of higher levels of education on entrepreneurship may be lower in less innovative countries, such as in Latin America (Alvarez and Urbano, 2011).

Education affects not only the likelihood of starting a business, but also its performance. Teruel and de Wit (2011) reported that a country's level of education (measured as the percentage of the population enrolled in higher education) was positively correlated with its percentage of high-growth companies.

Moreover, some authors argue that to encourage entrepreneurship in general, and TE in particular, specific training is needed. According to Van der Kuip and Verheul (2004), the most basic entrepreneurial skills, such as creativity, independence and perseverance, must be introduced in early education and developed through cross-wise training. In turn, in higher education the teaching of entrepreneurship-related topics such as management, finance and marketing (Van der Kuip and Verheul, 2004) may support TE, as a lack of technical and commercial skills can constrain entrepreneurs' ability to start a business (Alvarez and Urbano, 2011). But we must consider that the influence of teaching entrepreneurship varies between countries. In this sense, Ferreira and Fernandes (2017) showed that there were differences between Portugal, Spain and Brazil in a comparative study of the influence of teaching entrepreneurship to university students.

In addition to this role of entrepreneur 'trainers', universities can stimulate the creation of NTBFs by producing knowledge spillovers that, in turn, facilitates the emergence of business opportunities (Acs et al., 2009). Thus, according to the knowledge spillover theory of entrepreneurship, the knowledge producer may not necessarily be the agent who exploits it;

the exploiter is the entrepreneur who detects an economic opportunity to start a business based on the knowledge created. The agent or institution producing knowledge through R&D activities generates the basis that indirectly serves entrepreneurs (Acs et al., 2009; Audretsch et al., 2010).

Thus, empirical evidence shows that universities are a source of innovation for technology-intensive industrial sectors (Darby and Zucker, 2006) and for firms (Etzkowitz, 1998; Giuliani and Arza, 2009; Urban and von Hippel, 1988), because of their role in generating new knowledge (Mansfield, 1995; Pavitt, 2001; Farinha et al., 2016). In the same line of reasoning, El Harbi and Anderson (2010) conclude that in a country with research-oriented universities potential entrepreneurs can take advantage of them to create research-based companies; without this favourable climate entrepreneurs are more likely to imitate innovations developed in other countries.

Under the lens of the knowledge spillover theory of entrepreneurship, universities are not only seen as knowledge producers, but they also act as platforms for sharing knowledge, which is a critical factor of regional entrepreneurship (Xue and Klein, 2010). Opportunities to create a NTBF are strongly linked to the interactions that occur among the agents involved in the innovation ecosystem, such as talented people, government agencies, educational and research institutions, companies and investors, among others (Petti and Zhang, 2011). Particularly, prestigious educational institutions are able to attract talented young people from other geographical areas who have emigrated in order to benefit from studying or working in such institutions (Venkataraman, 2004). Hence the areas close to prestigious institutions will be the place where talent gathers and new ideas are produced (Venkataraman, 2004).

Nevertheless, to encourage TE is not enough with having universities in the surrounding area, but also they must be 'entrepreneurial' universities in order to obtain favourable results relating to the creation of NTBFs. The definitions of an entrepreneurial university are often generic; however, they all make reference to a dynamic institution that uses a variety of technology transfer mechanisms that speed the transformation of knowledge into marketable products and services.[1] One of the main mechanisms of knowledge and technology transfer is continuous collaboration with companies in the form of human resources exchange, competency development, joint research (Aceytuno and De Paz, 2008; Bramwell et al., 2012; Goel et al., 2017; Fernández-López et al., 2015) or the commercialization of academic knowledge, involving the patenting and licensing of inventions (Perkmann et al., 2013). This contributes to the efficient development of ecosystems of innovation, which are part of the framework required for the emergence of TE. Drawing on previous studies, we propose the following hypothesis:

Hypothesis: The presence of entrepreneurial universities will have a positive effect on the emergence of technology-based initiatives.

RESEARCH METHODOLOGY

Sample and Data

The research data in this chapter were drawn from four main sources: the Global Entrepreneurship Monitor (GEM) project, the Global Competitiveness Report, the World Bank (Doing Business and the statistical database), and the International Monetary Fund.

The GEM project[2] determined the choice of countries and the period of analysis. We analysed the period 2006–13, because prior to 2006 fewer than 30 countries were involved in the GEM project. Appendix Table 8A.1 lists the participating countries. In addition, because we used panel data methodology, countries for which there were fewer than three observations of the dependent variable over the analysis period were discarded. Thus, the final sample comprised 368 observations from 65 countries during the period 2006–13.

Definition of Variables

Data on the dependent variable, technology entrepreneurship (TE), were collected from the GEM project database. TE was measured as the percentage of the adult population (18 to 64-year-olds), including self-employed people, who had created a business or owned and managed a business no more than 3.5 years old, in what the Organisation for Economic Co-operation and Development (OECD) classifies as the medium- and high-technology sectors.

The entrepreneurial nature of universities was measured through two variables drawn from the Global Competitiveness Report. First, the variable 'university–industry relationship' represented responses to the question, 'To what extent do businesses and universities in your country collaborate on research and development (R&D)?'. Responses were given on a seven-point Likert scale ranging from 1 (do not collaborate at all) to 7 (collaborate extensively). University–industry relationship was expected to be positively related to TE. Second, the variable 'entrepreneurship education in business schools' represented responses to the question, 'How would you rate the quality of business schools in your country?'. Responses were given using a seven-point Likert scale ranging from 1 (very bad; among the worst in the world) to 7 (excellent; among the best in the world). Entrepreneurship education was expected to be positively related to TE. The independent and control variables used in the study are described in Table 8.1.

Model Specification

Linear models for panel data, and particularly, models of individual effects were used, based on the structure of the data:

$$y_{it} = \alpha_i + x'_{it}\beta + \varepsilon_{it} \tag{8.1}$$

where X_{it} are independent variables, α_i is the specific, time-invariant individual effect, and ε is the idiosyncratic error.

Random effects (RE) and fixed effects (FE) are two different models regarding α_i. The estimator of the parameters in the RE models uses both between- and within-country variation, whereas the estimator of the parameters in the FE models uses only the within-country variation. In this research we used RE models due to the nature of the variation across countries.

In RE models, it is assumed that the correlation of the composite error $u_{it} = \alpha_i + \varepsilon_{it}$ is constant across all delays (ρ_{tt}) (equicorrelated random errors). However, this assumption is often hard to satisfy. Then, more efficient estimates can be obtained by using population-average (PA) estimators with a better structure of error correlations (Cameron and Trivedi, 2010).

Similarly to the RE estimators, the PA estimators use both between- and within-country (time-series) variation, and are derived from the model of individual effects, rewriting eqation (8.1) as follows:

$$y_{it} = \alpha + x'_{it}\beta + (\alpha_i - \alpha + \varepsilon_{it}) \tag{8.2}$$

This second equation (8.2) explicitly includes a common intercept and the individual effects $\alpha_i - \alpha$ are now centred on zero. The consistency of the PA estimators entails that the error term ($\alpha_i - \alpha + \varepsilon_{it}$) and any individual-level effects are uncorrelated with regressors X_{it}, so they will be consistent if the RE models are appropriate. When PA estimators are obtained, it is necessary to specify a model for the error correlations. Calculation of cluster-robust standard errors is recommended, to protect against possible model misspecification related to error correlation. However, using robust standard errors might result in inefficient estimators, whilst specifying the best models for error correlation results in more efficient estimators. Cameron and Trivedi (2010) argue that assuming errors are unstructured

Table 8.1 Independent variables: description and source of information

Variable	Description	Source
University–industry collaboration	Weighted average of the evaluation of collaboration between university and business, on a scale ranging from 1 (do not collaborate at all) to 7 (collaborate extensively)	Global Competitiveness Report
Entrepreneurship education in business schools	Weighted average of the evaluation of the quality of business schools, on a scale ranging from 1 (very bad) to 7 (excellent)	Global Competitiveness Report
Entrepreneurship as a desirable career choice	Percentage of adults aged 18–64 years who regarded starting a new business in their country as a good career choice	GEM
Media attention to entrepreneurship	Percentage of adults aged 18–64 years who reported frequently seeing stories about successful new businesses in their country's public media	GEM
Social status of entrepreneurship	Percentage of adults aged 18–64 years who consider that successfully launching a new business garners high status and respect in their country	GEM
Personally know an entrepreneur	Percentage of adults aged 18–64 years who know someone who has started a business in the last two years personally	GEM
Innovation	Percentage of adults aged 18–64 years participating in the TEA who reported that their products were new to all or some of their customers	GEM
GDP growth	Annual gross domestic product (GDP) growth rates at market prices in local currency, expressed in US dollars at constant 2005 prices	World Bank
Informal venture capital	Percentage of adults aged 18–64 years who have personally provided funds for a new business started by someone else (acted as a 'business angel') in the last three years. Does not include the acquisition of stocks or mutual funds	GEM
Unemployment	The number of unemployed people as a percentage of the labour force	International Monetary Fund
Population density	The mid-year population divided by the territorial area in square kilometres.	World Bank

Table 8.1 (continued)

Variable	Description	Source
Procedures for starting a business	Natural logarithm of the product of the number of procedures that an entrepreneur must complete in order to start up and formally operate an industrial or commercial business and the duration of these procedures	Doing Business
Access to information	Weighted average of the evaluation of how easy it is for companies to get information on changes in government policies and regulations that affect their activities. Evaluations were given on a Likert scale ranging from 1 (extremely difficult) to 7 (extremely easy)	Global Competitiveness Report
Domestic market size	Sum of the value of GDP and imports minus the value of exports; normalized on 1–7 scale where 7 represents the largest market	Global Competitiveness Report
Investor protection	This indicator, on a scale 0–10 (better), is obtained by combining three indices: the disclosure index (transparency of related-party transactions), the director liability index (responsibility for self-negotiation) and the shareholder suits index (shareholder capacity for suing officials and directors for misconduct)	World Bank, Doing Business
Internet use	Number of Internet broadband subscribers with a digital subscriber line, cable modem or other high-speed technology (per 100 people)	World Bank
Access to credit	Domestic credit provided by financial sector as a percentage of gross domestic product (GDP); includes all forms of credit to various sectors	World Bank

might be the best model for error correlation when short panels (small t) are used. Therefore, as the panel used in this research is considered short ($t = 8$; 2006–13) we followed Cameron and Trivedi's (2010) suggestion. This model does not place any restriction on the correlation (ρ_{ts}); it only needs to be equal between individuals, in our case countries ($\rho_{i,ts}$).

RESULTS AND DISCUSSION

Univariate Analysis

The main descriptive statistics for the dependent and independent variables are summarized in Table 8.2. *TE*, the dependent variable, represents 0.46 per cent of total entrepreneurship. This low figure may partly explain why many national and regional economies are seeking ways of increasing the proportion of NTBFs among their new businesses. Table 8.2 reveals that most of the explanatory variables show more between-country variation than within-country variation.

Multivariate Analysis

Data analysis was carried out using RE models with PA estimators, as described above, assuming unstructured error correlation. Four different models, displayed in Table 8.3, were estimated to demonstrate the robustness of the results. Different independent variables were entered in separate analyses to avoid multicollinearity problems.

Two variables were used to capture the effects of entrepreneurial universities on TE: 'university–industry relationship' and 'entrepreneurship education in business schools'. Although the use of both was limited by the effects of the correlation, it was possible to obtain conclusive results that confirmed our hypothesis.

'University–industry relationship' had a positive effect on TE, supporting the arguments stemming from the knowledge spillover theory of entrepreneurship. Universities as knowledge producers and platforms for sharing knowledge positively impact the creation of NTBFs. Our findings are consistent with those by Aceytuno and De Paz (2008), Bramwell et al. (2012) and Petti and Zhang (2011) emphasizing the importance of collaborations between the university and industry to technology transfer. These collaborations are a key element in the innovation process as they help to develop competencies and research through the exchange of human resources, which in turn generate the knowledge base from which NTBFs emerge. The university–industry collaboration facilitates the creation of

Table 8.2 Descriptive statistics and breakdown of variance

Variable	Mean	Standard deviation		Minimum	Maximum	Observations
Technology entrepreneurship	0.46	overall	0.32	0.02	1.82	N = 368
		between	0.21	0.13	1.11	n = 65
		within	0.24	−0.36	1.41	T-bar = 5.66
University–industry collaboration	4.10	overall	0.92	1.85	5.93	N = 362
		between	0.89	2.22	5.76	n = 64
		within	0.26	3.19	5.23	T-bar = 5.66
Entrepreneurship education in business schools	4.67	overall	0.79	1.76	6.16	N = 362
		between	0.81	1.96	6.04	n = 64
		within	0.19	4.00	5.37	T-bar = 5.66
Entrepreneurship as a desirable career choice	65.46	overall	13.63	25.00	96.00	N = 347
		between	12.37	27.88	93.33	n = 65
		within	5.25	34.96	81.03	T-bar = 5.34
Media attention to entrepreneurship	59.28	overall	14.23	19.00	88.00	N = 348
		between	12.40	29.50	83.50	n = 65
		within	6.29	33.16	78.28	T-bar = 5.35
Social status of entrepreneurship	70.09	overall	10.24	31.00	94.00	N = 350
		between	9.37	48.00	93.67	n = 65
		within	4.96	40.34	83.29	T-bar = 5.38
Personally know an entrepreneur	39.21	overall	11.50	13.97	85.10	N = 368
		between	11.36	19.76	80.53	n = 65
		within	5.43	17.82	56.98	T-bar = 5.66
Innovation	5.13	overall	4.72	0.20	31.81	N = 368
		between	3.75	1.61	18.01	n = 65
		within	2.82	−4.46	22.60	T-bar = 5.66

GDP growth	2.55	overall	4.00	−14.19	20.94	N = 363
		between	2.58	−2.53	12.58	n = 64
		within	3.13	−13.55	12.26	T-bar = 5.67
Informal venture capital	4.97	overall	4.01	0.58	31.28	N = 368
		between	4.20	0.95	23.60	n = 65
		within	1.90	−9.84	20.02	T-bar = 5.66
Unemployment	8.94	overall	5.78	0.66	33.78	N = 345
		between	5.92	0.99	31.46	n = 59
		within	2.14	−0.08	21.75	T-bar = 5.85
Population density	206.34	overall	758.35	2.69	7713.14	N = 364
		between	901.03	2.82	7262.41	n = 64
		within	59.08	−714.00	657.07	T-bar = 5.69
Procedures for starting a business*	252.46	overall	389.97	4.00	2652.00	N = 368
		between	387.90	8.00	2313.67	n = 65
		within	119.91	−182.41	883.59	T-bar = 5.66
Access to information	4.40	overall	0.81	2.40	6.27	N = 362
		between	0.78	2.70	6.17	n = 64
		within	0.26	3.41	5.39	T-bar = 5.66
Domestic market size	4.48	overall	1.05	2.08	7.00	N = 362
		between	1.03	2.33	7.00	n = 64
		within	0.11	4.21	5.11	T-bar = 5.66
Investor protection	5.73	overall	1.42	2.30	9.30	N = 362
		between	1.40	2.57	9.30	n = 64
		within	0.30	4.06	7.06	T-bar = 5.66
Internet use	16.56	overall	11.78	0.01	42.52	N = 361
		between	11.17	0.01	37.59	n = 65
		within	4.16	−5.66	44.21	T-bar = 5.55
Access to credit	106.08	overall	71.21	−9.10	366.53	N = 345
		between	67.64	−3.17	327.85	n = 62
		within	12.97	43.23	184.32	T-bar = 5.56

Note: * Variable is not in log.

Table 8.3 Estimated population averages (PAs) with unstructured error correlation

	Model 1	Model 2	Model 3	Model 4
University–industry collaboration	0.06* (0.03)	0.07* (0.03)		
Entrepreneurship education in business schools			0.01 (0.03)	0.04 (0.03)
Entrepreneurship as a desirable career choice	−0.00 (0.00)	−0.00 (0.00)	−0.00 (0.00)	−0.00 (0.00)
Media attention to entrepreneurship	0.00† (0.00)	0.00* (0.00)	0.00** (0.00)	0.00* (0.00)
Social status of entrepreneurship	0.00 (0.00)	0.00 (0.00)	0.00 (0.00)	0.00 (0.00)
Personally know an entrepreneur	−0.00* (0.00)	−0.01** (0.00)	−0.00* (0.00)	−0.01** (0.00)
Innovation	0.01 (0.00)	0.01* (0.00)	0.01** (0.00)	0.01* (0.00)
GDP growth	0.02*** (0.00)	0.02*** (0.00)	0.02*** (0.00)	0.02** (0.01)
Informal venture capital	0.03*** (0.01)	0.03*** (0.01)	0.03*** (0.01)	0.03*** (0.01)
Unemployment	0.01 (0.00)	0.00 (0.00)	0.01† (0.00)	0.00 (0.00)
Population density	−0.00 (0.00)	−0.00 (0.00)	−0.00 (0.00)	−0.00 (0.00)
Procedures for starting a business		0.01 (0.02)	0.02 (0.02)	−0.00 (0.02)
Access to information	0.00 (0.00)			
Domestic market size		−0.05* (0.02)		
Investor protection		−0.01 (0.02)		
Internet use			0.01** (0.00)	
Access to credit				0.00 (0.00)
Constant	−0.08 (0.21)	0.19 (0.25)	−0.15 (0.22)	0.04 (0.23)
N	*319*	*319*	*319*	*303*
Hausman test	*0.6116*	*0.5598*	*0.5419*	*0.1784*

Note: Standard errors are given in parentheses. † $p < 0.10$; * $p < 0.05$; ** $p < 0.01$; *** $p < 0.001$.

new knowledge which promotes – to use the terminology of Teruel and De Wit (2011) – the emergence of new, high-growth companies, such as NTBFs.

In contrast, for 'entrepreneurship education in business schools' no effect was found on TE. We did not find support for the arguments about the importance of entrepreneurship training (Van der Kuip and Verheul, 2004). In other words, our data provide no evidence that having good business schools has a positive impact on development of TE. This lack of significance may partly be explained by the fact that the variable 'entrepreneurship education in business schools' is far from being an indicator of the extent to which training in entrepreneurship is included in educational curricula, as it just captures the perceived quality of a country's business schools. Another possible explanation is that the training offered by business schools relates more to the management of established companies than to the specific characteristics of TE.

With regard to the remaining regressors included in the models as control variables, our analysis indicated that the following variables had an effect on TE: 'media attention to entrepreneurship', 'personally know an entrepreneur', 'degree of innovation', 'GDP growth', 'informal venture capital', 'domestic market size' and 'Internet access'. All these variables, except 'personally know an entrepreneur' and 'domestic market size', had a positive effect on TE.

CONCLUSIONS AND FUTURE RESEARCH

This chapter explores whether university–industry relationships and entrepreneurship education in business schools have an effect on creation of NTBFs. More specifically, we applied panel data random effect models to a sample drawn from 65 countries over the period 2006–13 to shed some light on the role played by entrepreneurial universities in TE. We opted for RE models because most of the explanatory variables showed more between-country variation than within-country variation. PA estimators, which are consistent with RE estimators, were used assuming unstructured errors, which is better for short panels such as we used.

Our results corroborate the knowledge spillover theory of entrepreneurship and demonstrate the importance of interactions between universities and industry in producing and sharing knowledge which serves as a source of ideas for NTBFs. Academic authorities, politicians and decision makers must encourage links between university and industry through policies aimed at knowing each other. Hence, universities should make public and disseminate the knowledge produced by their departments, laboratories and faculties, since companies usually do not know the results of their research. Similarly, industry must make public its interests and innovation needs; these are mainly the services and products required for the markets and consumers, and the technologies and components needed to build them. In so doing, universities could focus their research on satisfying industry's needs. Industry PhD programmes may act as a catalyst for promoting applied research.

In order to increase collaboration between universities and industry, improvements in four main areas and in specific tools are required:

- Efficient management of technology transfer and projects: appropriate infrastructure for technology transfer; professional project management; clear strategy with respect to intellectual property rights.
- Marketing actions: promotion of scientific research to the private sector.
- Personal connections between universities and industry: common work spaces; exposure to real R&D problems; promoting the role of 'gatekeeper'.
- Financial support instruments: pre-competitive cooperative research grants; simplified procedures to research contracts; technological support and experimental development.

As a concluding remark regarding university–industry collaboration, it is particularly important to implement the above measures in countries where companies tend to be less interested in collaborating with universities, and to establish a certain degree of coordination among the different parties or stakeholders involved in the process of supporting entrepreneurship: governments, academia and firms. Thus, as Bergmann et al. (2016) point out, university programmes to support entrepreneurship among students will probably be more effective when coordinated with respective strategies of the region where the university is located.

Despite the fact that the variable 'entrepreneurship education in business schools' fails to exert a significant effect on technology entrepreneurship – which is probably due to the nature of the variable – the importance of entrepreneurship education is not negligible. In fact, entrepreneurship education was identified as a priority in the Europe 2020 Strategy and it constitutes an important issue in public policy. In this regard, the European Commission recognized that entrepreneurship must be embedded into the education system and should be available in different levels of the education system – not only in tertiary education – and proposed the inclusion of two main complementary actions into entrepreneurship education: the first one aimed at the development of attitudes and behaviours, such as problem solving, proactivity and creativity; and the second one aimed at the development of more managerial and technical competences, essential to run a business.

In this regard, Huber et al. (2014) conducted a randomized field experiment to evaluate a leading entrepreneurship education programme that was taught worldwide in the final grade of primary school. They concluded that this programme did not affect the knowledge of the students, but it did exert a positive effect on their non-cognitive entrepreneurial skills. Moreover, academic research has also shown that entrepreneurship education positively influences the entrepreneurial intention (Maresch et al., 2016).

Finally, this chapter has some limitations that suggest possibilities for further research. First, as different countries with diverse contexts are used in our analysis, the establishment of homogenous groups of countries could offer different results. Second, the variable 'entrepreneurship education in business schools' did not capture all the entrepreneurship-related training carried out by universities, and therefore the introduction of a new variable might provide a more accurate assessment of entrepreneurship education.

NOTES

1. For a characterization proposal of what might be considered an entrepreneurial and innovative university, see Fernández et al. (2017).
2. http://www.gemconsortium.org/.

REFERENCES

Aceytuno, M., and de Paz, M. (2008). La creación de spin-off universitarias. El caso de la universidad de Huelva (The creation of university spin-offs. The case of the University of Huelva). *Economía Industrial*, **368**, 97–111.

Acs, Z. (2006). How is entrepreneurship good for economic growth? *Innovations*, **1**(1), 97–107.

Acs, Z.J., Braunerhjelm, P., Audretsch, D.B., and Carlsson, B. (2009). The knowledge spillover theory of entrepreneurship. *Small Business Economics*, **32**(1), 15–30.

Alvarez, C., and Urbano, D. (2011). Environmental factors and entrepreneurial activity in Latin America. *Academia Revista Latinoamericana de Administración*, **48**, 126–139.

Audretsch, D. (1995). *Innovation and Industry Evolution*. Cambridge, MA: MIT Press.

Audretsch, D. (2014). From the entrepreneurial university to the university for the entrepreneurial society. *Journal of Technology Transfer*, **39**(3), 313–321. doi: 10.1007/s10961-012-9288-1.

Audretsch, D., Dohse, D., and Niebuhr, A. (2010). Cultural diversity and entrepreneurship: a regional analysis for Germany. *Annals of Regional Science*, **45**(1), 55–85.

Bergmann, H., Hundt, C. and Sternberg, R. (2016). What makes student entrepreneurs? On the relevance (and irrelevance) of the university and the regional context for student start-ups. Small Business Economics, 47(1), 53–76. doi: 10.1007/s11187-016-9700-6.

Bertoni, F., Colombo, M.G., and Grilli, L. (2011). Venture capital financing and the growth of high-tech start-ups: disentangling treatment from selection effects. *Research Policy*, **40**(7), 1028–1043. doi: 10.1016/j.respol.2011.03.008.

Bramwell, A., Hepburn, N., and Wolfe, D. (2012). Growing innovation ecosystems: university–industry knowledge transfer and regional economic development in Canada, knowledge synthesis paper on leveraging investments in HERD. Final Report to the Social Sciences and Humanities Research Council of Canada, Toronto, Ontario.

Cameron, A.C., and Trivedi, P.K. (2010). *Microeconometrics Using Stata*, Vol. 2. College Station, TX: Stata Press.

Coad, A., and Reid, A. (2012). The role of technology and technology-based firms in economic development: rethinking innovation and enterprise policy in Scotland. Technopolis Group, Scotland. Available at: http://www.evaluationsonline.org.uk/evaluations/Browse.do?ui=browse&action=show&andid=504&taxonomy=INO (accessed 23 May 2016).

Cohen, W.M., Nelson, R.R., and Walsh, J.P. (2002). Links and impacts: the influence of public research on industrial R&D. *Management Science*, **48**(1), 1–23.

Colombo, M.G., and Grilli, L. (2010). On growth drivers of high-tech start-ups: the role of founders' human capital and venture capital. *Journal of Business Venturing*, **25**, 610–626. doi: 10.1016/j.jbusvent.2009.01.005.

Colovic, A., and Lamotte, O. (2015). Technological environment and technology entrepreneurship: a cross country analysis. *Creativity and Innovation Management*, **24**(4), 617–628. doi: 10.1111/caim.12133.

Darby, M.R., and Zucker, L.G. (2006). Innovation, competition and welfare-enhancing monopoly. Cambridge, MA: NBER Working Paper.

El Harbi, S., and Anderson, A.R. (2010). Institutions and the shaping of different forms of entrepreneurship. *Journal of Socio-Economics*, **39**(3), 436–444. doi: 10.1016/j.socec.2010.02.011.

Etzkowitz, H. (1998). The norms of entrepreneurial science: cognitive effects of the new university–industry linkages. *Research Policy*, **27**(8), 823–833.

Farinha, L., Ferreira, J., and Gouveia, B. (2016). Networks of innovation and competitiveness: a Triple Helix case study. *Journal of Knowledge Economy*, **7**(1), 259–275. doi: 10.1007/s13132-014-0218-3.

Fernández, L., Fernández-López, S., Rey, L., Zapata, G.A., and Bobillo, M. (2017). Universidades Emprendedoras e Innovadoras: una propuesta de caracterización. In: *7th Conferência Ibérica de Empreendedorismo* (pp. 222–233). June, Esposende, Portugal.

Fernández-López, S., Pérez, B., Rodeiro, D., and Calvo, N. (2015). Are firms interested in collaborating with universities? An open-innovation perspective in countries of the South West European Space. *Service Business*, **9**(4), 637–662. doi: 10.1007/s11628-014-0243-0.

Ferreira, J.J., and Fernandes, C.I. (2017). The impact of entrepreneurship education programs on student entrepreneurial orientations: three international experiences. In: M. Peris-Ortiz, J. Alonso Gómez, J.M. Merigó-Lindahl, and C. Rueda-Armengot (eds), *Entrepreneurial Universities* (pp. 287–302). Cham: Springer International Publishing. doi: 10.1007/978-3-319-47949-1_20.

Giuliani, E., and Arza, V. (2009). What drives the formation of 'valuable' university–industry linkages? Insights from the wine industry. *Research Policy*, **38**(6), 906–921. doi: 10.1016/j.respol.2009.02.006.

Goel, R.K., Göktepe-Hultén, D., and Grimpe, C. (2017). Who instigates university–industry collaborations? University scientists versus firm employees. *Small Business Economics*, **48**(3), 503–524. doi: 10.1007/s11187-016-9795-9.

Hayes, D., and Wynyard, R. (eds) (2002). *The McDonaldization of Higher Education*. Westport, CT: Bergin & Garvey.

Huber, L.R., Sloof, R., and Van Praag, M. (2014). The effect of early entrepreneurship education: evidence from a field experiment. *European Economic Review*, **72**, 76–97. doi: 10.1016/j.euroecorev.2014.09.002.

Kuratko, D.F., and Menter, M. (2017). The role of public policy in fostering technology-based nascent entrepreneurship. In: J.A. Cunningham and C. O'Kane (eds), *Technology-Based Nascent Entrepreneurship* (pp. 19–52). Palgrave Advances in the Economics of Innovation and Technology. New York: Palgrave Macmillan. doi: 10.1057/978-1-137-59594-2_2.

Levy, R., Roux, P., and Wolff, S. (2007). An analysis of science–industry collaborative patterns in a large European University. *Journal of Technology Transfer*, **34**(1), 1–23. doi: 10.1007/s10961-007-9044-0.

Mansfield, E. (1995). Academic research underlying industrial innovations: sources, characteristics, and financing. *Review of Economics and Statistics*, **77**, 55–65.

Maresch, D., Harms, R., Kailer, N., and Wimmer-Wurm, B. (2016). The impact of entrepreneurship education on the entrepreneurial intention of students in science and engineering versus business studies university programs. *Technological Forecasting and Social Change*, **104**, 172–179. doi: 10.1016/j.techfore.2015.11.006.

Mosey, S., Guerrero, M., and Greenman, A. (2017). Technology entrepreneurship research opportunities: insights from across Europe. *Journal of Technology Transfer*, **42**(1), 1–9. doi: 10.1007/s10961-015-9462-3.

Pavitt, K.L.R. (2001). Public policies to support basic research: what can the rest of the world learn from US theory and practice? (And what they should not learn). *Industrial and Corporate Change*, **10**, 761–779.

Perkmann, M., Tartari, V., McKelvey, M., et al. (2013). Academic engagement and commercialisation: a review of the literature on university–industry relations. *Research Polity*, **42**(2), 423–442. doi: 10.1016/j.respol.2012.09.007.

Petti, C., and Zhang, S. (2011). Factors influencing technological entrepreneurship capabilities: towards an integrated research framework for Chinese enterprises. *Journal of Technology Management in China*, **6**(1), 7–25. doi: 10.1108/17468771111105631.

Slaughter, S., and Leslie, L. (1997). *Academic Capitalism: Politics, Policies, and the Entrepreneurial University*. Baltimore, MD: Johns Hopkins University Press.

Teruel, M., and De Wit, G. (2011). Determinants of high-growth firms: why do some countries have more high-growth firms than others? Working paper no. 2072/179670, Departament d'Economia-CREIP, Facultat d'Economia i Empresa.

Timmons, J. (1990). *New Business Opportunities: Getting to the Right Place at the Right Time*. Acton: Brick House Publishing Co.

Urban, G.L., and von Hippel, E. (1988). Lead user analyses for the development of new industrial products. *Management Science*, **34**(5), 569–582.
Van der Kuip, I., and Verheul, I. (2004). Early development of entrepreneurial qualities: the role of initial education. *International Journal of Entrepreneurship Education*, **2**(2), 203–226.
Venkataraman, S. (2004). Regional transformation through technological entrepreneurship. *Journal of Business Venturing*, **19**(1), 153–167.
Verheul, I., Van Stel, A., and Thurik, R. (2006). Explaining female and male entrepreneurship at the country level. *Entrepreneurship and Regional Development*, **18**(2), 151–183.
Wakkee, A.M., and Van der Sijde, P.C. (2002). Supporting entrepreneurs entering a global market. In P.C. Van Der Sijde, B. Wirsing, R. Cuyvers and A. Ridder (eds), *New Concepts for Academic Entrepreneurship* (pp. 129–150). Enschede: Twente University Press.
Xue, J., and Klein, P.G. (2010). Regional determinants of technology entrepreneurship. *International Journal of Entrepreneurial Venturing*, **1**(3), 291–308.

APPENDIX

Table 8A.1 Countries and number of participations in GEM, 2006–13

Country	Number of participations	Country	Number of participations
Argentina	8	Sweden	6
Brazil	8	Switzerland	6
Belgium	8	Ecuador	5
Chile	8	Iran	5
Croatia	8	Iceland	5
Slovenia	8	Jamaica	5
Spain	8	Malaysia	5
United States	8	Thailand	5
Finland	8	Algeria	4
France	8	United Arab Emirates	4
Greece	8	Guatemala	4
Hungary	8	India	4
Japan	8	Macedonia	4
Latvia	8	Portugal	4
Norway	8	Singapore	4
Netherlands	8	Taiwan	4
Peru	8	Angola	3
Russia	8	Australia	3
Uruguay	8	Egypt	3
Germany	7	Slovakia	3
China	7	Lithuania	3
Colombia	7	Nigeria	3
Denmark	7	Pakistan	3
Ireland	7	Palestine	3
Italy	7	Poland	3
United Kingdom	7	Dominican Republic	3
Romania	7	Czech Republic	3
South Africa	7	Serbia	3
Turkey	7	Trinidad and Tobago	3
Bosnia and Herzegovina	6	Tunisia	3
Korea	6	Uganda	3
Israel	6	Venezuela	3
Mexico	6		

9. Dynamics of student entrepreneurial teams: understanding individual coping strategies to build efficient teams*

Sandrine Le Pontois and Stéphane Foliard

INTRODUCTION

> Experience is the teacher of all things. (Julius Caesar, *Commentarii de Bello Civili*, 2.8)

With mounting complexity, interdependence and the increasing pace of change in organizational environments, entrepreneurial agility has become a much-needed meta-competency[1] for future entrepreneurs. According to the European Union, entrepreneurship education (EE) is a pillar for facilitating entrepreneurship. In 2013, the 'Entrepreneurship 2020 Action Plan' (European Commission, 2013) stated that we need increasing numbers of entrepreneurs to return to growth. To answer this need, universities have been developing entrepreneurial teaching programmes, providing continuous interactions with the business world since 1947 (Harvard MBA students; Katz, 2003). But by being embedded in this dynamic environment and increasing the relevance of learning by contact with the business world (Gartner et al., 2004; Edelman et al., 2008), universities also increase student difficulties because of the complexity of the task. To involve more and more students in entrepreneurial activities, those entrepreneurial teaching programmes concern more and more student entrepreneurial teams instead of individual projects. Entrepreneurship education literature is growing rapidly and it shows the need of a variety of methodological approaches, spanning interests in teaching, research and practices, and the need for additional and robust intellectual foundations (Fayolle, 2013).

Arising from the entrepreneurial learning model, focusing on the learner experiencing active pedagogy (Gibb, 1996), increasing numbers of programmes developed in higher education are focusing on entrepreneurial action. The student learns to be an entrepreneur by acting as an entrepreneur. More precisely, they learn entrepreneurship by acting in a student entrepreneurial team involved in the genuine context. In those situations, each student has to deal with the uncertainty coming from the entrepreneurial activities, with the uncertainty coming from the other members of the team and, finally, with the uncertainty coming from the little self-knowledge they have. The question of the effectiveness of these entrepreneurship education programmes then arises, and has many dimensions: how can we design a teaching model that fits the specificities of students (Béchard and Grégoire, 2007; Fayolle and Gailly, 2008)? What is the impact of a specific programme on entrepreneurial mindset, entrepreneurial intention (Ferreira et al., 2017), entrepreneurial competences (Lackéus, 2015), entrepreneurial action (Frese, 2009), and so on?

Furthermore, entrepreneurship education literature often focuses on the individual level. Very little is said about what happens in a student entrepreneurial team, at the individual and collective levels (Fayolle and Verzat, 2009). As stressed by Pöysä-Tarhonen et al. (2016), team dynamics and team aspects are passed over in favour of the task aspects of performance. Assessing whether the students are learning to work successfully as a team is most of the time impossible. This brings us to the question of the dynamics within the team and their impacts on both the global performance and the individual learning; that is, are all the members of a team developing the same level of skills and qualities? Once again, we do not know what happens in the black box.

So, the purpose of this chapter is to study what happens in the black box that constitutes an entrepreneurial student team. Our literature review gives us information about the benefits of teamwork in entrepreneurial activities, but little is said about entrepreneurial personal development within these student entrepreneurial teams. Using feedback on our experiences, we will question the performance of entrepreneurial learning-by-doing programmes regarding the personal dimension instead of the project dimension. To do that, a student entrepreneurial team allows us to open the black box that constitutes their team. We use an original qualitative approach to understand the team dynamics, the place of each student and, finally, the impact of the project on their personal development. Our results underline the coping strategies used by each student, the impact of leaderships, and the perceived individual place and the dynamics that impact the global performance of the project. Then, we explain the positive and negative impacts this programme can have on individual learning. We discuss our results and propose tools to structure those learning-by-doing programmes and a new perception of what the performance should be.

LITERATURE REVIEW AND PREVIOUS EXPERIENCES: WHAT DO WE KNOW ABOUT STUDENT ENTREPRENEURIAL TEAMS?

To respond to the authentic needs of the labour market or to be useful to meet the challenges of entrepreneurship, higher education programmes focus on the development of the entrepreneurial agility, the knowledge, skills and qualities expected to solve problems and to develop critical thinking, collaboration, and interpersonal communication. Because of the increased demand for teamwork in business, those programmes try to incorporate group projects into the curriculum, with the idea that students working in teams will learn teamwork, leadership and other key skills. It is also because higher education institutions need to maximize the number of students involved in these programmes that many utilize collaborative pedagogies such as learning in teams (Pöysä-Tarhonen et al., 2016).

Hernandez (2002) describes team learning as the creation of cooperative structures that promote active and higher-level learning or thinking. Teamwork provides many benefits when preparing students for practice, including improved leadership and communication skills (Hansen, 2006). Following Tarricone and Luca (2002), collaborating in student entrepreneurial teams requires much more than traditional entrepreneurial skills. Working in a team on an entrepreneurial project, in a learning-by-doing approach, results in active learning and a greater retention and comprehension of information. Some researchers underline that working in a team in such learning programmes results in higher levels of motivation and achievement, helps to develop critical thinking skills, and improves interpersonal and social skills (Ashraf, 2004; Williams et al., 1991[2]). For an entrepreneurial project, working in a team provides a larger workforce to face the challenge of starting and running a business. According to contemporary learning theories, knowledge is constructed in social interaction or even as a by-product of social interaction (Wenger, 1998). But that means that the learning programme should include working from a group to a team. For Pöysä-Tarhonen et al. (2016), teamwork is more difficult than working alone, because learning in teams tend to focus primarily on the task aspects of performance at the expense of the team aspects. Because they do not have time to develop specifically these general 'team skills', that are also difficult to train (De Hei et al., 2015), entrepreneurial programmes clearly focus on action. However, research shows that, in many classes, students are simply placed into team projects with no preparation, resulting in students being ineffectively prepared for work teams. Although higher education institutions have been placing students into teams for group projects for many years, the results are globally quite mixed.

Considering more precisely entrepreneurship, and compared to a solo entrepreneur, an entrepreneurial team appears to cope more successfully with uncertainties in a start-up, where flexibility and complexity of decision making is imperative (Vesper, 1990). But, on the other hand, when the team meets dysfunctions, this is the end of the project. Therefore, an understanding of entrepreneurial teams is essential in order to understand the creation and performance of new ventures (Khan et al., 2015).

Finally, this literature review focusing on student entrepreneurial teams shows that entrepreneurial higher education programmes have emphasized group and team work. What is also clear, though, is that group assignments are often made with little or no preparation to help the students function in the groups or teams. For Hansen (2006) this fundamental disconnect between the use of groups or teams and teamwork preparation is a significant problem. What the literature does not say is what happens in the team; what are the relationships and individual behaviours that students adopt to deal individually and collectively with the uncertainty provided by entrepreneurship. Even if the entrepreneurial project is a success, there is no highlighting of the impact of the project at the individual level. Because, as a team, students are able to start and run a business, teachers think that the entrepreneurial education programmes are efficient. But even if the team manages to start and run a business successfully, it does not mean that the programme is efficient at the individual level.

In 2012 in the University of Lyon, we started with the Roanne Chamber of Commerce a learning-by-doing programme called Campus for Entrepreneurs. Widely adapted from the JA Worldwide approach, this teaching programme leads a group of students in working over a period of ten months on the creation and the daily management of a company. Campus for Entrepreneurs is an organization that offers a simplified framework in which students can immediately focus on the entrepreneurial approach without having to deal with time-consuming administrative procedures. The programme is divided into three main phases: creativity and development of a business idea; feasibility and business plan; and operational management. All these steps are themselves divided into complementary modules, some of which enable students to act, while others bring methodological elements that align the approach to their needs in a non-linear way. 'Autonomy' is the keyword for the approach. Since 2012, 11 student teams have started and run their businesses. Nine of them were successful; they have reached the quantitative criteria to be recognized as effective. Two of them crashed and burned at an early stage of the process because the students were not able to work together. Although we have good feedback from most of the 60 students involved in this programme, the impact seems poor. For some of them, it has changed their higher education path to include more entrepreneurial experiences. But as far as we can tell, no one has already started their own business, and some of those students think that they will never do so. This is not the kind of performance that we are expecting from the entrepreneurial education programmes we are developing.

Filling this gap is crucial to understand why so few students involved in entrepreneurial programmes in teams go further in entrepreneurship. To improve the performance of entrepreneurial education programmes, we need to open the black box and start to discover and understand the team dynamics and explain this contradiction: how can a team perform in an entrepreneurial project when, individually, some students have a bad experience? Discovering what they are looking for when they start and run the project could also change our perception of the performance of an entrepreneurial learning programme. The stakes are high.

METHODS, GROUNDED THEORY AND INTERSUBJECTIVITY

Because we knew little about the student team dynamics in an entrepreneurial context when we began this study, we chose to open the black box and to pursue our investigation inductively, relying on a qualitative, interpretive approach (Corley and Gioia, 2004). An interpretive research focuses on building an emergent theory from a perspective that gives voice to the interpretations of the students living the experience of starting and running a business in an entrepreneurial student team. To discover and understand team dynamics and how it can impact upon the team and its performance, we needed to identify a group of students in which those issues were open and apparent, and thus possible for those students to acknowledge and discuss. The group of student we chose had been constituted for a training project based on entrepreneurial activities: Campus for Entrepreneurs.

Every year, two or three student teams choose this programme as an option in their curriculum. During a period of ten months, the students have to form a group, to imagine a concept, to design a business model and to write a business plan, and to find all the stakeholders they need to start their business; then, they can run their business, focusing on sales and daily management. Entrepreneurship is challenging, being a student is challenging and working in a brand new team is challenging too. Facing these challenges, most of the entrepreneurial student teams seem to be efficient with respect to quantitative criteria. We can say that our programme is efficient as well, but we finally know very little regarding the impact of this programme at the individual level. In the wake of such ambiguity, 'What happens in the student entrepreneurial team?' is a salient question. When students are working in a team, the place of each student arises, and questions follow about the commitment of each one in the team, of the sharing of responsibilities, of internal communication, and so on.

We (the authors) are both members of the pedagogical team. One is the founder of the programme, and the other joined the team when we decided to start the study. Because we are also researchers, we consider this programme as an ongoing process, and we try every year to improve the courses, the activities and tools to improve performance. We chose for our study a freely constituted group of five dynamic students (three men, denoted M, and two women, denoted F, between 19 and 22). We chose their entrepreneurial project as a unit of analysis. Because we followed this student entrepreneurial team throughout the ten months by occupying the roles of teachers, coaches or facilitators, we have knowledge about the global functioning of the group. We also have access to the reporting of all the activities carried out, and the way of carrying out the tasks within the entrepreneurial framework but also in an academic context.

This group achieved the whole of the entrepreneurial process one month ahead of what other groups are accustomed to requiring. In our mind, the team was quite successful. They surpassed their business objectives, achieved a consistent turnover, wrote excellent reports to obtain excellent marks. The group seemed cohesive during their oral presentations and overall to be happy with their performances. We also had excellent feedback from all the businessmen, suppliers and customers who had the opportunity to work with them. But we also heard about, without witnessing, many tensions in the group. This was a great opportunity to understand how a group of students in which tensions exist managed to overcome them to succeed in their entrepreneurial project. Identifying the elements that enabled them to continue the project is likely to consolidate our learning programme, to allow future teams to continue to move forward. We have observed in the past students unable to work in their team, and we want to develop entrepreneurial team management tools to be able to act in those situations, to fix the problems in the team and allow the students to move forward.

Apart from the advance completion of the programme, the team we chose to study is not different from the other teams we have followed. The training followed by the students was the same as for the other groups; their number, age and geographical origin do not differ either. A priori, this group seems to be prototypical in many dimensions (Pratt, 2009). It is a good opportunity for us to open the black box and to understand the existing dynamics and their impact both on the team performance and on each student.

Data Collection

Following Gioia et al. (2013), we consider that the students constructing their entrepreneurial realities are 'knowledgeable agents'. They know what they are trying to do and can explain their thoughts, intentions and actions. To explore the team dynamics of our students and their personal representations of what happened, and why and how they acted, we used a methodology derived from grounded theory (Glaser and Strauss, 1967; Corbin and Strauss, 1990). Because we can collect a lot of data coming from this student team, we design a unique case study research. Even if we take into account the precepts, the advice and the boilerplates produced by famous authors (Yin, 1984; Eisenhardt, 1989; Miles and Huberman, 1994), our purpose is the capturing and the modelling of informant meanings, and doing that, we are closer to the 'Gioia method' (Gioia et al., 2013) that Langley and Abdallah (2011) propose as a template.

Because we teach and coach this team, we had previous information about their relationships or task divisions in the team. We used that information, coming from observations, student oral presentations or written reports, to prepare the core of our studies: the semi-structured interviews. To be sure that the students, the informants, would agree to reveal what we might have considered to be proprietary information (Gioia et al., 2013), we explained the following process and promised anonymity.

We used the following strategy to collect data. Our protocol is designed to collect data about the team's dynamics, and it also works perfectly well to help students to verbalize the skills and qualities they have developed during the project. We asked each student about what they have done or not during the project following the entrepreneurial process. More precisely, we tried to understand the personal perception of what they had done, but also why, and how those actions took place. Then, we asked each student about their perception of what the members of the team had done, why, and how they did it. Knowing what they have precisely done, with a lot of detail, is very useful to express the skills they have developed. To be clear on our data exploitation and to include a tool in the teaching programme that enables students to describe their new skills and qualities,[3] we asked them to verbalize all they had done. This part is very important, because to gain objectivity and depth, we chose an intersubjective approach. Each student had their own feelings about the progress of the project, their place, and so on. We opted for a system of collecting data derived from the psychology

BOX 9.1 THE SEMI-STRUCTURED INTERVIEW PROTOCOL

1. Preconceptions, psychological capital and perception of risk (individual).
2. Intention, desirability, initial grounds of motivation (individual and team).
3. Business idea, feasibility (individual and team).
4. Starting the business, marketing, communication (individual and team).
5. Daily management and sales (individual and team).
6. Reasons of motivation (individual and team).
7. Adaptability, trial-and-error method (individual and team).
8. Qualities, skills developed (individual and team).
9. The work–life balance (individual).

of work and organization practised in clinical activity: the method of crossed self-confrontation (Clot, 1999: 131–151). The first part of the data collection was individual semi-structured interviews filmed in a neutral space. For the second part of the data collection, a video was shown to a duo consisting of the student concerned and another member of the team. This intersubjective and contradictory step of our methodology allowed us to gain insight about those individual and collective perceptions.

To explore what happened in the team, in this black box that the students opened for us, we decided to design our interview protocol around the entrepreneurial process followed by the students during the ten months. Focusing on their experience rather than starting from theory allowed us to capture their sensemaking (Gioia et al., 2013). The interview protocol includes nine sections (Box 9.1) covering the entrepreneurial process, starting from the preconceptions, and leading to the qualities and skills developed during the project. Most of the sections are divided, to obtain information about the student's perception of what they have done and information about their perception of the group (Appendix Box 9A.1). We used this interview guide in the five one-to-one semi-structured interviews. We also prepared probing questions in order to have a better understanding of what the students really think or feel. We adopt a maieutic approach to make the students talk, because it is clearly not an easy exercise for them.

For the second part of the data collection, the crossed self-confrontation, we formed pairs according to common and opposite points of view. Because the crossed self-confrontation is designed to gain depth and objectivity, we formed the pairs according to our perception of their individual subjectivities. Shifting, opposing points of view makes it possible to gain depth by understanding the ins and outs of these points of view. It also allows us to diminish subjectivity, with each student integrating the point of view of the other to obtain a shared point of view closer to reality.

During those one-to-two interviews, the researcher in the position of a 'psychologist' accompanies the students as they exchange views about their activity. The students and the researcher can stop the video to react to what has been said as well as the attitudes or expressions seen. This confrontation of points of view makes it possible to widen certain aspects. Above all, it allows us to confront subjective points of view and thus gain objectivity and depth. Approximately 14 hours of recorded material were collected.

Data Analysis

As we collected the data, we also inductively analysed it, adhering closely to the guidelines of constant comparison techniques (Glaser and Strauss, 1967). These approaches provide the basis for rigorous collection and analysis of qualitative data, and for clearly delineating themes and aggregate dimensions (Corley and Gioia, 2004) through the examination and comparison of the ideas discussed by the informants. Because we had previous information about this team and how they had worked individually and as a group, we did not need to change our interview protocol.

We began the analysis by identifying initial concepts in the data and grouping them into categories (open coding). To perform this initial data coding, we tried to maintain the integrity of first order conceptual coding (Gioia et al., 2013) using *in vivo* codes (Corbin and Strauss, 1990). When the language used by the informants was not available, we used a simple description phrase (Corley and Gioia, 2004). This part of the analysis allows us to start a comprehensive compendium of the first order terms. At this stage, the information provided by the informants was surprising. The first order conceptual coding shows very different individual perceptions and behaviours in the group. It concerns the global performance of the project as well as the perception of what had been done individually and collectively, the place of each student in those achievements, the power balance, and so on.

To gain depth, we decided to partly organize the first order codes into the second order themes using a theoretical grid of what was not initially foreseen. This return to literature led us to use in our analysis the theories of self-managed team leadership, more specifically the theories of distributed leadership (Barry, 1991) and coping strategies (Ionescu et al., 1997; Côté, 2013). The distributed leadership model emphasizes the development of leadership abilities within all members of a team; each member has certain leadership qualities that will be needed by the group at some point. The coping strategies refer to all the processes that an individual implements between themself and a perceived threat (stressor) in order to control, tolerate or diminish the impact on their psychological and physical well-being (Lazarus and Folkman, 1984). We chose these theories because they fitted particularly well to our data and can explain the team dynamics, even if other theoretical frames could have been used. We completed this second order analysis with themes coming inductively from the informants.

Finally, we gathered similar themes into several overarching dimensions that make up the basis of the emergent framework. This process was not linear: we made some returns to theory to organize and reorganize the themes into aggregate dimensions. Our interviews were structured around what the informants actually did, and how, individually and collectively. It was easy to understand their personal strategy within the group and how the leaderships took place.

The final data structure is illustrated in Figure 9.1. We used the second order themes to build our model of entrepreneurial student team performance. Following Gioia's method, we took several steps to ensure the trustworthiness of our data. First, we were careful to manage our data meticulously. To gain in consistency, all the interviews were led by the same researcher. All the interviews were recorded and integrally transcribed. We used NVivo 11 software. The two authors started with individual coding, before joining and discussing their results. Second, and following Gioia's boilerplates, we used peer debriefing. Because we were involved in the project as teachers and in the field as researchers, we needed other points of view to discuss emerging patterns in the data as well as our methodology and analysis. We presented our project, and the methodology of data collection we planned to use, to an experienced qualitative researcher familiar with the grounded procedures.[4] Then, we asked many opinions from researchers. In this study, the peers were department colleagues and members of our research centres using qualitative methods and were not involved in this entrepreneurial programme. Finally, we attended a conference to solicit critical questions about our analysis procedures. As illustrated in Figure 9.2, there are three main dimensions to the model of student entrepreneurial team performance: coping strategies, distributed leaderships and skills development.

RESULTS

Three specific themes relating to the performance of a student entrepreneurial team characterize our informants' experiences: (1) the coping strategy each student adopted; (2) distributed leadership and the place and role perceived by each student; and (3) skills development. In this presentation of our results, we coordinate and integrate four data displays:

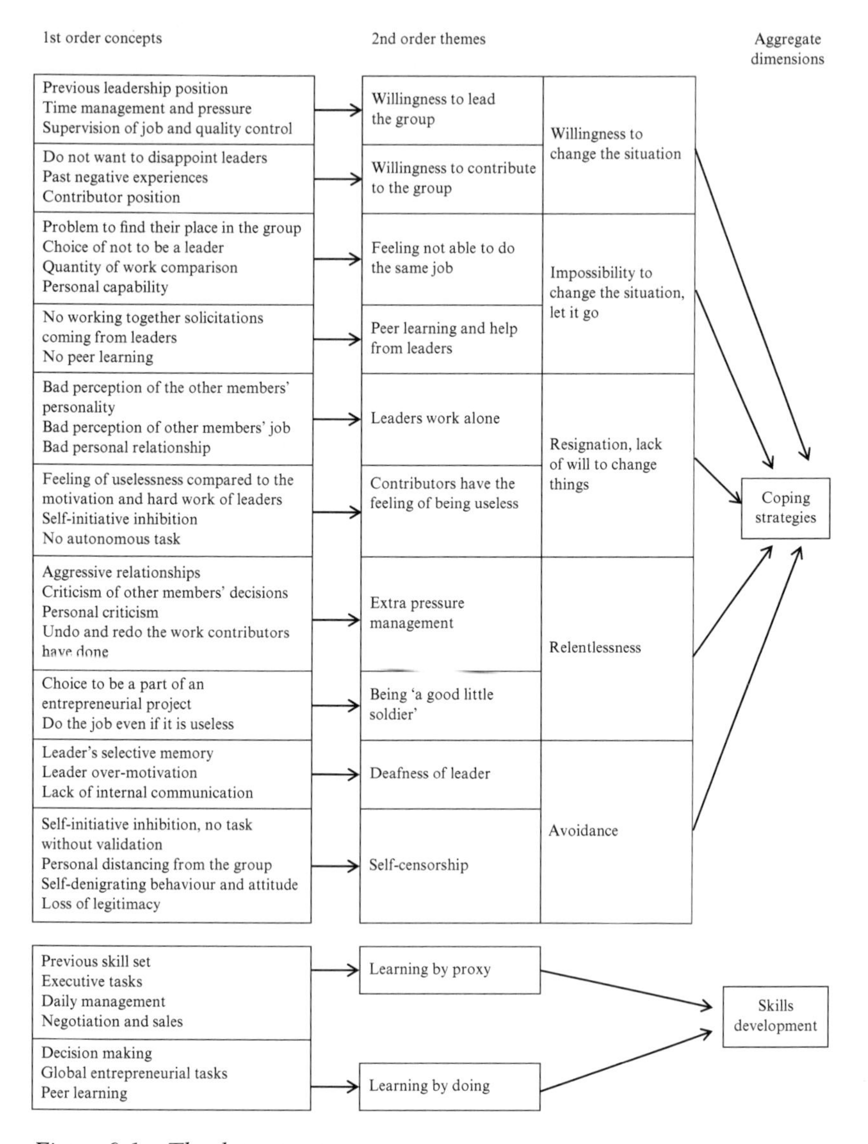

Figure 9.1 The data structure

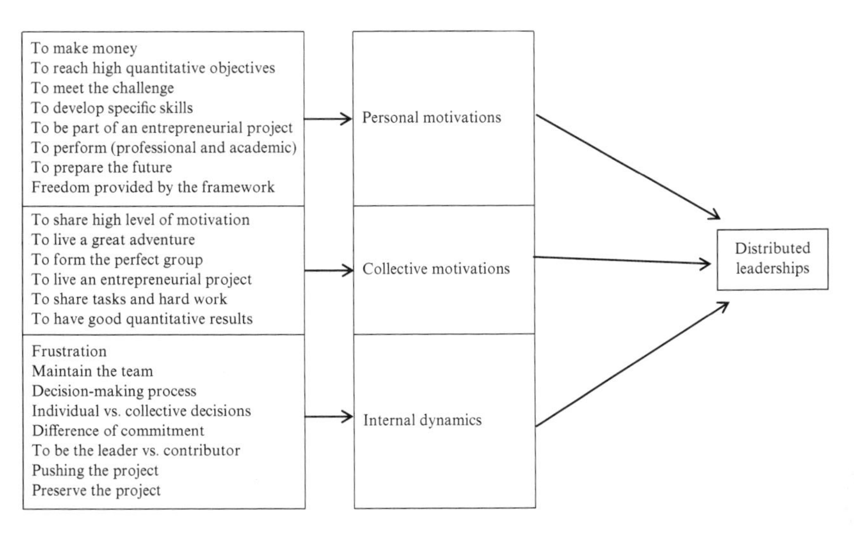

Figure 9.1 (continued)

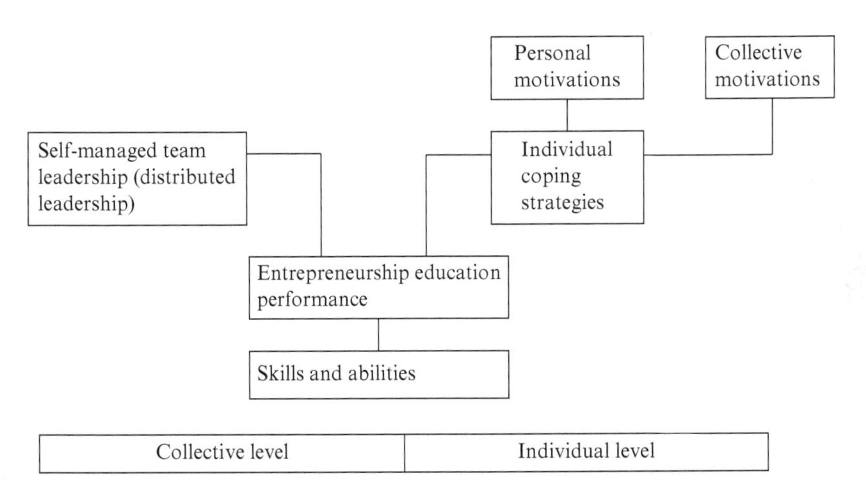

Figure 9.2 Team dynamics and EE performance

the progressive data structure (Figure 9.1), the emergent model (Figure 9.2), and additional supporting data (Tables 9.1 and 9.2).

The Coping Strategies

Asking about and discussing the perception of each student of what they have done, why, and how they have have done it, and about the perception

Table 9.1 Data supporting the coping strategies (following Côté, 2013)

The coping strategies				
Controllability of the situation				
	YES		NO	
Coping +	**CHANGING THE SITUATION** Increase resources and capacities: seek relevant information and develop skills.Act in practice: communicate, analyse, plan and organize time, tasks and environment, make the necessary efforts to accomplish their tasks and persevere.Obtain instrumental support from the social network: receive direct help, resources or advice to identify and apply concrete solutions. Mainly: F1 (Group-oriented) M1 (Project-oriented)		**LET IT GO** Accept serenely to deal with reality: self, others, the situation. Feeding realistic expectations and expectations, accepting the limits of one's power and abilities as well as those of others. Focus on the positive, relativize the importance of a problem and de-dramatize its consequences. Choose your battles and stop wanting to change a situation in which one has no power. Mainly: F1, F2, M2	
M1	**Entrepreneurial family** 'My father pushed my brothers and me, he pushed us and he will push us to create our own stuff, our own business' **Leader position** *Accepts implicitly sharing the leadership with F1 as he wanted to be the leader*	M2	**Cold calling** (supplier research) *'I stopped calling because M1 and F1 called all the suppliers'*	
M2	'It was impossible because we are both leaders and so we have understood that we had to work together'	M3	**Quantity of work** *Not enough work?* 'M1 said: "you've done nothing"' . . .but 'after reflection, I said to myself: M1 is taking rubbish, I have worked.' **M1 annoyed when M3 focused on risks** *M3 plays downs the effects* 'it was not a waste of time' **No (good) results (to sell boxes)** *Distancing*	
M3	**M1 and F1 supervision and quality control** 'I was doing my best after having listened to what they had to say' **Risk of disappointing M1 and M2** 'I didn't want to be a deadweight'; 'we had to be at their' level'			

Role played within the group
'It is useless to insist on imposing yourself'; 'it's better to position yourself as a good worker/contributor'
M1's strategy to appropriate M3's choice to be part of this project
Communicates
'I said to myself, entrepreneurship, that's great'; 'I said to F1: 'who is working together?'; 'entrepreneurship was a thing to do, something better than other projects'
Negative experience in another group (previous year)
Time management

F1 'the time pressure was tiring but stimulating'
M1 position towards M3 (and M2/F2)
Explains and argues her vision
'you can't take away what he has done'

Negative experience in another group (previous year)
F2 'last year, relationships were tense, we didn't have the same workload, I really wanted to share the work fairly'; 'In the end, I have done a lot of work but without talking about it, I have had no acknowledgement'; 'I want to work with motivated and efficient people'; 'the same workload'
Time management
'we were working a lot, a lot'; 'entrepreneurial lectures when the other students had free time'; 'our project and classes'
Risk of disappointing M1 and M2
'we gave everything we had so they [M1 and F1] would not be disappointed with us'

'that doesn't matter'
Impossibility to find his place within the group
Less involvement
'When F2 and I proposed doing something, it was too late, we heard: "that's already been done"'
Reviewing the essay about the project
Revision without changing what M2 and F2 had written (M3 chooses not to rewrite even if he is good at this task)
'I didn't do the rewriting, I just made some corrections'
Cold calling (supplier research)
Stop calling/M1 and F1 call suppliers

F1 **Tensions within the team**
Goes along with it, that's normal
'even if each person's involvement was different, we advanced the project'; 'I was ok with that'

F2 **No 'working together' solicitations coming from M1, M2 and F1**
Doing nothing
'if you didn't call me, that's because you didn't need me'
No driving licence
Didn't go to meet suppliers
'you had cars, it was easier for you three'
Role to play within the group
Chooses not to be a leader (as F2 is usually)
'I couldn't be a leader at the same level'; 'Personally I was not embarrassed about it'

Table 9.1 (continued)

The coping strategies			
Controllability of the situation			
	YES		NO
Coping –	**RESIGNATION/DISEMPOWERMENT** To complain, to pity, to blame others without recognizing his own faults or failures. Undergo the situation, feeling helpless to change it even though, in reality, it could be. Removing responsibility for what can be done, letting others find solutions or dealing with problems, procrastinating. Mainly M3, F2 (recriminations sustained by M1) M1 (low perceived commitment level of F2 and M3)		**RELENTLESSNESS** Continue to pursue ineffective strategies of action, as there is no possible control over the situation. To persist in trying to achieve an unrealistic, if not impossible, result. Take responsibility for problems that belong to others. Mainly M1
M1	**Relationship with M2, M3 and F2** 'They brought nothing of their own'; 'in this case F2 will feel overwhelmed all her life' **Relationship with M3** *Blames M3* 'F1 and I, we killed ourselves over this thing, it took a lot of time, I gave it everything, and you didn't show us any appreciation' **M3 idea generation** *Criticizes M3* 'unrealistic'; 'you took a long time to share your ideas, I was angry'	**M1**	**Aggressive relationship with M3** *Doesn't want to work with him* 'I would have preferred another student from another department'; 'all his initiatives were bad'; 'he made a box and it was shit'; 'I gave him an ultimatum, we had 15 boxes, you sell the 15 boxes because you have to work, it's normal' **Undo and redo the work M2, M3 and F2 had done** 'we had to follow up on everything'; 'perhaps because they realized they couldn't keep up'; 'who takes his car to negotiate with the suppliers?'

M3 **Aggressiveness from M1 about the incapacity of M3 to explain something clearly**
Humour 'That's right, you [the researcher] didn't say anything to help me when I was talking in this video'

F2 **M1 and F1 strong motivation**
Feels helpless about being as motivated and hard working as M1 and F1
Feeling of uselessness

M2 'we were here, I don't know [why]. . .'
Decision making
Doesn't give his opinion/ he's shocked because F1 decided the box price by herself
'we were shocked and after that, we didn't discuss it'

F2 personality and tastes
Criticizes F2 personality and skills
'F1 loved it, I found it really hideous'; 'you have to review your strategy class [about innovation]'; 'you know you are the only one who thinks like that'; 'you are too kind' (12 occurrences); 'they will eat you up' (5 occurrences); 'you should think about how you behave'

Stand location at the Christmas market
'It didn't work, because this location is lost in no-man's land between two big pedestrian streets; there's the traffic'

M2, M3 and F1 don't keep abreast of what is happening, what needs to be done
Stops giving information
'they couldn't keep up, they knew where the tools were on our FB page'; 'I don't want to hear about him, them, M3'

Financial losses
Tries to demonstrate that losses at the end of the project are caused by F1
'you made bad decisions'

F2 **Cold calling** (town halls, to sell boxes) 1 month
Calling even if it is useless
'I kept going'; 'we knew every time that the answer would be negative'

Table 9.1 (continued)

The coping strategies	
Controllability of the situation	
YES	NO
AVOIDANCE Numbing emotions and feelings: addiction or abuse of drugs, alcohol or drugs, hypersomnia. Block unpleasant thoughts and excessively practice compensatory activities: impulse buying, food, electronic games or gambling. Moving away from sources of stress: some places, people or aversive activities. Mainly M3	

M1	*Refuses to remember what positive work M3 has done* 'I don't remember'; 'I don't know'
M2	**Self-initiative inhibition** *No autonomous tasks (without validation from M1 and F1 – quantity and quality)* **Decision making** *Not getting involved by choosing M1 or F1's point of view* 'If I agreed with F1, I was afraid that my friendship with M1 . . .'
M3	**Role played within the group** *Distancing himself from the group* 'I was fed up'; 'that doesn't matter' **Quantity of work** *Works less and less as the project goes on* 'I've really done less than all of you!' **Selling boxes to relatives** *Chooses not so sell to relatives (ethical reasons)* **Shares with M1 perceived relational difficulties** *Self-denigrating behaviour and attitude* 'sometimes I just say things that don't mean anything' **Lack of internal communication** *Doesn't try to know what is happening by the end of the project* 'there were things, ok, we didn't know how to use these tools you had made'; 'great things were done but we didn't know it'; 'ok, you have done things: share the information. M1 has answered: you have to show your interest' **M1 and F1 over-motivation** *Doesn't want to be like them* 'you are crazy'; 'it was ridiculous sometimes' **Idea proposal** *Stop proposing ideas* 'we knew our ideas would never be chosen because M1 and F1 expressed their point of view' **Strong motivation of M1 and F1** *Not able to be as motivated as they are* 'regarding M1 and F1's work, it was difficult to do
F2	better, so we couldn't feel effective'; 'they were doing everything so it was difficult to make something new or anything' **Self-initiative** *No autonomous tasks (without validation – quantity and quality)* **Legitimacy** *Doesn't speak* 'we couldn't say anything because we had not achieved as much as they [M1 and F1] had'

Table 9.2 The coping strategies used in the team following Ionescu's model (following Ionescu et al., 1997)

Coping strategies/defence mechanisms	
Coping centred on emotion: • Minimizing risks or taking distance M1, F2 • Positive reassessment F1, M2, M3 • Self-accusation M3, F2	Avoiding coping: • Passive strategies (avoidance, escape, denial, resignation) M3, M2, F2, M1
Coping centred on the problem: • Problem solving and information retrieval F1, M2 (M2 for the project, F1 for the relations of M1 with the group and for the project) M1 (for the project) • The fighting spirit or the acceptance of confrontation M1, F1	The vigilant coping: • Active strategies to confront the situation: information, social support, medium, etc. M1, F1/M2 (concerning its mission as communication manager)

of what the others have done, why and how, during the project gives us a lot of information about the respective places of each member of the team. To understand team dynamics and their impact on the performance, we here underline the importance of why and how this team was formed.

On the one hand, F1 and F2 decided to work together because they knew their respective work capacity. The year before, they were respectively involved in other student projects and had to take the lead because of the lack of work from the other members of the team. For F2: 'last year, relationships were tense, we didn't have the same workload, I really wanted to share the work fairly'; 'In the end, I have done a lot of work without talking about it, and nobody has recognized the value of my work'. F1 had the same bad experience: (in M3's words) 'that was the same problem with F1, at the beginning she didn't say a lot and by the end she was tense in "karate" mode'. F2 gave a good illustration of her first motivation to form a group, whatever the subject of the project: 'I want to work with motivated and efficient people'; 'the same workload'. On the other hand, M1 and M2 had worked together on a previous project. M1 was really interested in entrepreneurship and wanted to form the best possible group to reach such an ambitious goal. F1 contacted M1 because she knews his work capacity. Both agreed to work together, but for M1 only on the entrepreneurial project. At the same time, M3 had joined F1 and F2: 'I said to myself, entrepreneurship, that's great'; 'I said to F1: "Are we working together?"'; 'entrepreneurship was a thing to do, something better than other projects'.

In fact, every member of the team had the same vision about the constitution of the group: building the perfect group. This initial positioning led quickly to differences in the perception of the project. For M1 and F1 it was no longer a traditional student project, it was a real business and, mainly for M1, they had to reach the objectives to run their business and make money. Gaining a good mark was no longer their priority, while it remained a priority for F2 and M2. These differences of perception about the nature of the project, added to the uncertainty involved in every project of starting and running a business, led each student to cope with those unexpected situations. 'Coping strategies' refer to all the processes that an individual implements between themself and a perceived threat (stressor) to control, tolerate or diminish the impact on their psychological and physical well-being (Lazarus and Folkman, 1984). In Table 9.1, we use mainly the model of Côté (2013) to analyse the strategies used by students and to understand the impacts on team dynamics.

Whether the controllability of the situation was effective or not, we observe that the strategies of positive coping were used mainly by F1 who thus ensured cohesion of the team. M3 left the project about midway through the process by adopting the strategy of avoidance against M1, which embodied for him a situation of over-aggressive entrepreneurship. M1 sought to control the entire process and the team, which he wanted to create in his image in terms of commitment, motivation and quality of achievement. He adopted negative coping regarding the other members of the team: resignation about what the others were able to inject, or relentlessness regarding the tasks they had done. Because the pace was not high enough, he started to work alone or only with F1 as a co-leader. F2 was protected by a 'let-it-go' strategy ('only' part of a tutored project where students work seriously) linked to a strategy of resignation (she did not feel she was an entrepreneurial leader and left this role to M1; she felt unwilling and unable to assume responsibility).

In brief, M1 was 'overinvolved' in the project, which he considered as his own business. He also considered F2, M2 and M3 as employees and not as students. To develop this activity and create a huge turnover, he put a lot of pressure on the other members of the team, and most of his strategies were negative coping strategies. But his motivation and commitment were so high that he inspired a kind of respect from the other members of the team who felt unable to do the same. He only accepted F1 as a co-leader because she took good initiatives and she sold a lot. The only remaining function was commercialization of the products. Because of their initial motivations (being in a good group and gaining good marks) F2 and M2 adopted project-oriented coping strategies (Table 9.2). They acted as 'good little soldiers', following the decisions of M1 and F1. They also knew that their personal motivations would be satisfied in this way, even if it was frustrating. In a way, they acted to protect the project and their leaders: 'we gave everything we had so they [M1 and F1] would not be disappointed with us' (F2). M3 initially thought that he could be a leader. Because it was difficult for him to find his place, he just chose to work less. Finally, this project was an entrepreneurial success in terms of quantitative criteria (turnover, sales, contacts, and so on) because every member of the team protected the project and chose a project-oriented coping strategy even if they knew that their personal benefits were not as high as promised.

The Ionescu model (Table 9.2) sheds light on the fact that the team encountered difficulties in implementing problem-oriented adjustment strategies, and the emotional aspect remained prevalent. Avoidance coping formed a majority, but the quality of the vigilant coping allowed the team to carry out their project on a short-term (operational phase: three months). In the medium term – that is to say, in the sixth month of the project – relationships between the team members deteriorated significantly, which the teaching team did not necessarily perceive, even though the entrepreneurial project was experienced as a real success at all levels (acquisition of skills by students, creation of business, creation of added value, recognition of socio-economic actors).

Understanding the coping strategies adopted by the student members of an entrepreneurial team highlights some threats that could impact upon any team, and negative coping is undoubtedly the cause of many student project failures. Our analysis shows that positive coping strategies are essential in team dynamics and can overcome tensions between people. We also show that those strategies derive from personal and collective motivations: why the student is a part of the project. Starting from this point, a student adapts their behaviour and adopts a strategy to cope with uncertainty and recurrent stressors. Our comprehension of team dynamics underlines the interrelationships between personal strategy and how the place within the team is found. Understanding coping strategy dynamics enables us to understand how and why every student has found their place. The distributed leadership model (Barry, 1991; see Table 9.3) provides a good lens through which to understand the place of each student in the project and how predispositions to certain strategies visible in the initial motivations are supported by the distributed leadership dynamics.

Table 9.3 Self-perceived leadership, perceived leadership from peers and from the pedagogical team, based on Barry's model (Barry, 1991)

Student leadership (below) evaluated by (row):	M1	M2	M3	F1	F2
M1 **Envisioning leadership** **Organizing leadership** **Spanning leadership**	*<u>Envisioning</u>* *<u>Organizing</u>* *<u>Spanning</u>* *LEADER with the help of F1*	Envisioning Organizing Spanning	'manager' Envisioning Organizing Spanning	'project leader' Envisioning Spanning	Envisioning Spanning
M2 **No leadership** (on communication and marketing topics: Envisioning leadership Spanning leadership)	No leadership	*<u>No leadership</u>* *CONTRIBUTOR*	Envisioning (on communication and marketing topics)	Envisioning (on communication and marketing) topics)	Envisioning (on communication and marketing topics)
M3 **No leadership**	No leadership	No leadership	*<u>Envisioning</u>* *Social (with F2)* *CONTRIBUTOR*	No leadership	No leadership
F1 **Envisioning leadership** **Organizing leadership** **Social leadership**	Organizing	Envisioning leader (business idea)	Organizing	*<u>Organizing</u>* *CO-LEADER*	Envisioning leadership
F2 **Social leadership**	No leadership	Social ('third leader')	Social	No leadership	*<u>No leadership</u>* *CONTRIBUTOR*

Note: Italic underlining refers to the student self-perception; bold type refers to the teacher perception; normal type refers to the peer perception.

The Self-Managed Team Leadership: A Distributed Leadership

When they form their team to engage in an entrepreneurial project, students do not know exactly what they are going to do and who will be in charge of what. They start as self-managed teams and, following Barry (1991), those teams require even more leadership than conventional organizational units. They need task-based leadership (project management, scheduling, resource gathering, and so on) but they also require leadership in the team building and team development processes including cohesiveness, establishing effective communication patterns, and so on. In a student entrepreneurial team, there is no formal authority at the beginning, and power struggles and conflicts surface more often. Understanding the underlying leadership dynamics can explain the performance of a student entrepreneurial team. Students only receive theoretical information in group process skills, and that could lead to unstable groups, with more fission than fusion. Two of the 11 teams involved in Campus for Entrepreneurs experienced this misadventure.

To be effective, leadership roles and behaviours required for proper student entrepreneurial team functioning fall into four basic types of leadership: envisioning leadership, which revolves around creativity and development of overall business vision; social leadership, which centres on the interpersonal dealings within a group; spanning leadership, which is concerned with acquiring and disseminating resources external to a group; and organizing leadership, which involves developing and maintaining task structures and plans, information management systems and control systems.

Understanding leadership dynamics highlights the performance of the team as regards the place and the role occupied by each student. Because those perceptions are subjective – and as F2 said, 'Finally, no one in the group experienced the project in the same way' – we report in Table 9.3 three perceptions of how leadership was distributed (or not) in the team. The first perception is the personal one: what leadership each student thought they had; the second is the perception of student leadership by all other teammates; and the third is the perception of student leadership by the pedagogical team.

Our results underline the predominance of a strong leader, M1, and a co-leader, F1. In their previous student projects, M1, M3, F1 and F2 were leaders. In this entrepreneurial project, M1 and F1 clearly expressed their willingness to be the leader, and they drew lots to know who would be the 'official' project manager. Because M1 and F1 were so much involved in this entrepreneurial project, they undertook many tasks, took many decisions with little consultation and feedback, assigned tasks and work to the other students, checked the quantity and quality of work done, and actually assumed the major part of leadership. Because they were under time pressure, they chose to act instead of consulting, to take decisions alone without informing others about what they had done. They did not leave any room for others.

M1 was seen by everybody (including himself) to assume envisioning leadership, organizing leadership and spanning leadership. He concentrated most of the leadership to be sure that this entrepreneurial project would reach his personal objectives. F1 was perceived as assuming organizing leadership and envisioning leadership because she had the business idea and she dealt with daily management. For the pedagogical team, she was also perceived as assuming social leadership. At the midway point of the project, she understood that, from the beginning, their over-involvement and their over-motivation had not left any room for other students to find their place and to be more active. She took time to consult every student (except M1), but it was too late for others to regain a place in the project. M2 thought he was only a contributor, without leadership. The other members of the team and the pedagogical team perceived envisioning leadership on communication and marketing topics. M3 thought he assumed envisioning leadership when the other members thought he had no leadership. F2 assumed social leadership because, when M1 and F1 started to work alone, she talked a lot with M2 and M3. They were frustrated, and she pushed them to keep going and to stay motivated. By doing this, she preserved the project.

Because leadership had not been discussed, the team's dynamic and the prevalence of M1 and F1 acting under pressure of time led to tensions and issues. On the one hand, M1 and F1 engulfed the project, leaving nothing but crumbs to the other teammates. This generated a lot a frustration, especially for M3 who clearly adopted a withdrawal strategy. M1 was also frustrated because the other members of the team were not as involved as he was. M2 and F2 found it hard that they had not been more involved in steps such as negotiation or creativity. M2 wanted to be more involved and got frustrated: 'I was ready to get into his [M1] car and you [F1] came, you left together and I was alone on the sidewalk. So I said to myself: "Ok, never mind . . .". The lack of internal communication, the directivity of the leaders and the lack of room for F2, M2 and M3 to express themselves, was very difficult to live with.

On the other hand, the previous motivations to form the perfect group counterbalanced this frustration and the bad experiences. F2, M2 and partially M3 accepted a contributor position to preserve the group and the project. But in doing this, they did not benefit from the whole learning-by-doing process, and their perception of self-efficacy (Bandura, 1994 [1998]) decreased: F2, 'When I worked with them, if I had an idea, I did not say it', 'Unintentionally, they do not walk on you, but you really feel inferior'; M2, 'I know that I am not great at doing it'; M3, 'the lack of self-confidence'. Even if this project was a real success in terms of quantitative criteria, the personal development of every student involved was not attained.

DISCUSSION: WHAT ARE WE TALKING ABOUT WHEN WE TALK ABOUT ENTREPRENEURIAL EDUCATION PERFORMANCE?

> Placing students into groups for class projects is not the same as developing teams, even when the term 'team' is applied. (Barker and Franzak, 1997)

For most entrepreneurial projects, the question of performance refers to quantitative data because it is easy to assess: turnover, number of sales, of customers, diversity of the activities carried out, originality of the steps taken, daily management, communication, and so on. If the team manages to launch an organization that perfectly suits the entrepreneurial objectives, they have certainly developed the skills that make them able to turn an idea into a company. Less is said about the impact of those programmes on the development of entrepreneurial skills for each student involved in the team, about the impact of the team on the development of the individual entrepreneurial intention, about the performance of the team, or about pleasure or well-being at work. In the same way, the feedback from our pedagogical experience is not really fruitful.

Entrepreneurial education is seen as a good response to the increasing pace of change our societies are experiencing. The learning-by-doing programmes embedded in a genuine business context usually concern teams of students facing the challenge of starting and running a business from scratch. They have to deal with multilevel uncertainty: self-knowledge; uncertainty coming from the other members of the team in terms of personality, motivation, involvement, and so on; and uncertainty related to the entrepreneurial process. The main purpose of this study was to better understand what happens in the black box: the student entrepreneurial team dynamics. This qualitative study provides insights on the relations between the leadership system, the individual coping strategies, and individual and collective motivations. The leadership system and the initial motivation have an impact on the coping strategies used by each student to deal with recurrent stressors. Those strategies have protected the students and the project. Regarding quantitative criteria (academic and entrepreneurial), the team we studied was successful. However, most of the individual objectives were not attained, and there was frustration. The project performance concentrated all the students' energy, instead of their personal development.

At the epistemological level, we need to redefine the objective of our entrepreneurship education programme, Campus for Entrepreneurs. Living an entrepreneurial experience within a team is a very good way to develop entrepreneurial abilities, but we have to be careful that it benefits all the students. For Karanian et al. (2012), to collaborate in an entrepreneurial team leads the participants to develop specific characteristics. The students will be self-motivated, which refers to the capacity of each student member of the entrepreneurial team to go above and beyond the tasks they are charged with. Being together will increase the 'ambiguity readiness', which refers to the capacity of a student to deal with the entrepreneurial ambiguity. 'Passionate social awareness' includes responses that express a sense of intrigue, and an interest in problem solving. A team relies on the cooperation of all the parts; it is essential that there is a constant feedback loop between team members. And finally, a student entrepreneurial team needs empathy within the team and with all the stakeholders. Each teammate must be aware of the inputs and contributions of each other person, and ensure that people feel valued and appreciated to improve team dynamics.

Campus for Entrepreneurs is designed to be a secure environment for entrepreneurship, and we have to take care of our students. The balance between not enough and too much structure can be difficult to strike. Even if the students are free to choose their project, the frame is wide enough to run it as they want. The results of this study highlight the necessity to be aware of the dynamics within the team so that everyone finds their place. This place is relevant if: (1) the individual objectives meet the collective ones; and (2) the place is negotiated and accepted by all the members. To improve the Campus for Entrepreneurs programme, we discuss several proposals, as follows.

First is team building. To go from a group to an effective team, students are free to select their team members, and then the programme will include team building and team training workshops starting from their needs: (1) entrepreneurial basics; and (2) what it means to work in a team (self-knowledge, leadership and team dynamics, personal and collective motivations and objectives, skills to develop, how to communicate within a team). Communication is a general foundation upon which teams' task- and team-related processes are built (Bradley et al., 2013). The quality of communication improves team performance, for example, as information is shared and assessed in a collaborative climate (Woolley et al., 2010). This study underlines some of those needs within the team: non-violent communication tools, life group common rules (Verzat et al., 2015), discussing and agreeing the decision making process, understanding the place of each member, and using peer learning to develop relevant skills.

Second is the team contract. To limit the impact of the negative coping strategies, we propose a team contract including why every student wants to be a part of the team project, how they want to contribute, and what they are ready to do for the project (objective, motivation, skills, qualities and place). This contract is a third space in which to discuss, negotiate and understand the willingness of each member to be part of the project. The impact of emotions and moods on behaviour is greater when the task is relevant to the individual (Forgas, 1999). It will be useful to avoid misunderstanding coming from different individual levels of implication, and with different perceptions regarding the project (academic versus entrepreneurial project). Because entrepreneurial projects are dynamic, this contract could be renegotiated if needed to improve the performance of the team and the project.

Third is peer learning, action based. To improve the individual skills of each student, we propose to include in the contract a systematic peer learning method. Every student has to share their skills with the others. According to their level of skills they can start, for example, as simple observers and step by step become actors. Based on action theories (Frese, 2009), we propose a six-step process:[5] (1) asynchronous observation (they explain to each other how to act); (2) synchronous *in vivo* observation; (3) 'number two' in the pair (a student acts in support of a skilled teammate); (4) 'number one' in the pair (the skilled teammate only helps if needed and debriefs after the task); (5) action done autonomously and result assessment; (6) double-loop action (the student analyses the result and the way they act to improve their practice).

All of these tools seem relevant and useful to improve the performance of an entrepreneurial education programme. This study raises the epistemological question of performance in entrepreneurship education. Traditional quantitative criteria measure a kind of figured performance, and we think this is not enough. The team we studied was a real quantitative success, but all the teammates were frustrated. Our question is: entrepreneurial education, or education by entrepreneurship? Also, we need other criteria to improve our programme and reach our original objective: to develop individual entrepreneurial skills for all the students involved in the project. We propose another lens focusing, first, on individual developments within the team; and second, on the project's success. Moving away from the *Homo oeconomicus* model, Campus for Entrepreneurs has become an alternative to traditional programmes and an emancipating space where turnover is not the main goal. Focusing on team dynamics will lead to greater teams in which students will cooperate, learn from each over and develop their individual skills to reach a high level of performance.

CONCLUSION

Contributions

The contributions of this chapter can be given in three main points. At the theoretical level, we provide elements to understand the dynamics within an entrepreneurial student team by identifying the strategies used individually and their impact on motivation and involvement. We also provide elements of reflection on the definition of the performance of entrepreneurship education, by exceeding the purely quantitative criteria mainly used. We show above all that it is not because these quantitative goals have been reached that the programme has had the expected effects on the students' desire to pursue the entrepreneurial adventure, or on the pleasure they may have had to be part of this type of project. At the methodological level, we use an intersubjective approach, the crossed self-confrontation, to gain depth and objectivity. This allows us to understand what the students are doing in the team, but above all why they act or do not. At the managerial level, our results can help teachers to improve their entrepreneurial programme by being vigilant to team dynamics, and consolidating activities through teambuilding exercises and an effort of reflexivity on the functioning of the team and the satisfaction of each student in their place.

Limits and Transferability of Findings

A reasonable question often arises concerning the transferability of case study findings, including grounded theory models, to other entrepreneurial education programmes (Corley and Gioia, 2004). Even if it is always difficult to argue for extensions from case studies, our study has a number of features that suggest that the team dynamics we have observed are likely to share commonalities with other student entrepreneurial teams. Clearly, motivations have an effect on the coping strategy and the commitment of each student in the project, but there is nothing unusual in this team. In fact, the dynamics for this specific student entrepreneurial team (coping strategies to deal with entrepreneurial uncertainty, and personal and collective perceptions of distributed leaderships) are common, and we have observed (and we will study) some similar patterns in the other teams involved in Campus for Entrepreneurs, which lends confidence that similar processes are likely in other settings. More generally, it seems fair to say that in a genuine entrepreneurial context, and facing all the complexity of the task (starting and running a business from scratch), members of a student entrepreneurial team adapt their personal behaviour regarding their motivation, the commitment they inject into the project, and the distributed leaderships that the interactions with the others allow them.

Although specific characteristics might differ, the processes associated with these uncertainties and their resolution resulting from the team organization that surfaced in this study would seem to apply to other student teams as well. Overall, it is apparent that our informants' experiences have commonalities with other domains, so the model seems plausibly transferable to other student teams involved in projects embedded in a genuine environment. There is little that is unique in the team we observed concerning the differences in personality, the differences in the perception of the nature of the project (student project or real business creation), the power takeover by a student, and the problem-focused coping strategies to save the common project at the expense of the personal situation of some students. In addition, the concepts present in the grounded theory point up another advantage of the model. Even if the performance of an entrepreneurship education programme includes quantitative criteria, the model consolidates many issues and ideas around the personal impact of those programmes and how team dynamics impact upon motivation, involvement, emotion, skills development and self-efficacy. According to the OECD's (2009) evaluation of entrepreneurship education programmes, it is important to understand the performance of the student entrepreneurial teams, but also the reasons why things did not work. Our results underline one of this report's conclusions:

> given that the aim of programmes is to generate a shift in attitudes towards entrepreneurship, it becomes difficult to ascribe quantifiable measures, so that, instead of 'hard' outcome evidence (such as the numbers initiating a business start-up), an attempt has to be made to gauge 'softer' outcomes (such as changes in attitude). (OECD, 2009)

Because the pace of change is increasing incredibly, entrepreneurship education programmes need to improve learning-by-doing in genuine entrepreneurial contexts. Because teamwork in crucial, and requested by employers, higher education has to enhance the way in which student entrepreneurial teams generate internal dynamics. Lastly, to produce new insights on entrepreneurial efficacy in higher education curricula, future research could: (1) identify how team efficacy and individual efficacy within a team are related and could be improved; (2) determine whether team efficacy increases the expected individual learning outcomes; and (3) understand and measure the impact of our teaching model on entrepreneurial intention after the training.

NOTES

* These authors contributed equally.
1. Including continuous improvement and adaptation in context, alignment with stakeholders, creativity and emotional agility.
2. Quoted by Hansen (2006).
3. This process of verbalization is very interesting because it underlies the fact that students have developed qualities and skills during this entrepreneurial project, even if they are not able to express this in a simple way. See an example in Appendix Table 9A.1. This will be the subject of a publication by the authors.
4. The authors would like to thank Professor Martine Hlady-Rispal for her valuable guidance.
5. The same authors, to be published.

REFERENCES

Ashraf, M. (2004), 'A critical look at the use of group projects as a pedagogical tool', *Journal of Education for Business*, **79** (4), 213–217.

Bandura, A. (1982), 'Self-efficacy mechanism in human agency', *American Psychologist*, **37** (2), 122–147.

Bandura, A. (1994 [1998]), 'Self-efficacy', in V.S. Ramachaudran (ed.), *Encyclopedia of Human Behavior*, Vol. 4 (pp. 71–81). New York: Academic Press. Reprinted in H. Friedman (ed.) (1998), *Encyclopedia of Mental Health*, San Diego, CA: Academic Press.

Barker, R.T., and Franzak, F.J. (1997), 'Team building in the classroom: preparing students for their organizational future', *Journal of Technical Writing and Communication*, **27** (3), 303–315.

Barry, D. (1991), 'Managing the bossless team: lessons in distributed leadership', *Organizational Dynamics*, **20** (1), 31–48.

Béchard, J.P., and Grégoire, D. (2007), 'Archetypes of pedagogical innovation for entrepreneurship education: model and illustrations', in A. Fayolle (ed.), *Handbook of Research in Entrepreneurship Education*, Vol. 1 (pp. 261–284). Cheltenham, UK and Northampton, MA, USA: Edward Elgar Publishing.

Bradley, B.H., Baur, J.E., Banford, C.G., and Postlethwaite, B.E. (2013), 'Team players and collective performance: how agreeableness affects team performance over time', *Small Group Research*, **44**, 680–711.

Carré, P. (2001), *De la motivation à la formation*. Paris: Editions L'Harmattan.

Clot, Y. (1999), *La fonction psychologique du travail*. Paris: PUF.

Corbin, J., and Strauss, A.L. (1990), 'Grounded theory research: procedures, canons, and evaluative criteria', *Qualitative Sociology*, **13** (1), 3–21.

Corley, K.G., and Gioia, D.A. (2004), 'Identity ambiguity and change in the wake of a corporate spin-off', *Administrative Science Quarterly*, **49**, 173–208.

Côté, L. (2013), 'Améliorer ses stratégies de coping pour affronter le stress au travail', *Psychologie Québec*, Dossier, **30** (5), 41–44.

De Hei, M.S.A., Strijbos, J.W., Sjoer, E., and Admiraal, W. (2015), 'Collaborative learning in higher education: lecturers' practices and beliefs', *Research Papers in Education*, **30** (2), 232–247.

Deci, E.L., and Ryan, R.M. (2010), *Self-determination*. Hoboken, NJ : John Wiley & Sons.

Dubard Barbosa, S. (2008). La perception du risque dans la décision de création d'entreprise. Doctoral dissertation, Grenoble 2.

Edelman, L.F., Manolova, T.S., and Brush, C.G. (2008), 'Entrepreneurship education: correspondence between practices of nascent entrepreneurs and textbook prescriptions for success', *Academy of Management Learning and Education*, **7** (1), 56–70.

Eisenhardt, K.M. (1989), 'Building theories from case study research', *Academy of Management Review*, **14** (4), 532–550.

European Commission (2013), 'The Entrepreneurship 2020 Action Plan', accessed 6 July 2017 at http://eur-lex.europa.eu/legal-content/EN/TXT/?uri=CELEX:52012DC0795.

Fayolle, A. (2013), 'Personal views on the future of entrepreneurship education', *Entrepreneurship and Regional Development*, Special Issue: *The Myths of Entrepreneurship? Exploring Assumptions in Entrepreneurship Research*, **25** (7/8), 692–701.

Fayolle, A., and Gailly, B. (2008), 'From craft to science: teaching models and learning processes in entrepreneurship education', *Journal of European Industrial Training*, **32** (7), 569–593.

Fayolle A., and Verzat, C. (2009), 'Pédagogies actives et entrepreneuriat: quelle place dans nos enseignements?', *Revue de l'entrepreneuriat*, **2** (8), 1–15.

Ferreira, J.J.M., Fernandes, C.I., and Ratten, V. (2017), 'The influence of entrepreneurship education on entrepreneurial intention', in M. Peris-Ortiz, J. Gómez, J. Merigó-Lindahl and C. Rueda-Armengot (eds), *Entrepreneurial Universities: Innovation, Technology, and Knowledge Management* (pp. 19—34). Cham: Springer.

Forgas, J.P. (1999), 'Network theories and beyond', in T. Dalgleish and M.J. Power (eds), *Handbook of Cognition and Emotion* (pp. 591–611). Chichester: Wiley.

Frese, M. (2009), 'Towards a psychology of entrepreneurship – an action theory perspective', *Foundations and Trends® in Entrepreneurship*, **5** (6), 437–496.

Gartner, W.B., Shaver, K.G., Carter, N.M., and Reynolds, P.D. (eds) (2004), *Handbook of Entrepreneurial Dynamics: The Process of Business Creation*. Thousand Oaks, CA: SAGE Publications.

Gibb, A.A. (1996), 'Entrepreneurship and small business management: can we afford to neglect them in the twenty-first century business school?', *British Journal of Management*, **7** (4), 309–321.

Gioia, D.A., Corley, K.G., and Hamilton, A.L. (2013), 'Seeking qualitative rigor in inductive research: notes on the Gioia methodology', *Organizational Research Methods*, **16** (1), 15–31.

Glaser, B.G., and Strauss, A. (1967), *The Discovery of Grounded Theory: Strategies for Qualitative Research*. Chicago, IL: Aldine.

Hansen, R.S. (2006), 'Benefits and problems with student teams: suggestions for improving team projects', *Journal of Education for Business*, **82** (1), 11–19.

Hernandez, S.A. (2002), 'Team learning in a marketing principles course: cooperative structures that facilitate active learning and higher level thinking', *Journal of Marketing Education*, **24** (1), 73–85.

Ionescu, S., Jacquet, M.D., and Lhote, C. (1997), *Les mécanismes de défense. Théorie et Clinique*. Paris: Nathan université.
Julius Caesar (1856), *Commentarii de Bello Civili* (The Commentaries of Caesar). William Duncan. St Louis, MO: Edwards & Bushnell.
Karanian, B.A., Eskandari, M., Aggarwal, A., et al. (2012), 'Open process for entrepreneuring team collaboration: parallels from an academic research team to the start up they studied', paper presented at the 2012 ASEE Annual Conference and Exposition, San Antonio, Texas, June. Accessed 10 June 2017 at https://peer.asee.org/21768.
Khan, M.S., Breitenecker, R.J., Gustafsson, V., and Schwarz, E.J. (2015), 'Innovative entrepreneurial teams: the give and take of trust and conflict', *Creativity and Innovation Management*, **24**, 558–573.
Katz, J.A. (2003), 'The chronology and intellectual trajectory of American entrepreneurship education, 1876–1999', *Journal of Business Venturing*, **18**, 283–300.
Lackéus, M. (2015), 'Entrepreneurship in education. What, why, when, how', accessed 4 May 2017 at https://www.oecd.org/cfe/leed/BGP_Entrepreneurship-in-Education.pdf.
Langley, A. and Abdallah, C. (2011), 'Templates and turns in qualitative studies of strategy and management', in D.D. Bergh and D.J. Ketchen (eds), *Building Methodological Bridges* (pp. 201–235), Research Methodology in Strategy and Management, Volume 6. Bingley: Emerald Group Publishing.
Lazarus, R.S., and Folkman, S. (1984), *Stress, Appraisal and Coping*. New York: Springer.
Luthans, F., Luthans, K.W., and Luthans, B.C. (2004), 'Positive psychological capital: beyond human and social capital', *Business Horizons*, **47** (1), 45–50.
Miles, M.B., and Huberman, A.M. (1994). *Qualitative Data Analysis: An Expanded Sourcebook, Second Edition*. Thousand Oaks, CA: SAGE Publications.
OECD (2009), 'Evaluation of programmes concerning education for entrepreneurship', report by the OECD Working Party on SMEs and Entrepreneurship, OECD.
Pöysä-Tarhonen, J., Elen, J., and Tarhonen, P. (2016), 'Student teams' development over time: tracing the relationship between the quality of communication and teams' performance', *Higher Education Research and Development*, **35** (4), 787–799.
Pratt, M. (2009), 'From the editors: for the lack of a boilerplate: tips on writing up (and reviewing) qualitative research', *Academy of Management Journal*, **52** (5), 856–862.
Tarricone, P., and Luca, J. (2002), 'Employees, teamwork and social interdependence – a formula for successful business?', *Team Performance Management: An International Journal*, **8** (3/4), 54–59.
Verzat, C., O'Shea, N., and Raucent, B. (2015), 'Réguler le leadership des étudiants en APP', *Revue Internationale de Pédagogie de l'Enseignement Supérieur*, **31** (1), 1–20.
Vesper, K.H. (1990), *New Venture Strategies*. University of Illinois at Urbana-Champaign's Academy for Entrepreneurial Leadership Historical Research Reference in Entrepreneurship. Champaign, IL: University of Illinois.
Wenger, E. (1998), *Communities of Practice: Learning, Meaning, and Identity*. Cambridge: Cambridge University Press.
Williams, D.L., Beard, J.D., and Rymer, J. (1991), 'Team projects: achieving their full potential', *Journal of Marketing Education*, **13**, 45–53.

Woolley, A.W., Chabris, C.F., Pentland, A., Hashmi, N., and Malone, T.W. (2010), 'Evidence for a collective intelligence factor in the performance of human groups', *Science*, **330** (6004), 686–688.

Yin, R.K. (1984), *Case Study Research: Design and Methods*, Beverly Hills, CA: SAGE.

APPENDIX

BOX 9A.1 THE INTERVIEW PROTOCOL

Semi-Structured Interview Grid (V4) – Feedback on Student Entrepreneurial Experience

Preconceptions/psychological capital/risk perception
What did you know about entrepreneurship before integrating this project?
What was your vision/perception of entrepreneurship?
Entrepreneurship: threat (marks . . .) or opportunity?
What risks did you feel/identify before starting the project, individually collectively?
4 dimensions of risk – global, financial, personal and social

Intention/desirability/initial motivations
Why did you choose an entrepreneurial (initially) tutored project?
What were your personal expectations?
How was your group formed? (professional/friendly affinity)
What were your collective expectations?
What were your personal goals?
What were your group goals?
Intrinsic/extrinsic motivations (Deci and Ryan, 2010)

Business idea/feasability
How did you find your idea?
What have you brought to your customers (value proposition, new product, cheaper, more beautiful, innovative . . .)?
How did you turn it into a business idea?
What were the key steps?
What were the key encounters?
How did you identify your key partners?
Concretely:
How did you get in touch with stakeholders (partner companies, suppliers, customers, communication . . .)?
What did you need and how did you get it?
What did you think was easy? difficult?
Have these contacts influenced your business idea? If so, on what? How?

Creation/marketing/communication
Business model:
What communication strategies have you implemented? How?
What business strategies have you developed? What distribution policy? How did you sell the products? + Follow-up
How did you 'market' your products (mix marketing)? (Design, name, logo, visual . . .)
How did you organize the group? (Equity in workload, same tasks?)

Daily management

Describe the activities you have undertaken (tasks) during the operational part of your project:

Contacts, sales area (negotiation, commercial communication . . .), treasury, logistics, customer relationship management

How? Who?

Select a recurring activity and describe it as accurately as possible

Clinic of activity, ergonomics of work (Clot, 1999)

Purposes of motivation

What motivated you (individual) before, during and after the project?

What motivated you (the team) before, during and after this project?

Has this experience changed your educational and/or professional projects? In what? Why, in your opinion?

Intrinsic/extrinsic motivations (Carré, 2001)/experiential link

Adaptability (try and fail demarch)

Group:

What difficulties have you faced?

Team dynamics communication, task division, customer negotiation

Operational management, daily management, place in group

How did you overcome these difficulties? What corrections have been made? How? With whom?

Individual:

Did you feel effective during the conduct of this project? Did the others teach you things, allow you to improve? Vicarious experience (Bandura, 1982)

Personal effectiveness (Bandura, 1994 [1998])

What difficulties have you encountered?

Team dynamics communication, breakdown of tasks, negotiation

Daily management, place in group

How did you overcome these difficulties? What solutions have you found? How? With whom?

Qualities/skills/psychological capital

What did this experience bring you?

- As an individual (personal dimension)
- Collectively (interpersonal dimension)
- What qualities do you think you have developed through this entrepreneurial project?

Solidarity, responsibility, trust, teamwork, resourcefulness, perseverance, initiative, motivation and determination . . .

- What cross-curricular competencies can be transposed into another non-entrepreneurial context?

To think creatively, to work in teams, to manage risks and to take account of uncertainty . . .

- What specific skills (entrepreneurial) have you developed?

What has 'moved' in your personality following this experience? What do you think?
Resilience, optimism, hope, self-efficacy
Psychological capital (Luthans et al., 2004)

Work–life balance
How did you manage the spaces 'personal life', 'student life'/'professional life'?

Table 9A.1 Example of skills verbalization

Skills	Expression of what they have done
Team work	To help each other, the idea of solidarity, to generate a collective dynamic. Share common goals, participate in the decision. Create friendliness, a good working atmosphere. Manage collective discussions, time management, listening to others, and openness to others' opinions. Manage collective time vs. individual working time. Be open to others without a priori, be understanding, be able to self-regulate, challenge personal according to the opinion of others, need to compromise, negotiation. Work in mutual adjustment (depending on the personalities, desires, skills, qualities, apprehensions of each one) when the 'who does what' is difficult to predict. Managing tensions in the group, mediation, no stake taking to preserve the group, search for third-party objectives for information helping the decision. Pay attention to the feelings of others (empathy), support them when they are in difficulties. Adapt communication to preserve the group (assertiveness). Appreciate the work of others at its true value. Assume and realize what has been agreed by the team. Organize work, distribution of tasks, follow-up tools accepted by all. Have tolerance in relation to different ways of working. Communicate internally to keep everyone involved. Participate willingly in less rewarding tasks

10. The role of entrepreneurship education and its characteristics in influencing the entrepreneurial intention: a study based on India and the UK

Kavita Panwar Seth, Fintan Clear, Tariq Khan and Sharmaine Sakthi Ananthan

INTRODUCTION

'Entrepreneurship education can influence the thinking and acting of the academic or student' (Davey et al., 2016: 173). According to Davey et al. (2016) and Gibb and Hannon (2006), entrepreneurship education may influence the entrepreneurial mindset in different ways; for example, in some cases students may decide to start their own venture after completing entrepreneurship education.

Mandel and Noyes (2016). state that there is a causal link between entrepreneurial training and the tendency to be an entrepreneur. Furthermore, it is fascinating that entrepreneurship classes might alter entrepreneurial aims if an individual considers the financial significance of entrepreneurial activity pointed out by numerous experts. It turns out that more people consider altering their plans and the financial relevance of this when the advancement of entrepreneurship is required to be included in education programmes (Brown and Hanlon, 2016). There are some studies which propose that entrepreneurship education should be studied in more depth (Fayolle and Gailey, 2015; Lorz, 2011; Lackeus, 2015), and that duration of the programme is an important element which is related to students' ability to remember and retain information, which consequently affects learning.

Intentions have been recognized as being the best interpreters of planned behaviour, particularly if the behaviour is 'rare, hard to observe, or involves unpredictable time lags' (Krueger et al., 2000). For this reason, entrepreneurship might be demonstrated as a kind of planned attitude which might be examined with the support of intention models. The current research makes use of an Ajzen's intention model; that is, a theory of planned behaviour.

In the next section of the chapter, key aims and objectives of the study are given. Then, the background of the study along with key hypotheses and the conceptual model will be discussed. In the following sections, the research methodology, results and discussion are included. Finally, a valid conclusion is made.

This chapter aims to discover how elements of entrepreneurship education programmes (for example, business plans, role models, entrepreneurial networks and feedback) relate to entrepreneurial intention and its antecedents, such as perceived behavioural control, subjective norm and attitude. It seeks to advance the theoretical discussion on the relationship between entrepreneurship courses and entrepreneurial intention, and to seek its practical relevance. Specifically, its objectives are:

1. To determine how specific characteristics of entrepreneurship education influence one's intention to become an entrepreneur.
2. To determine what specific set of characteristics the entrepreneurial courses should have, to be effective in increasing a student's entrepreneurial intention.

Research Question: What entrepreneurship education course (duration only 10–12 weeks) characteristics may positively increase the intention (and antecedents) of participants to start their own ventures?

BACKGROUND OF THE STUDY

According to the theory of planned behaviour, intentions have three independent determinants (or antecedents of intentions): attitudes toward behaviour, perceived behaviour control and subjective norm (Ajzen, 1991, 2002). The theory states that the behaviour of a person is a result of their intention to perform the said behaviour, and the intent is influenced by their outlook towards the behaviour as well as their individual standards. The intention is said to be the immediate precursor of the behaviour.

Another key part of the research is related to the entrepreneurship education course characteristics, hence Müller's (2011) work has also been taken into account. Müller (2008), in her study, sought to know the effect of entrepreneurship course characteristics on entrepreneurial intention. Her study aimed to achieve both theoretical discussion advancement and

BOX 10.1 CATEGORY SCHEME: THE INFLUENCE OF ENTREPRENEURSHIP COURSE CHARACTERISTICS

1. General impact of entrepreneurship courses.
2. Course characteristics with influence on attitude:
   – role models;
   – practical experiences.
3. Course characteristics with influence on perceived subjective norms:
   – provide a platform to build an entrepreneurial network.
4. Course characteristics with influence on perceived behavioural control:
   – reveal what it takes to be an entrepreneur;
   – practical knowledge;
   – business planning;
   – role models;
   – entrepreneurial networks;
   – explorative and interactive elements;
   – feedback;
   – supportive infrastructure.

Source: Müller (2008).

its practical relevance. According to Müller (2011), the course characteristics which influence intention antecedents are as shown in Box 10.1.

In this chapter the focus is on only three key characteristics – that is, role models, entrepreneurial networks and feedback – to analyse the significance of these elements in more depth.

Entrepreneurial Network

If opportunities of entrepreneurial networking are provided during the course then it may play a key role for influencing intention to start a business (Laviolette et al., 2012; Dyer, 1994; Scott and Twomey, 1988); also, although few studies understand that how individuals successfully create and manage new ventures through networks and learning, these are increasingly popular in the entrepreneurship literature (Hoang and Antoncic, 2003; Politis, 2005; Rae, 2005; Rae and Carswell, 2001; Ravasi and Turati, 2005; Wang and Chugh, 2014; Soetanto, 2017). Although some literature argues the importance of networks in entrepreneurship (Hoang and Antoncic, 2003; Jack et al., 2010; Ostgaard and Birley, 1994), few studies focus on the role of networks in entrepreneurial learning (Pittaway and Cope, 2007; Rae, 2005; Romano and Secundo, 2009; Taylor and Thorpe, 2004). A recent study by Soetanto (2017) confirms that networking with entrepreneurs helps in entrepreneurial learning; however, the limitation of the study is that a very small sample size was considered, therefore the research done for this chapter will be helpful to address that gap. Soetanto also suggests that the importance of networking in entrepreneurial learning has been overlooked. This research will include this element and explore the ways it can influence the intention. Studies of Müller (2008) suggest that entrepreneurial networks may influence the subjective norms and perceptions of students to start their own venture.

Role Model

New graduates' behaviour and orientations regarding entrepreneurship are influenced by a number of personal and environmental factors. Researchers have demonstrated the importance in various societies of role models of entrepreneurial activities and situations in the participant's environment (Begley et al., 1997), and the impact cultural values and norms through role models may have on entrepreneurial attitudes, intention or behaviour (Fayolle et al., 2011; Hayton et al., 2002; Turker and Sonmez Selcuk, 2008).

Müller (2008) suggests that role models can be responsible for influencing the participant's attitude, perception and also their intention. If participants can see there are entrepreneurs in their own network, or can meet the entrepreneurs or speak with them, this can influence their intentions. A course which includes role models or introduces entrepreneurs in the courses can be more attractive to students, and hence can influence their entrepreneurship intentions; therefore this aspect is relevant in studying entrepreneurship course characteristics.

Feedback

According to Laurillard (2002), feedback processes are also a part of interactive aspects and reflective aspects; feedback gives the opportunity to reflect back and take corrective actions wherever required. However, feedback always comes after the act, and therefore students need to act. Feedback provides the opportunity of continuous improvement and it can be given at various stages. Evaluation and assessment form a key part of the quality cycle and hence should be taken very seriously. Further progress of teaching and learning depends on assessment and evaluation.

Tummons (2007) suggests that 'Evaluation of assessment is about judging the extent to which assessment does what it is supposed to do.' The assessment process is about making appropriate judgements and giving proper feedback with evidence. Appropriate assessment methods – for example, formative and descriptive assessment methods – also help to provide appropriate information to the learners and maximize opportunities to improve further. Müller (2008) also suggests that if students get their feedback during their course it may influence their perception to start their own venture.

RESEARCH METHODOLOGY

Quantitative research focuses on trying to quantify a problem and understand how prevalent it is, by looking for projectable results to a larger population or examining the data to test the theory (Saunders et al., 2016). Based on Ajzen's model we try to understand the association of attitude to behaviour, perceived behaviour control and subjective norm to the entrepreneurial intention and entrepreneurial behaviour. To do so, the Hypotheses 1, 2 and 3 (see below) have been formulated. These hypotheses are used to test these relationships in the context of Indian as well as United Kingdom (UK) students in an attempt to understand the differences in the impacts of entrepreneurial education of the two countries. The relationships have been identified using bivariate Pearson correlation in SPSS (Ver 21.0). The results have checked at $p < 0.05$.

Further, as per the conceptual model created in Figure 10.1, entrepreneurial network, role model and feedback are antecedents to the

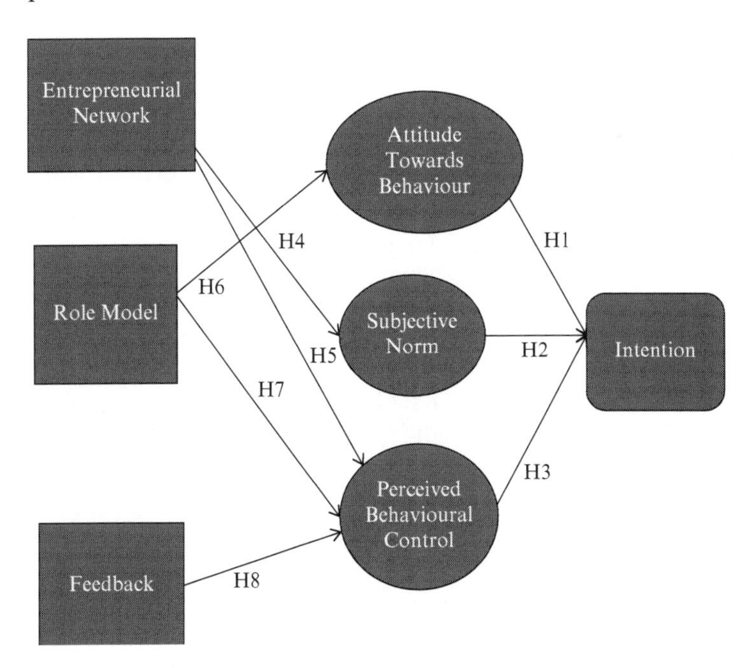

Figure 10.1 Conceptual model

factors of attitude toward behaviour, perceived behaviour control and subjective norm, which impact upon the entrepreneurial intention as well as behaviour. These antecedents are tested through bivariate Pearson correlations in Hypotheses 4–8 at $p < 0.05$ significance.

Selection of Sample

To select the sample we used purposive sampling which helped in choosing relevant students who were undertaking the entrepreneurship course for the given duration (10–12 weeks) only. According to Etikan et al. (2016), the purposive sampling technique, also called judgment sampling, is the deliberate choice of a participant due to the qualities the participant possesses. The total sample universe was more than 10000 students from each country, but due to budgetary, time and logistical constraints it was impractical to collect data from all final-year university students. Therefore, a small representative sample from final-year students was undertaken. It was collected from the ten established universities in the UK, and five universities in India (that is, those that had been in existence for more than five years). Data from 100 respondents will be discussed in the chapter: 50 students of each country.

RESULTS AND DISCUSSION

The conceptual model created in Figure 10.1 shows nine different hypotheses which would be tested on the data collected from UK and Indian students (50 each). The first three hypotheses check for the relationship between the determinants of planned behaviour and the entrepreneurial intention, while the other six hypotheses check for the influence of the antecedents of the determinants on the determinants of planned behaviour. The various variables which have to be tested through these hypotheses and their genesis through the data of the questionnaire have been listed in Appendix Table 10A.1. The correlation between these variables is tested at $p < 0.05$. The hypothesis which has a positive and significant correlation between the variables is accepted, while those which do not have a significant correlation have been rejected:

Hypothesis 1: Positive attitudes to start their own venture increase the level of entrepreneurial intention.

Table 10.1 shows $r = 0.122$, $p < 0.05$, $N = 50$ for UK students; that is, a positive and significant relationship between the attitude of the students

Table 10.1 Correlations: attitude and entrepreneurial intention

		Attitude	Entrepreneurial intention (UK students)	Entrepreneurial intention (Indian students)
Attitude	Pearson correlation	1	0.122*	−0.117

Note: * $p < 0.05$; N = 50.

towards starting their own venture with respect to the level of the entrepreneurial intention of UK students.

The students with a positive attitude towards starting their own venture would also already have an intention to start their own venture. These students would want to be their own bosses and use the market opportunities to establish their own venture within first five years of the completion of the course.

As compared to UK students, for Indian students it can be observed from Table 10.1 that r = – 0.117, p = n.s., N = 50, which implies that there is no significant relationship between the attitude of the students and their intention to start their own entrepreneurial venture. Thus, while in the case of UK students there was a positive relationship between the positive attitude of the student and entrepreneurship intention, in the case of Indian students there is no relationship.

Hypothesis 2: Subjective norm concerning starting own venture positively influences the level of entrepreneurial intention.

In Table 10.2 it can be observed that r = – 0.029, p = n.s., N = 50 for UK students. This implies that the subjective norm concerning starting

Table 10.2 Correlations: subjective norm and entrepreneurial intention

		Entrepreneurial intention	Subjective norm (UK students)	Subjective norm (Indian students)
Entrepreneurial intention	Pearson correlation	1	−0.029	−0.318*

Note: * $p < 0.05$; N = 50.

one's own venture does not have any significant impact on UK students. This indicates that most UK students are free from the social pressure to perform, and partake in entrepreneurial activity only when they feel it is right, and not because it is socially expected of them

On the other hand, for Indian students Table 10.2 shows $r = -0.318$, $p < 0.05$, $N = 50$, which is a significant negative influence of subjective norm concerning starting one's own venture on the level of entrepreneurial intention with respect to Indian students. It can be clearly seen that the relationship between the two parameters is not positive. This implies that, in the given case, the increase in subjective norm to start one's own venture has a mildly negative influence on level of entrepreneurial intention. The social pressure to perform and become an entrepreneur does not always positively motivate the student. It also has a negative impact, and may be detrimental to the intensity with which a student might want to open a new venture of their own.

Hypothesis 3: Strong perceptions about one's ability to successfully found one's own company positively influence the level of entrepreneurial intention.

In Table 10.3, we can see that $r = 0.237$, $p < 0.05$, $N = 50$ for UK students; that is, there is a strong positive relationship between the perceptions of the students towards their ability to be successful, and the level of entrepreneurial intention, for the students of the UK. This further suggests that students who had perceptions towards success were able to start their own ventures shortly after completion of their course.

Table 10.3 shows the influence of the perceptions about one's ability to be successful on the level of entrepreneurial intention in the case of Indian students. Here one can observe that $r = -0.025$, p = n.s., $N = 50$, which implies that a student's perception about their ability to succeed does not significantly influence their intention to start up their own venture. In the

Table 10.3 Correlations: perceptions and entrepreneurial intention

		Perceptions	Entrepreneurial intention (UK students)	Entrepreneurial intention (Indian students)
Perceptions	Pearson correlation	1	−0.237*	−0.025

Note: * $p < 0.05$; $N = 50$.

Table 10.4 Correlations: entrepreneurship network and subjective norm

		Entrepreneurial network	Subjective norm (UK students)	Subjective norm (Indian students)
Entrepreneurial network	Pearson correlation	1	0.341*	0.204*

Note: * $p < 0.05$; N = 50.

case of Indian students the perception about their ability to succeed in not in sync with their intention to actually start an entrepreneurial venture.

The next group of research hypotheses is based on the impact of course characteristics on attitudes, perceived subjective norm and subjective norm. Hence research hypothesis 4 is formulated as:

Hypothesis 4: Entrepreneurship courses that provide opportunities to build an entrepreneurial network positively influence the perceived subjective norm.

The entrepreneurship courses in the UK that provide the opportunity to meet people who may tomorrow act as potential co-founders to the organization, or those people who could help in getting through initial hiccups in establishing one's own business, have a significantly positive influence on the perceived subjective norm of the students. For UK students, Table 10.4 reflects $r = 0.341$, $p < 0.05$, N = 50 with a positive significant correlation between the two variables. It shows that an increase in networking would also increase the social pressure that a student faces to establish themself as an entrepreneur

Similar to the behaviour of UK students, the Indian students reflect $r = 0.204$, $p < 0.05$, N = 50. Hence they also show a positive and significant relationship between the courses that help students build an entrepreneurial network, and the subjective norm or social pressure that the student faces to establish themself as an entrepreneur.

Hypothesis 5: Entrepreneurship courses that provide opportunities to build an entrepreneurial network influence participants' perception towards starting their own company.

Table 10.5 shows $r = 0.250$, $p < 0.05$, N = 50 for UK students, which implies that entrepreneurship courses that provide the opportunity to the

Table 10.5 Correlations: entrepreneurial network and perception

		Perception	Entrepreneurial network (UK students)	Entrepreneurial network (Indian students)
Perception	Pearson correlation	1	0.250*	−0.048

Note: * $p < 0.05$; N = 50.

students to meet the right people and build strong networks also positively and significantly influence the perception of the students to start their own venture. The networking opportunity helps them in meeting potential co-founders, and to obtain the key resources that would help them to establish their business in the initial phase.

In the case of Indian students, $r = -0.480$, p = n.s., N = 50, which shows that the entrepreneurial network that is built through the entrepreneurship courses has no significant impact on the students' perceived behaviour to succeed. This also indicates that students are not able to value the opportunity that is provided to them by the institute to build networks. These students are more reliant on their own abilities to build their own networks, and are comfortable with the concept that they would be able to start their own venture within five years based on their own ability.

Hypothesis 6: Entrepreneurship courses that provide opportunities to meet role models positively influence participants' attitude towards starting their own venture.

All students have certain role models which they aspire to become, and for such students success is a measure of how closely they have been able to imitate their role models. Entrepreneurship courses which provide the opportunity to students to meet their role models help in building a strong attitude towards starting their own venture. The interaction with the role models helps and inspires the students and hence establishes a strong positive attitude towards starting their own network. This has been verified in Table 10.6, in which a strong significant relationship between the variables for UK students shows $r = 0.574$, $p < 0.001$, N = 50.

Contrary to the behaviour of UK students, as seen in Table 10.6 for Indian students, $r = 0.196$, p = n.s., N = 50, so there seems to be no significant relationship between the students' attitude towards starting their own

Table 10.6 Correlations: attitude and role model

		Attitude	Role model (UK students)	Role model (Indian students)
Attitude	Pearson correlation	1	0.574*	0.196

Note: * $p < 0.05$; N = 50.

Table 10.7 Correlations: perception and role model

		Role model	Perception (UK students)	Perception (Indian students)
Role model	Pearson correlation	1	0.227*	0.037

Note: * $p < 0.05$; N = 50.

business soon after the course and the opportunity to meet role models during the entrepreneurship course.

Hypothesis 7: Entrepreneurship courses that provide opportunities to meet role models positively influence participants' perception towards starting their own venture.

Table 10.7 clearly shows $r = 0.227$, $p < 0.05$, $N = 50$ for UK students; that is, students who were enrolled in entrepreneurship courses that provided the opportunity to meet and interact with their role models had a significant and positive perception towards starting their own venture. These students benefited from the opportunity of being able to connect with their role models, and hence had a clear and strong perception that they would be able to establish their own venture within the first five years of completing their courses.

Table 10.7 shows $r = 0.037$, p = n.s., $N = 50$ for Indian students, which means that exposure which they received by interacting with their role models during the entrepreneurship course did not have any significant impact on their perceived behaviour to succeed. It can be observed in the previous hypothesis as well that in the context of the Indian students, the opportunity to meet their role models did not significantly impact upon their attitude and hence their perception towards starting their own venture soon after the course.

Table 10.8 Correlations: perception and feedback

		Feedback	Perception (UK students)	Perception (Indian students)
Feedback	Pearson correlation	1	0.030	0.185

Note: * $p < 0.05$; N = 50.

Hypothesis 8: Entrepreneurship courses that provide feedback positively influence participants' perception towards starting their own venture.

Table 10.8 shows r = 0.030, p = n.s., N = 50 for UK students; that is, there is no significant relationship between feedback provided to the students during the course and the perception of the students towards starting their own venture.

This basically highlights the fact that the feedback which the students received for their class activities remained focused on their behaviour and performance in class and was not able to affect the perception of the student towards starting their own venture within the next five years. Hence this hypothesis is rejected. It also shows that the perception of the student towards their own success is predefined, and feedback from the faculty of the course during the classes is not able to affect it. It is heavily affected by networking with relevant industry experts and the students' own role models in their domain.

Just like the UK students, for Indian students Table 10.8 highlights r = 0.185, p = n.s., N = 50, which means that they also do not see any significant impact on their perception towards starting a new venture, based on the feedback they received during the course. The presence of feedback from the faculty seems to neither motivate nor demotivate the students in building their perception towards starting their own new venture.

Discussion

As per the theory of planned behaviour, the entrepreneurial intentions after the completion of the course should have been affected by the three independent determinants (antecedents of intentions): attitude toward behaviour, perceived behaviour control and subjective norm (Ajzen, 1991, 2002). The data collected showed results which deviated slightly from the theory, and also differed between UK and Indian students, showing

Table 10.9 Relationship of determinants of planned behaviour on entrepreneurial intention

	UK students	Indian students
Attitude	0.122*	−0.117
Subjective norm	−0.029	−0.318*
Perception about behaviour	0.237*	−0.025

Note: * $p < 0.05$; N = 50.

the impact of ethnicity on the course. The hypotheses which pertain to the theory of planned behaviour (H1, H2 and H3) were tested at $p < 0.05$ significance, and the impact of the determinants of intention on entrepreneurial intention are summarized in Table 10.9 after testing the hypothesis.

Table 10.9 indicates that in the case of Indian students, their entrepreneurial intention does not bear any significant relationship with attitude or perception towards opening up their own new venture. They only have a negative relationship with the social pressure or social norm, which means that the more the pressure the lower their intention towards starting their own new venture. On the other hand, one can observe that for UK students, intention to start their own venture is primarily governed by their attitude and perception to succeed in their entrepreneurial venture. Intentions of the UK students are not affected by the social pressure to perform.

Following this, the study also tries to connect the antecedents of these determinants and their impact on the three determinants of intention. The study attempts to determine why the entrepreneurial intention between the two set of samples is different. For this, the following hypotheses (H4, H5, H6, H7 and H8) were formulated and tested.

In trying to understand the antecedents of the entrepreneurial behaviour and intention, the relationship between important factors was observed for Indian and UK students. Table 10.10 highlights the various areas which were tested through the hypotheses mentioned above, and indicates the difference of behaviour that was observed amongst the two groups of UK and Indian students.

Table 10.10 shows that while UK students are significantly impacted upon by the antecedents of entrepreneurial network and role model, Indian students on the other hand are not affected by the presence of the opportunity to interact with their role models during the course. It is also clear that the presence of feedback on performance from the faculty of the course does not have any significant impact on the perception of the

Table 10.10 Impact of antecedents on determinants of planned behaviour

		UK students	Indian students
Entrepreneurial network	Perceived behaviour control	0.341*	0.204*
	Subjective norm	0.259*	−0.048
Role model	Attitude towards behaviour	0.574*	0.196
	Perceived behaviour control	0.227*	0.037
Feedback	Perceived behaviour	0.030	0.185

Note: * $p < 0.05$; N = 50.

students about their ability to achieve entrepreneurial success within the first few years of completing the course.

CONCLUSION

The key objective of the research was to contribute to providing effective entrepreneurship education to students through identifying the relevance of three key elements of entrepreneurship education: that is, role models, entrepreneurial network and feedback. In order to explore the relevance of these elements in a broader way the research was conducted in two different countries, that is, India (Delhi) and the UK (London). The differences in culture and ethnicity change the relationship of these variables and also their impact on the determinants of planned behaviour.

It has been observed that the UK students showed a positive attitude and perception towards their ability to succeed in their own venture after the course, and this helped in increasing their entrepreneurial intention. On the other hand, in the case of Indian students their entrepreneurial intention was mostly affected negatively by the increase in subjective norm and social pressure. The entrepreneurial intention of the Indian students was not affected by the positive attitude and perception towards their ability to succeed in their own venture. The Indian students were observed to be more self-reliant, and did not depend much on the presence of entrepreneurial networks or interactions with role models during the course. The UK students, on the other hand were inspired by these interactions and due to them they showed a positive attitude and behaviour towards entrepreneurship. One of the common reactions of the students was towards the feedback provided by the faculty. Both the groups seemed unaffected by the feedback from the faculty, and it did not change their perceived behaviour towards entrepreneurship.

There were a few limitations to the study, such as time and unavailability of other key content of entrepreneurship education such as business plan activities. Overall, this chapter will be a good contribution in designing the course curriculum of entrepreneurship courses based on the ethnicity of the participants.

REFERENCES

Ajzen, I. (1991) The theory of planned behaviour. *Organizational Behavior and Human Decision Processes*, **50** (2), 179–211.

Ajzen, I. (2002) Perceived behavioral control, self-efficacy, locus of control, and the theory of planned behavior. *Journal of Applied Social Psychology*, **32**, 665–683.

Begley, T.M., Tan, W.L., Larasati, A.B., Rab, A., Zamora, E., and Nanayakkara, G. (1997) The relationship between socio-cultural dimensions and interest in starting a business: a multi-country study. *Frontiers of Entrepreneurship Research*, Babson Conference Proceedings, http://www.babson.edu/entrep/fer.

Brown, C.T., and Hanlon, D. (2016) Behavioral criteria for grounding entrepreneurship education and training programs: a validation study. *Journal of Small Business Management*, **54** (2), 399–419.

Davey, T., Hannon, P., and Penaluna, A. (2016) Entrepreneurship education and the role of universities in entrepreneurship: introduction to the special issue. *Industry and Higher Education*, **30**(3), 171–182.

Dyer, W.G. (1994) Toward a theory of entrepreneurial careers. *Entrepreneurship Theory and Practice*, **19**(2), 7–21.

Etikan, L., Musa A.S., and Alkassim, S.R. (2016) Comparison of convenience sampling and purposive sampling. *American Journal of Theoretical and Applied Statistics*, **5**(1), 1–4. doi: 10.11648/j.ajtas.20160501.11.

Fayolle, A., Basso, O., and Bouchard, V. (2011) Three levels of culture and firms' entrepreneurial orientation: a research agenda. *Entrepreneurship and Regional Development*, **22**(7), 707–730

Fayolle, A., and Gailly, B. (2015) The impact of entrepreneurship education on entrepreneurial attitudes and intention: hysteresis and persistence. *Journal of Small Business Management*, **53**(1), 75–93.

Gibb, A.A., and Hannon, P.D. (2006) Towards the entrepreneurial university. *International Journal of Entrepreneurship Education*, **4**, 73–110.

Hayton, J.C., George, G., and Zahra, S.A. (2002) National culture and entrepreneurship: a review of behavioral research. *Entrepreneurship Theory and Practice*, **26**(4), 33–52.

Hoang, H., and Antoncic, B. (2003) Network-based research in entrepreneurship: a critical review. *Journal of Business Venturing*, **18**(2), 165–187.

Jack, S.L., Moult, S., Anderson, A.R., and Dodd, S. (2010) An entrepreneurial network evolving: patterns of change. *International Small Business Journal*, **28**(4), 315–337.

Krueger, N.F., Reilly, M.D., and Carsrud, A.L. (2000) Competing models of entrepreneurial intentions. *Journal of Business Venturing*, **15**(5/6), 411–432.

Lackeus, M. (2015) Entrepreneurship in education: what, why, when, how. Entrepreneurship Background Paper, https://www.oecd.org/cfe/leed/BGP_Entrepreneurship-in-Education.pdf.

Laurillard, D. (2002) *Rethinking University Teaching: A Conversational Framework for the Effective Use of Learning Technologies*. New York: Routledge/Falmer.

Laviolette, M.E, Lefebvre, R.M., and Brunel, O. (2012) The impact of story bound entrepreneurial role models on self-efficacy and entrepreneurial intention. *International Journal of Entrepreneurial Behavior and Research*, **18**(6), 720–742, https://doi.org/10.1108/13552551211268148.

Lorz, M. (2011) The impact of entrepreneurship education on entrepreneurial intention. PhD thesis, University of St Gallen, Germany.

Mandel, R., and Noyes, E. (2016) Survey of experiential entrepreneurship education offerings among top undergraduate entrepreneurship programs. *Education + Training*, **58**(2), 164–178. DOI: 10.1108/ET-06-2014-0067.

Müller, Susan (2009) Encouraging future entrepreneurs: the effect of entrepreneurship course characteristics on entrepreneurial intention. Doctoral thesis, Universität St. Gallen.

Müller, Susan (2011) Increasing entrepreneurial intention: effective entrepreneurship course characteristics. *International Journal of Entrepreneurship and Small Business*, **13**(1), 55–74.

Ostgaard, T.A., and Birley, S. (1994) Personal networks and firm competitive strategy – a strategic or coincidental match? *Journal of Business Venturing*, **9**(4), 281–305.

Pittaway, L., and Cope, J. (2007) Simulating entrepreneurial learning integrating experiential and collaborative approaches to learning. *Management Learning*, **38**(2), 211–233.

Politis, D. (2005) The process of entrepreneurial learning: a conceptual framework. *Entrepreneurship Theory and Practice*, **29**(4), 399–424

Rae, D. (2005) Entrepreneurial learning: a narrative-based conceptual model. *Journal of Small Business and Enterprise Development*, **12**(3), 323–335.

Rae, D., and Carswell, M. (2001) Towards a conceptual understanding of entrepreneurial learning. *Journal of Small Business and Enterprise Development*, **8**(2), 150–158.

Ravasi, D., and Turati, C. (2005) Exploring entrepreneurial learning: a comparative study of technology development projects. *Journal of Business Venturing*, **20**(1), 137–164.

Romano, A., and Secundo, G. (2009) *Dynamic Learning Networks: Models and Cases in Action*. New York: Springer.

Saunders, M., Lewis, P., and Thornhill, A. (2016) *Research Methods for Business Students*. Harlow, UK: Pearson Education.

Scott, M., and Twomey, D. (1988) The long-term supply of entrepreneurs: students' career aspirations in relation to entrepreneurship. *Journal of Small Business Management*, **26**(4), 5–13.

Soetanto, D. (2017) Networks and entrepreneurial learning: coping with difficulties. *International Journal of Entrepreneurial Behavior and Research*, **23**(3), 547–565.

Taylor, D.W., and Thorpe, R. (2004) Entrepreneurial learning: a process of co-participation. *Journal of Small Business and Enterprise Development*, **11**(2), 203–211.

Tummons, J. (2007) *Becoming a Professional Tutor in the Lifelong Learning Sector*, 2nd edition. Exeter: Learning Matters.

Turker, D., and S. Sonmez Selcuk (2008) Which factors affect entrepreneurial intention of university students? *Journal of European Industrial Training*, **33**(2), 142–159.

Wang, C.L., and Chugh, H. (2014) Entrepreneurial learning: past research and future challenges. *International Journal of Management Reviews*, **16**(1), 24–61.

APPENDIX

Table 10A.1 Genesis of variables

Role model	*Ex post* questionnaire, Part B, nos 9, 9a, 9b and 19 B9) During the class I had the chance to listen to entrepreneurs' field reports (e.g., entrepreneurs' speeches, lecturer's reports). B9a) Among these entrepreneurs was at least one whose work I appreciate and admire. B9b) I understood and it was discussed extensively why the entrepreneur and the company have been successful. B19) During the class I heard about entrepreneurs or got to know entrepreneurs with whom I could identify.
Entrepreneurial network	*Ex post* questionnaire, Part B, nos 11, 12, 13 B11) During the class I was able to establish a network which will be helpful when I start an own company. B12) During the class I was able to get to know potential co-founders. B13) During the class I learned who to refer to when I want to start my own business.
Feedback	Source: *Ex post* questionnaire, Part B, 5, 5a, 5b B5) During the class I frequently received feedback on my ideas, contributions to the discussion and/or on my work (e.g. written business plan). B5a) If you received feedback, please evaluate the following statement: The feedback was given by a qualified person. B5b) If you received feedback, please evaluate the following statement: I was able to draw on the feedback during the rest of the course.
Subjective norm index	Source: *Ex post* questionnaire, Part D: D1, D2, D3, D4, D5 D1) My family thinks that I will become an entrepreneur. D2) People whose opinion I value have become entrepreneurs within 5 years of finishing their studies. D3) People who are important to me think that I should become an entrepreneur. D4) The opinion of my family is very important to me. D5) The opinions of people who are important to me influence me a lot.
Attitude index	Source: *Ex post* questionnaire, Part C: C1–C17 C1) My intention is to become an entrepreneur within 5 years after finishing my studies useful for me. C2) It is important to me to have a secure job. C3) I want to take decisions on my own.

Table 10A.1 (continued)

	C4) I would enjoy becoming an entrepreneur within the first 5 years after finishing my studies.
	C5) I want to have freedom during my work.
	C6) I want to have a stimulating job.
	C7) It is important to me to have social contacts during my work. (get to know new colleagues and friends).
	C8) I want to use market opportunities to have economic success.
	C9) I want to avoid taking responsibility during my work.
	C10) I want to be my own boss.
	C11) It is important to me to get promoted and to advance my career.
	C12) Becoming an entrepreneur within 5 years after finishing my studies would advance my career.
	C13) I would like to take part in the whole working process.
	C14) I want to have a challenging job.
	C15) It is important not to work overtime.
	C16) I want to have authority at work.
	C17) Self-actualization is important to me.
Perceived behaviour control	Source: *Ex post* questionnaire, Part E: E1–E6
	E1) Whether I become an entrepreneur within 5 years of finishing my studies is entirely up to me.
	E2) I know enough to start my own business within 5 years of finishing my studies.
	E3) I have enough self-confidence to start my own business within 5 years of finishing my studies.
	E4) If I started my own business I would be overworked.
	E5) Starting a company within the first 5 years after finishing my studies would be very easy for me.
	E6) Starting a company within the first 5 years after finishing my studies would be very easy for me.

11. Building technology entrepreneurship capabilities: an engineering education perspective

Kari Kleine, Ferran Giones, Mauricio Camargo and Silke Tegtmeier

INTRODUCTION

Much has been discussed about the changing role of universities in society, in particular when examining the contribution of universities to economic growth and societal development (Audretsch, 2014). The transition from universities as research centres to universities as innovation drivers has left many co-existing models in place (Schmitz et al., 2017), which makes it difficult to identify and articulate valid response mechanisms to new societal challenges.

The demand to respond to societal challenges contrasts with the research-focused nature of most universities that have traditionally left the role of technology innovation and entrepreneurship to other agents. Thus, the function of science and technology commercialization has often required the activation of specific actors such as technology transfer offices (TTOs) linked to the government, universities or research centres (Fitzgerald and Cunningham, 2015). Prior research has identified the existing constraints to activating academic engagement, highlighting the distance between science and technology research activities with industry-related innovation and entrepreneurship initiatives (Perkmann et al., 2013).

An alternative path to respond to the divergence between the new demands imposed by the societal challenges and the existing science and technology development focus of universities is to transform the offered educational programmes. Instead of aiming to modify consolidated structures through directed interventions, such as entrepreneurship incentives for established researchers, efforts would be focused on building the student's skills and capabilities for technology entrepreneurship and innovation.

To study this alternative path, we explore the case of two European universities. Prior research has observed that in the European context there have been additional challenges and difficulties for successful academic entrepreneurship in the form of university spin-offs, compared to the United States (Fini et al., 2017). Therefore, the exploration of alternative paths or mechanisms to promote technology entrepreneurship and innovation could be particularly relevant. We identified the engineering programmes of two universities based in France and Denmark as two especially suitable cases that serve the purpose of illustrating responses to the demand of activating science and technology education with a focus on science-based entrepreneurial activity.

The two cases of science and technology entrepreneurship education (STEE) share common elements; for instance, there are similarities in the overall design, content, pedagogical methods, learning environment and intended learning outcomes. Nevertheless, each programme has specific characteristics in relation to those categories, and unique features in driving STEE. A comparative analysis of the two cases provides insights on potential guidelines to structure programmes that foster technology entrepreneurship through education and training.

Both programmes, one at Lorraine University (UL) in France and the other at the University of Southern Denmark (SDU), were developed as a response to a strong regional demand for professionals with an entrepreneurial mindset and engineering capacities. The regional actors see the universities as collaborative partners for research and education in the field of science and technology. The strong connection with the region's industry becomes an influencing factor on the design and implementation of the specific approach to STEE.

The overall theme for the pedagogical model at UL and SDU is organized around the student–subject–project triangle. Supporting problem-based learning is the preferred approach. In more detail, the DSMI model (acronym for *Den Syddanske Model for Igeniøruddlannelser*) used at SDU requires that students work on problems proposed by companies in the region during their studies, introducing company visits and the participation of company employees as guest lecturers as part of the regular course activities.

The development of attitudes towards entrepreneurial behaviour is also activated through internal projects. For instance, as part of a master's degree, engineering students enrol in a business venturing course (the course has different names in each institution), where either researchers or company representatives pitch their ongoing projects to the students. Those projects then build the basis for the ongoing course or semester focus. The course offers a safe environment to apply technology commercialization practices through a real case exercise; although the learning outcomes of the course are focused on analysing and applying methods, the real-life outcomes have been the creation of student-led start-ups in the region.

A significant catalyst of the technology entrepreneurship education for both programmes has been the creation of a specific learning environment, and communities of knowledge and practice related to it. In the case of UL it has been the creation of the Lorraine Fab Living Lab, and at SDU the Innovation Lab facility. These communities in their innovation spaces have become a centrepiece of the training programmes as they have different properties compared to other engineering or research labs. Instead of replicating industry labs at a smaller scale, they are a tangible representation of the often abstract entrepreneurship process. The intense use of these facilities in the educational programmes aims to modify the self-efficacy perception of the students regarding entrepreneurial behaviour (Piperopoulos and Dimov, 2015).

Taking this context into account, we aim to investigate the phenomenon of STEE in these two engineering degrees. This enables us to provide answers to the following questions: How is entrepreneurship education being introduced in engineering programmes? What specific considerations are being taken into account, and what are the characteristics of current programmes?

The key findings of our work are threefold. Firstly, the two educational programmes show that a pedagogic approach that emphasizes interactive teaching and problem-based learning is mostly applied in STEE-related courses. The respective programme coordinators perceive that to be essential in involving the students and in motivating them to be proactive. Self-directed learning plays a fundamental role to complete the students' knowledge and skills by taking initiatives, based in curiosity, definition of learning goals, and the identification of resources to achieve these goals. Secondly, creating a context where theoretical knowledge can be applied in a real-world setting is crucial to achieve specific learning outcomes. These real-world collaborative projects serve as a staging ground where the specific knowledge acquired in scientific modules makes practical sense and feeds the emergence and improvement of new concepts. At the same time, within those projects, students learn to manage the complexity of dealing with compromises between technical implications, human resources and business aspects. Thirdly, it is important to provide the students with self-directed access to communities of knowledge and practice and innovation spaces. The collaboration with such incubational infrastructures allows students to demystify the difficulties and challenges of taking entrepreneurial risk, and enhances their motivation to pursue their own start-ups. This happens through an increased awareness of methods, tools and competences that enables them to overcome challenges which they would otherwise perceive to be beyond their capabilities.

Following this introduction, we provide a reference framework for science and technology entrepreneurship education. This includes the reasoning for the research questions that guide our work. Then we describe the method we pursued. As the aim is to provide illustrative examples that can be used as a guide to propose alternative paths to activate technology entrepreneurship, we then present findings related to the two cases we have investigated. To finish, a discussion section that includes implications for research and practice is proposed, prior to our concluding remarks.

REFERENCE FRAMEWORK

The debate on the role of universities in the generation of innovation and entrepreneurial activity remains an active subject of discussion. The concept of an entrepreneurial university with the mission of 'creating, disseminating and applying knowledge for economic and social development' (Schmitz et al., 2017: 17) signifies the evolution of the role of universities in society. Furthermore, this debate is now moving towards the idea that in an entrepreneurial society the university mission will also be to 'contribute and provide leadership for creating entrepreneurial thinking, actions, institutions, and entrepreneurship capital' (Audretsch, 2014: 314).

The broader and extended expectations on the universities' contribution to innovation and entrepreneurship have been responded to with the introduction of new educational programmes and entrepreneurial activities in the academic setting (Støren, 2014; Kuratko, 2005). There has been a diversity of approaches in both the introduction and delivery of entrepreneurship education programmes, and in the activation of entrepreneurial activities. While entrepreneurship education approaches range from teaching about what entrepreneurs do, to actually helping students learn how to think and behave as entrepreneurs (Neck and Greene, 2011), entrepreneurial activity in universities has been promoted with a diversity of initiatives such as support mechanisms to knowledge and technology transfer using TTOs (Fitzgerald and Cunningham, 2015), and the introduction of academic entrepreneurship programmes (Meoli and Vismara, 2016; Perkmann et al., 2013).

The disconnection between the entrepreneurship education and the entrepreneurial activities in the academic setting is particularly relevant in the science and technology fields. Although entrepreneurship and innovation courses have gradually moved beyond business management programmes, we still know little about the impact that specific pedagogic approaches might have on science and technology students (Nabi et al., 2017). With notable exceptions (see Souitaris et al., 2007), we know much more about the impact of different approaches on business or management students (see Piperopoulos and Dimov, 2015) than on those pursuing engineering or other technical studies. Similarly, research on academic entrepreneurship and technology transfer activities has often overlooked the participation of students, and their training, in the innovation and entrepreneurship activities (Siegel and Wright, 2015), focusing instead on the involvement of faculty members and their efforts to disseminate knowledge and new technologies to society.

We aim to address this research gap by exploring how universities have introduced entrepreneurship education programmes in science and technology fields, focusing on how they balance the duality between scientific knowledge and entrepreneurial education. We review recent research findings on entrepreneurial education to complete the theoretical framework that guides the analysis of a selection of engineering degree programmes.

Advances in Entrepreneurship Education

The field of entrepreneurship education has matured and gained legitimacy in the last decade, and it has also gained centrality in the curriculum in education programmes across disciplines, as envisioned by Katz (2008). Although there is a diversity of pedagogical approaches and programme designs labelled under 'entrepreneurship education', the maturity in the field has also made preferred approaches visible that would fit better with recent years' research insights. Two dominant characteristics of these programmes are the focus on learning to behave like an entrepreneur (Neck and Greene, 2011) and the use of action-based learning approaches (Rasmussen and Sørheim, 2006).

As entrepreneurship education programmes have progressively abandoned their attachment to the business plan as the core element in their curriculum (Honig, 2004), a shift in the expected learning outcomes has also occurred. Learning about entrepreneurship or the characteristics of entrepreneurs has become a marginal part of modern courses; instead it is now more common to dedicate time to achieve learning outcomes related to developing skills and competences related to entrepreneurial thinking and decision making (Neck and Greene, 2011). The evolution in the content of the programme also reflects the progress in entrepreneurship research. Thrane et al. (2016) describe how the entrepreneur–opportunity nexus reconceptualization (Davidsson, 2015) impacts upon present and future educational programmes. Thrane and colleagues argue that educational programmes should aim to follow an entrepreneurial learning process, focusing on the building blocks of entrepreneurial identity, opportunity creation and the activation of the new venture (Thrane et al., 2016).

The second interrelated aspect is the introduction of action-based learning approaches. Thus, we have seen a migration from passive to active entrepreneurship education programmes. The traditional teaching, with a passive involvement of students, was suitable for knowledge learning outcomes related to studying what entrepreneurs do. To achieve learning outcomes related to thinking and behaving like entrepreneurs, the activation of the students becomes a central aspect of the educational programme (Rasmussen and Sørheim, 2006). Again, such changes in the pedagogical approach go hand in hand with research insights on entrepreneurs' behaviours, habits and heuristics (Aldrich and Yang, 2014). The active-learning approaches have also opened the door to the introduction of specific contexts for entrepreneurial learning. As also observed in research, context has an influence on the activation of entrepreneurial behaviour (Autio et al., 2014). Therefore, it is not surprising that specific learning contexts provide a more or less favourable environment for entrepreneurial learning. In fact, recent research is already exploring how specific spaces (such as 'maker' spaces) might impact upon entrepreneurs' actions and decisions (Mortara and Parisot, 2018, 2016).

As entrepreneurship education keeps being transferred to new fields, new questions and challenges emerge. A potential concern is to ensure that the best practices in entrepreneurship education are visible enough when educators aim to adapt existing programmes to a new context or field. We aim to explore the specific challenge that science and technology engineering programme coordinators face when they aim to bring entrepreneurship into their curriculum. How is entrepreneurship education being introduced in engineering programmes? What specific considerations are being taken into account, and what are the characteristics of current programmes? To answer these research questions we study two cases of engineering programmes that educate science and technology entrepreneurs.

METHOD

We identified two engineering programmes that focus on science and technology entrepreneurship within their curriculum. One is the MSc in Engineering – Innovation and Business at the University of Southern Denmark, and the other is the MSc Global Design – Management of Innovation and Design for Industry at the French Université de Lorraine.

As our research questions aim to provide answers to specific characteristics of educational programmes that have not been investigated regarding STEE prior to this study, we consider it appropriate to use a document analysis and interviews with programme coordinators as our research method. Since these programmes have not been analysed before, and we intend to make an in-depth analysis of them (addressing mainly the 'how' and 'why'), we assume that an inductive qualitative research method is appropriate (Edmondson and McManus, 2007; Eisenhardt, 1989). We therefore focus on a methodological approach that enables us to identify the specifics of the educational programmes and their STEE-related courses, such as general content, job profiles, competences and applied pedagogical approaches, in detail. Further, we intend to identify key characteristics of the programmes that foster science and technology entrepreneurship education and to investigate commonalities and differences of the two cases.

We proceeded as follows: first, we analysed the official documents of the two faculties that describe the programmes and teaching approaches in detail. This includes curricula, syllabi and documents on teaching models of the respective universities. We identified major concepts related to STEE in the documents and sorted the available material accordingly. This produced the following categories: pedagogical approach, learning processes, programme objectives, job profiles, core competences, knowledge, skills, courses and content.

As the documents cannot tell us in detail how these categories apply in practice, we triangulated the identified content with semi-structured interviews of the programme coordinators of both programmes (see the Appendix for the Interview Guide). The interviews revolved around the major themes previously described and were organized accordingly: introduction and framing, job profiles, pedagogical approach and learning processes, programme objectives and learning outcomes, programme structure, programme content, teaching staff and assets. In total, the interview guide contained 32 open-ended questions. Open-ended questions find suitable application in exploratory research as recommended by Edmondson and McManus (2007). The audio-recorded interviews, which lasted 58 and 59 minutes, were transcribed and content-analysed by an iterative approach of inductive category building as well. This allowed a triangulation of the data gathered in the document analysis and allowed us to simplify focal categories to the following: general content, job profiles, competences and pedagogical approaches.

Although the documents and the interviews provided us with large amounts of data on the two educational programmes, we are currently in the process of establishing other units of analysis in investigating this context by interviewing current students and teaching staff of both programmes. This will allow a more in-depth understanding of the programme specifics in relation to STEE and will serve to evaluate current findings in the future. Other focal groups are alumni who have gained professional experience or launched a start-up after completing their education in one of the two programmes.

CASES

This chapter gives a brief introduction to the context of the two educational programmes at their respective universities, before identifying commonalities and differences in relation to STEE. We conclude this chapter by providing an overview of the key findings, which serves as the basis for the subsequent parts of this study.

University of Southern Denmark: MSc in Engineering – Innovation and Business

The University of Southern Denmark (SDU) is a multi-campus university with approximately 30 000 students and 2000 researchers. The educational programme MSc in Engineering – Innovation and Business (hereafter named IB) is located at the Sønderborg campus in southern Denmark and is taught in the English language. The hosting section is SDU Technology Entrepreneurship and Innovation which is part of the Faculty of Engineering. Courses contain usually 15–25 students and the two-year master's education consists of 120 points according to the European Credit Transfer and Accumulation System (ECTS). A specific characteristic of the programme is the high degree of internationality and the interdisciplinary nature of study collaboration, as the students have completed an engineering degree in different disciplines in various countries at bachelor level prior to being admitted to the master's programme. Courses focus in general on either business or engineering aspects, or a mixture of both. In line with local industry and the general research focus of the technical institute, there is an emphasis on mechatronics in the engineering courses that are part of the education. The programme has been the starting point of several student-driven technology-based start-ups in recent years since it provides substantial support to start-ups through various incubators. Although this is not defined as a success criterion in evaluating the educational programme, it serves as an additional incentive for investigating this course and its context.

Université de Lorraine: MSc Global Design – Management of Innovation and Design for Industry

The University of Lorraine is likewise a multi-campus university with approximately 52 000 students and 3800 researchers. The educational programme MSc Global Design has a specialty named MIDI (Management of Innovation and Design for Industry), is located at the Nancy campus in eastern France and is taught in the French language. The hosting department is the Ecole Nationale Superièure en Genie des Systèmes et de l'Innovation (ENSGSI), which is part of the Engineering College. On average courses of 25–30 students, the two-year master's education consists of 120 ECTS.

Similar to the IB education at SDU, there exists a high degree of internationality, and as the students have completed engineering degrees in different disciplines in various countries at the bachelor level prior to being admitted to the master's programme, study collaborations are often of a very interdisciplinary nature. In general, there is a course emphasis on business, design or engineering aspects, or a mixture of these, which corresponds to local industry and the general research focus of the ERPI research laboratory (Research Team on Innovation Processes), which is an industrial engineering lab focusing on innovation. The MIDI programme produces several student start-ups every year and provides substantial support to start-ups through various incubators.

Case Commonalities and Differences in Relation to STEE

In line with the semi-structured interview guide there has been a strong focus on STEE-related aspects of the educational programmes. The following investigates both commonalities and differences between the programme cases. Corresponding to the primary focus of this study, and as the analysis of documents and interviews delivered large amounts of content for the categories of general content, job profiles, competences and pedagogical approaches, they have been summarized in a table format. Other significant findings will be described in text form before the key findings are synthesized in graphics which will conclude this chapter.

In describing the general purpose of their respective education, the IB programme coordinator stated the following:

> The basic idea was always to create growth in the region by having more start-ups . . . we also just educate engineers for the industry, but with the kind of an entrepreneurial mindset more or less, so they can go into companies and still be the creative employees who then benefit the organization.

The general focus on educating both entrepreneurs and employees for various tasks in industry was similarly mentioned by the MIDI programme coordinator. Another similarity that both interviewees emphasized when introducing their programmes was a strong focus on innovation and the implications thereof. The MIDI programme coordinator said, 'By definition innovation processes are complex processes, you are dealing with multiple stakeholders; every stakeholder is autonomous, having different goals individually'. This statement is reflected in the description of competences of graduating students which follows subsequently.

Table 11.1 provides a comprehensive summary of the findings for specific core categories of the two educational programmes. The table includes findings that resemble commonalities in both programmes, and differences that are listed separately for each programme. It clearly shows many similarities and the interdisciplinary nature of the two approaches to science and technology entrepreneurship education.

According to the programme coordinators there are no specific teaching staff utilized in STEE-related courses. Rather, lecturers are typically researchers of related fields, and although the pedagogical model defines a certain approach, the lecturers are free to apply it according to their preferences. At both universities training programmes are available that facilitate tools and methods to apply open and problem-based teaching that engages students to participate actively and to relate knowledge to practical contexts.

Students are in principle free to pursue start-ups during their studies. While the IB programme coordinator mentioned there is nonetheless a conflict of interest and a time management issue if they decide to launch a venture during the studies, the MIDI programme coordinator stated that students in their programme are encouraged to engage in start-ups should they desire to do so.

Key Findings in Relation to Science and Technology Entrepreneurship Education

Based on Table 11.1 and the emphasis of the programme coordinators, there are three key findings that will receive more attention in the following, and simultaneously build the foundation for the contribution of this research.

Pedagogic approach in STEE-related courses

A pedagogic approach that encourages interactive learning, active involvement of students and self-directed learning is more applied in STEE-related courses compared to pure engineering courses, and is of special

Table 11.1 Summary of empirical findings

	University of Southern Denmark: MSc in Engineering – Innovation and Business	Université de Lorraine: MSc Global Design – Management of Innovation and Design for Industry
General content	Holistic view on innovation Ideation and creativity Product development processes and prototyping Business models and market specifics Innovation as a contextual and complex phenomenon Real-life cases as the basis for semester projects with the objective of creating innovation	
	Operations and manufacturing processes Internship in the form of an in-company period or an entrepreneurial training course	Holistic view on technology systems in taking technology, competences and stakeholders into account Personal development Methodologies and tools for innovation Usability studies
Job profiles	Entrepreneurs Project managers Industrial engineers Innovation managers	
	Consultants (primarily within information technology)	Product manager
Competences	Project management abilities Creating or adapting products Managing multidisciplinary resources and implications Reflecting on the context of technologies and companies Integrating technical, managerial and human dimensions	
	Starting up new businesses based on technical products Creating value propositions for existing or new markets and stimulating innovations in a given context Identifying entrepreneurial opportunities	Product development Design, launch and management of innovation projects in a practical context Design and operationalization of processes within a practical context

Table 11.1 (continued)

	Group and team-related dynamics Knowledge sharing across disciplines Taking responsibility for decisions and results	Self-directed learning Flexibility and adaptability Creativity and an ability to manage creative processes
Pedagogical approach	Open and interactive learning Active involvement of students through exercises, project work, etc. Dialogue-based teaching	Self-directed learning Problem-based learning Learn to learn
	Involvement in projects with 'real-life' context Input from multidisciplinary sources Offering advice for entrepreneurs through collaboration with external partners (both on a business and a technology level)	

importance, according to the interviewees. In explaining why self-directed learning is important, the MIDI program coordinator stated:

> There is one philosophy behind our pedagogy; that is learn to learn. And as you're able to address your self-directed strategy, so you are more able to be adaptive . . . You must be able to learn new things, because every single day new tools, new approaches are available, so you have to be able to learn.

The interactive teaching approach can be put into practice in different ways. According to the IB programme coordinator:

> You can do this interactive teaching in many, many ways, it is just that you understand, how can you create exercises, how can you use, for example online systems to facilitate a learning process, whatever you can use in order to make the students think and reflect, instead of just lecturing like feeding the students.

Figure 11.1 includes the pedagogical approach as a dimension and illustrates the key finding that active involvement of students is higher in technology entrepreneurship-related courses than in pure engineering courses or practical engineering exercises.

Context is of high importance in STEE-related courses

Both programme coordinators stressed the importance of 'real-life' projects where theoretical knowledge finds application in a complex context in

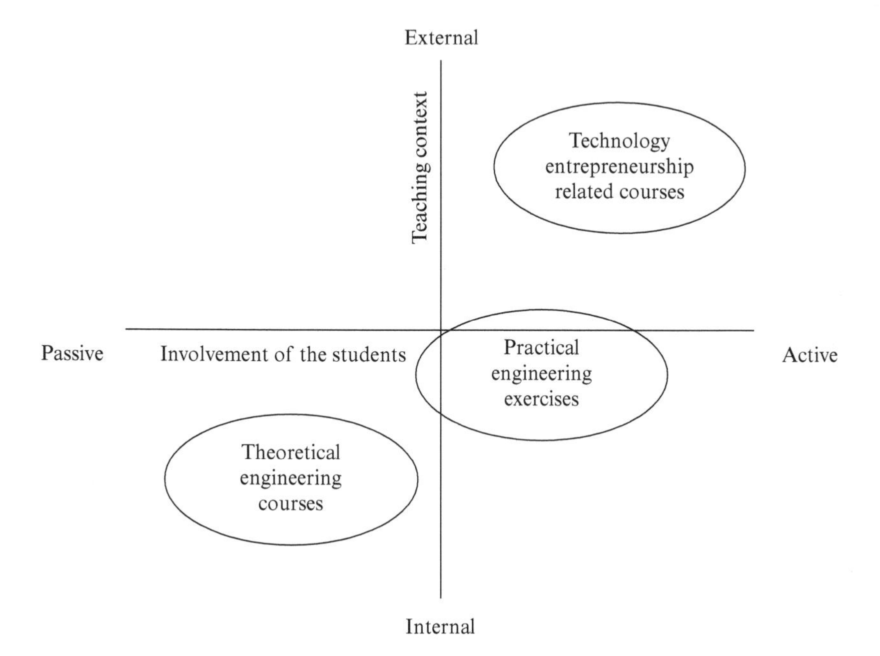

Figure 11.1 Teaching context and pedagogical approach in the form of student involvement in different courses

order to achieve specific learning outcomes. In describing some general but important learnings, the IB programme coordinator explained:

> These general things are the softer things, how you interact with your group for example, if you work in a team later on, how do you deal with complexity, how do you take responsibility for your work, how do you organize your work and all these kind of things are things that you learn because you work in groups and you work on real-life projects and I think they are very important for the life afterwards.

The importance of real projects was also emphasized by the MIDI programme coordinator when stating:

> There is interesting thinking, we're working on an entrepreneurial project or more enterprise linked project so the students along the courses they have a project linked with a company, could be a start-up, could be an already existing company, but they have to create a new product, new services, new business model, so the fact that they interact with real companies, I guess let's allow them to have a better understanding on the priorities of an entrepreneur and

> the dynamics in this entrepreneurial process. So participating in real projects is an important fact.

The teaching context is primarily internal in both theoretical and practical engineering courses. In contrast, technology entrepreneurship-related courses are occurring in a much more external context, as Figure 11.1 illustrates.

The importance of access to communities of knowledge and related physical spaces

Both interviewees stated that access to communities of knowledge is critical in building STEE capabilities such as creativity, prototyping skills and the ability to solve complex issues in specific contexts. Furthermore, physical spaces facilitate access to those communities through common use of machinery, joined projects or workshops, or a stimulating collaboration environment. When asked about support structures for students who pursue a start-up, the IB programme coordinator stated the following:

> We collaborate with different external organizations, public organizations or incubators where there is the possibility to get support or getting a mentor. So there is access, we kind of tell them about the possibilities . . . And in this network or in this incubator environment there are other companies that are also technical. So you get kind of access to a network through these incubators so there you could get your technical sparring basically.

Using suitable physical spaces like Fablabs or SDU's Innovation Lab and connected communities enables students to solve issues that they perceive to be beyond their capabilities. 'Fablabs' are fabrication laboratories; spaces that offer fabrication devices in the form of conventional tools and machinery based on digital technologies, such as 3D printers (Walter-Herrmann and Büching, 2014). The MIDI programme coordinator stressed especially the importance of communities of knowledge and practice:

> Space matters, it's important, having machines is important, but it's not the most important thing for me. For me the most important is having communities of people working in those spaces . . . The same space is shared by communities and as far as we have problems, sometimes we go through these communities, because you know the competences are not the same . . . So next we are sharing competences and helping each other. For me that is the secret . . . So this crosslinking of communities is so important!

While the educational programme at SDU involves mainly one external partner in offering additional advice for student entrepreneurs, the MIDI

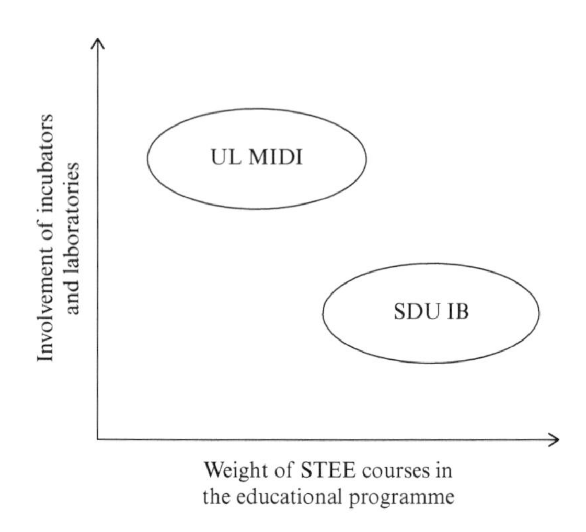

Figure 11.2 Comparison of the MIDI and the IB programmes regarding involvement of incubators and laboratories in educational activities and the weight of STEE-related courses in the educational programmes

programme utilizes three different communities that the students gain access to. Both programmes offer laboratories for product development, access to machinery, and so on, to a similar extent, although the MIDI programme has access to larger relevant infrastructures.

Figure 11.2 compares the IB programme at SDU and the MIDI programme at UL regarding the extent of involvement of incubators and laboratories, as well as the overall ratio of courses with a strong relation to STEE. In the MIDI programme the ratio of STEE-related courses in the context of all courses is approximately 30 per cent. For the IB programme the ratio is at least 30 per cent and can reach up to 60 per cent, depending on electives chosen by the students.

DISCUSSION AND IMPLICATIONS

The development of entrepreneurial education has been accompanied by the introduction of entrepreneurship training in a diversity of programmes and scientific fields. The evolution of entrepreneurship education research has provided evidence on the adequacy of action-based approaches where the student takes a central role in driving the learning process (Rasmussen and Sørheim, 2006). As a result, this is now considered as the first option design for new entrepreneurship courses. Our research findings suggest that as entrepreneurship education has been transposed to new education and training fields, such as engineering programmes, there have been unexpected consequences for both the overall education programme design and the students' learning outcomes.

First, the introduction of action-based approaches, popular now in entrepreneurship but not so much in other science and technology fields, often generates a shock for the students. Engineering education programmes still have a substantial number of courses that rely on passive engagement of the students, following a more traditional teaching model, where exercises or computer simulations are the closest that the student gets to reality. Action-based approaches favour the introduction of active learning activities that can occur in the classroom context, but also outside of the university boundaries; this puts the student in situations of high uncertainty, often without a clear final output in mind besides engaging with an iterative process to unlock the potential product market fit of a new technology.

Second, the introduction of action-based training for entrepreneurship competences requires a supportive and collaborative environment. It is a different approach, and in some cases it requires a transition process, similar to the process of activating entrepreneurial cognition aspects (Gregoire et al., 2009). The students benefit from interactions with internal and external actors that help them to build self-efficacy perceptions of the entrepreneurial behaviour (Piperopoulos and Dimov, 2015). An unexpected finding from the cases studied is the low degree of control that the faculty maintained over the type and content of the interactions that the students had with internal and external stakeholders in their entrepreneurial activities. These generated unexpected results through the activation of unpredictable ideas, on a smaller scale, but we could argue that this is a process that resembles the construction of entrepreneurial social capital (Stam et al., 2014) in the context of an educational programme.

Lastly, the interaction with individual but also groups of stakeholders is activated in specific contexts, helping the technology entrepreneurship students to cross thresholds in their learning process. Entrepreneurship researchers have increasingly been interested in exploring contexts, from incubators and innovation labs to the more recent Fablabs or similar experimentation spaces (Aernoudt, 2004; Mortara and Parisot, 2018; Moultrie et al., 2007). We observed that the education programmes for technology entrepreneurship naturally bring in aspects such as structured design approaches and tools, prototyping, and other techniques that are common in engineering but not in business or management courses. The tangible and evidence-based approach to problem solving in the engineering programmes enriches the transposition of action-based entrepreneurship training by further accelerating and making visible the learning and progress of the students. This is a promising contribution of technology entrepreneurship programmes in science and technology to the overall entrepreneurship education research.

The findings of our study are built upon a small selection of cases, as we narrowed our focus to two programmes in Europe. Therefore, further research efforts to generate findings from other programmes and other locations would enrich and complement the insights presented here. Additionally, other units of analysis (other actors) and their perspectives, for example alumni and teaching staff, should be emphasized in future studies. This would offer to the researchers a more comprehensive understanding of the impact and effect of specific approaches and contexts. Future research should also investigate the meaning of incubational infrastructures in the academic setting, and characteristics and details of physical spaces and related communities of knowledge and practice in this regard. Another avenue for future work is the impact assessment of STEE through various measures that go beyond the reductionist measure of the number of technology start-ups.

CONCLUSION

As universities perform additional functions in their contribution to society, new challenges emerge. There is an increasing societal demand to universities, as they should not only produce and disseminate new knowledge, but also generate entrepreneurial capital (Audretsch, 2014). This demand introduces a novel challenge in the academic setting, where innovation and entrepreneurship are only starting to progressively permeate and transform the academic logics (Schmitz et al., 2017). Our study on how engineering education programmes are introducing science and technology entrepreneurship education is an illustration of this transformation.

The cases of two engineering master's degrees in Europe suggest that the integration of science and entrepreneurship education benefits from a combination of pedagogical approaches. Our cases show that the education design focus shifts from the 'what' to the 'how' of students' learning. STEE aims to build on the technical knowledge and skills of the students while also activating entrepreneurship competences. Therefore, the application of science and technical knowledge is done through entrepreneurial behaviour, which introduces a new source of uncertainty to students. This new source of uncertainty requires action-based learning, as the experiences that the students collect will be the drivers of their learning. As learning becomes experiential, the context gains importance. Therefore, our findings show how physical spaces become enablers of intense learning experiences, in particular if they are embedded in communities of practice. To sum up, the introduction of entrepreneurship education implies an overall revision of the teaching model of the engineering master's degree. This revision emphasizes the importance of the use of external contexts and action-based learning, which in turn requires a higher tolerance for uncertainty of both students and teachers.

The popularization of entrepreneurship education programmes in universities is a global phenomenon. But the generation of high-impact science and technology entrepreneurship remains an elusive goal. Policy makers have struggled to find adequate mechanisms that convert academic researchers into successful science-based entrepreneurs (Siegel and Wright, 2015). Our findings support the idea that students can close this gap by becoming science and technology entrepreneurs that bridge the distance between new technological developments and application markets. As a result, STEE initiatives can render part of the much sought-after impacts to policy makers. However, STEE initiatives require: (1) the introduction of action-based pedagogical approaches that put the student in the centre and build on continued student–student and student–teacher interaction; and (2) access to physical spaces (as learning settings) that enable individual experimentation of entrepreneurial activities and tasks with the involvement of external communities of practice.

Since science and technology entrepreneurship has the potential to make a substantial contribution to society, policy efforts that support an interdisciplinary education of science and technology students with the aim to acquire, even if only partially, an entrepreneurial identity can potentially have a direct effect on the generation of entrepreneurial capital in society.

REFERENCES

Aernoudt, R. (2004). Incubators: tool for entrepreneurship? *Small Business Economics*, **23**(2), 127–135. doi:10.1023/B:SBEJ.0000027665.54173.23.

Aldrich, H.E., and Yang, T. (2014). How do entrepreneurs know what to do? Learning and organizing in new ventures. *Journal of Evolutionary Economics*, **24**(1), 59–82. doi:10.1007/s00191-013-0320-x.

Audretsch, D.B. (2014). From the entrepreneurial university to the university for the entrepreneurial society. *Journal of Technology Transfer*, **39**(3), 313–321.

Autio, E., Kenney, M., Mustar, P., Siegel, D., and Wright, M. (2014). Entrepreneurial innovation: the importance of context. *Research Policy*, **43**(7), 1097–1108. doi:10.1016/j.respol.2014.01.015.

Davidsson, P. (2015). Entrepreneurial opportunities and the entrepreneurship nexus: a re-conceptualization. *Journal of Business Venturing*, **30**(5), 674–695. doi:10.1016/j.jbusvent.2015.01.002.

Edmondson, A.C., and McManus, S.E. (2007). Methodological fit in management field research. *Academy of Management Review*, **32**, 1246–1264.

Eisenhardt, K.M. (1989). Building theories from case study research. *Academy of Management Review*, **32**, 532–550.

Fini, R., Fu, K., Mathisen, M.T., Rasmussen, E., and Wright, M. (2017). Institutional determinants of university spin-off quantity and quality: a longitudinal, multilevel, cross-country study. *Small Business Economics*, **48**(2), 361–391.

Fitzgerald, C., and Cunningham, J.A. (2015). Inside the university technology transfer office: mission statement analysis. *Journal of Technology Transfer*, **41**(5), 1235–1246. doi:10.1007/s10961-015-9419-6.

Gregoire, D.A., Barr, P.S., and Shepherd, D.A. (2009). Cognitive processes of opportunity recognition: the role of structural alignment. *Organization Science*, **21**(2), 413–431. doi:10.1287/orsc.1090.0462.

Honig, B. (2004). Entrepreneurship education: toward a model of contingency-based business planning. *Academy of Management Learning and Education*, **3**(3), 258–273.

Katz, J. (2008). Fully mature but not fully legitimate: a different perspective on the state of entrepreneurship education. *Journal of Small Business Management*, **46**(4), 550–566. doi:10.1111/j.1540-627X.2008.00256.x.

Kuratko, D.F. (2005). The emergence of entrepreneurship education: development, trends, and challenges. *Entrepreneurship Theory and Practice*, **29**(5), 577–598.

Meoli, M., and Vismara, S. (2016). University support and the creation of technology and non-technology academic spin-offs. *Small Business Economics*, **47**(2), 345–362. doi:10.1007/s11187-016-9721-1.

Mortara, L., and Parisot, N.G. (2016). Through entrepreneurs' eyes: the Fab-spaces constellation. *International Journal of Production Research*, **54**(23), 7158–7180.

Mortara, L., and Parisot, N. (2018). How do fab-spaces enable entrepreneurship? Case studies of 'makers' –entrepreneurs. *International Journal of Manufacturing Technology and Management*, **32**(1), 16–42.

Moultrie, J., Nilsson, M., Dissel, M., Haner, U.-E., Janssen, S., and Van der Lugt, R. (2007). Innovation spaces: towards a framework for understanding the role of the physical environment in innovation. *Creativity and Innovation Management*, **16**(1), 53–65. doi:10.1111/j.1467-8691.2007.00419.x

Nabi, G., Linan, F., Krueger, N., Fayolle, A., and Walmsley, A. (2017). The impact of entrepreneurship education in higher education: a systematic review and research agenda. *Academy of Management Learning and Education*, **16**(2), 277–299.

Neck, H.M., and Greene, P.G. (2011). Entrepreneurship education: known worlds and new frontiers. *Journal of Small Business Management*, **49**(1), 55–70. doi:10.1111/j.1540- 627X.2010.00314.x

Perkmann, M., Tartari, V., McKelvey, M., Autio, E., Broström, A., D'Este, P., et al. (2013). Academic engagement and commercialisation: a review of the literature on university–industry relations. *Research Policy*, **42**(2), 423–442. doi:10.1016/j.respol.2012.09.007.

Piperopoulos, P., and Dimov, D. (2015). Burst bubbles or build steam? Entrepreneurship education, entrepreneurial self-efficacy, and entrepreneurial intentions. *Journal of Small Business Management*, **53**(4), 970–985.

Rasmussen, E.A., and Sørheim, R. (2006). Action-based entrepreneurship education. *Technovation*, **26**(2), 185–194. doi:10.1016/j.technovation.2005.06.012.
Schmitz, A., Urbano, D., Dandolini, G.A., de Souza, J.A., and Guerrero, M. (2017). Innovation and entrepreneurship in the academic setting: a systematic literature review. *International Entrepreneurship and Management Journal*, **13**(2), 369–395.
Siegel, D.S., and Wright, M. (2015). Academic entrepreneurship: time for a rethink? *British Journal of Management*, **26**(4), 582–595. doi:10.1111/1467-8551.12116.
Souitaris, V., Zerbinati, S., and Al-Laham, A. (2007). Do entrepreneurship programmes raise entrepreneurial intention of science and engineering students? The effect of learning, inspiration and resources. *Journal of Business Venturing*, **22**(4), 566–591. doi:10.1016/j.jbusvent.2006.05.002.
Stam, W., Arzlanian, S., and Elfring, T. (2014). Social capital of entrepreneurs and small firm performance: a meta-analysis of contextual and methodological moderators. *Journal of Business Venturing*, **29**(1), 152–173. doi:10.1016/j.jbusvent.2013.01.002.
Støren, L.A. (2014). Entrepreneurship in higher education. *Education + Training*, **56**(8/9), 795–813. doi:10.1108/ET-06-2014-0070.
Thrane, C., Blenker, P., Korsgaard, S., and Neergaard, H. (2016). The promise of entrepreneurship education: reconceptualizing the individual–opportunity nexus as a conceptual framework for entrepreneurship education. *International Small Business Journal*, **34**(7), 905–924. doi:10.1177/0266242616638422.
Walter-Herrmann, J., and Büching, C. (eds) (2014). *FabLab: Of Machines, Makers and Inventors*. Wetzlar: Transcript Verlag.

APPENDIX: SEMI-STRUCTURED INTERVIEW GUIDE

Introduction and Framing

In two sentences, how do you describe your educational programme?
What are the general objectives of your educational programme? Amount of start-ups as a success criterion?
What is your understanding of the term 'science and technology entrepreneurship education'? What is STEE? What is it not?
In general, how do you define the learning outcomes of STEE?
Are there any STEE-related requirements for the students admitted to your educational programme?

Job Profiles

Which job profiles are relevant for your educational programme?
What are specific learning outcomes of STEE-related courses that are relevant for those job profiles?
Which core competences are graduates supposed to possess at the end of the education in order to qualify for those job profiles?
Any other insights into knowledge and skills that graduates are supposed to possess?

Pedagogical Approach

Which pedagogical approach is being used/recommended in STEE-related courses? Why?
Which teaching model(s) is pursued? Why?
How is that teaching model communicated and implemented? Are there any instructions on specific activities that are designed to implement that teaching model?
What could be the best and most appropriate pedagogies in STEE? Why?

Programme Structure

How is the programme structured? What is the underlying reasoning?
Structure-wise: how to balance theoretical knowledge and practice-based knowledge in STEE?
Is there a specific learning process? How does the programme structure correspond to it?

Programme Content

Which content is communicated in STEE-related courses? Why?
Which stages of entrepreneurship play a role in the educational programme?
Are there any activities/courses that aim at identifying entrepreneurial opportunities? Are there any attempts to get the students 'out into the real world'?
How does the education support the intentions and abilities to start-up a business after the educational programme? (*investigate separately for intentions and abilities*)
Are there any specific activities that challenge students to pursue an actual start-up already during their studies? How is this supported through the programme (structure, activities, mentors, etc.)? Is it desired that students work on the education and their start-up in parallel? How do you deal with this conflict?
Content-wise: how to balance theoretical knowledge and practice-based knowledge in STEE?

Teaching Staff

Is there specific teaching staff for STEE related courses? If yes, which one? Why?
Do you use mentorship? Technical or entrepreneurial?

Assets, etc.

Which physical spaces/environments/assets are used in your educational programme? Other labs, etc.?
What is the impact of those spaces/environments/assets? How does it affect entrepreneurial mindset, self-efficacy, etc.?
Do incubators/accelerators play a role in your STEE-related courses? How about funding/investment contacts? Is there any financial support for creating technical prototypes?
What are resource implications for universities attempting to develop interdisciplinary STEE?

Conclusion

What is the weight of STEE-related courses in your educational programme?
What are strengths and weaknesses of your programme in relation to STEE?
What is the future meaning of STEE for your educational programme?
What are the most important things in STEE in your opinion?

12. Entrepreneurial actions towards the success of exponential technologies*

Sandro Battisti, Eduardo Giugliani, Rafael Prikladnicki and Paolo Traverso

INTRODUCTION

Entrepreneurial education could be central for the success of the innovation ecosystem in terms of value creation, technology transfer from research to the market, as well as business impact (e.g., Kuratko, 2005; Guerrero et al., 2015). Generation, attraction and transfer of talented people and technology from research to the market is a successful driving factor for economic growth and local development (e.g., Bramwell and Wolfe, 2008).

From this perspective on high-impact entrepreneurial actions, this chapter addresses the topic of organizing innovation to enable the creation of high impacts by entrepreneurs, on both business and society. It is an emerging issue for researchers and managers, where the role of key actors can be crucial for the results of innovation and entrepreneurial activities, an argument supported by Pisano and Verganti (2008). Innovation parks and business ecosystems seem to be the most effective ways to create environments capable of delivering both business and societal impact towards sustainability, which is also supported by Seebode et al. (2012) and Adner (2017).

This chapter uses as reference the definition of innovation proposed by Baregheh et al. (2009), which is: 'Innovation is the multi-stage process whereby organizations transform ideas into new/improved products, service or processes, in order to advance, compete and differentiate themselves successfully in their marketplace'. This definition is particularly relevant because it is based on an in-depth analysis of 60 definitions of innovation from a multidisciplinary perspective.

Towards understanding the development of a complex innovation process, this chapter explores the collaborative innovation models capable of delivering measurable results to companies (e.g., Bogers et al., 2017) and society, in particular by addressing key drivers and exploring the innovation ecosystems around living labs. Additionally, this chapter adopts the definition of Katzy et al. (2012) for living labs: 'innovation intermediaries that coordinate network partners for the execution of innovation processes with the engagement of end-users for which they provide the technical and organizational infrastructure', which is based on the research of Howells (2006) and Almirall and Wareham (2008).

Innovation ecosystems are a powerful way of creating conditions to catalyse economic growth and entrepreneurial activities (Urbano and Guerrero, 2013), and there is a need to explore their success factors (Oh et al., 2016), in particular towards high societal impact by increasing the employment rate and the quality of life of local citizens. From this perspective, Winter et al. (forthcoming) look at the success factors of mobile ecosystems by analysing the role of technology in creating platforms of collaboration for companies and users. Additionally, Van Looy et al. (2011) argue that the scientific productivity of the researcher is positively associated with the success of entrepreneurial activities.

This chapter expands the theory by creating new drivers for performance measurement in innovation ecosystems, as suggested by Ritala and Almpanopoulou (2017). It also explores new opportunities for identifying new constructs to be measured, which could be directly related to ecosystem performance and capability (e.g., Adner, 2017). From this perspective, the research question is:

Research Question: What are the main entrepreneurial drivers for the collaboration of innovation ecosystems that enable the high impact of technology-based initiatives on business and society?

LITERATURE REVIEW

The background research used to understand this phenomenon lies at the intersection between organizational innovation and innovation platforms (e.g., Gawer and Cusumano, 2014). Furthermore, the organizational innovation body of knowledge focused on living labs (e.g., Battisti, 2014) leverages information and communication technology (ICT) as the central mechanism of support for high impact creation, based on the exponential capacity of such technology for scaling up business growth and societal impact. Ismail et al. (2014) defined this exponential characteristic as the capacity of a technology to be diffused and adopted by the final end-user in an exponential way, rather than a classical diffusion model based on linearity as founded by Rogers (2003).

From this perspective, exponential organizations are capable of achieving high impact in business and society by enabling the participation of organizations and groups of people (e.g., Stewart and Hyysalo, 2008) in the innovation process, and the adoption of exponential technologies by the target market of knowledge-based start-ups (e.g., Battisti, 2013). Furthermore, Hellebrand (2017) suggests that the entrepreneurs of tomorrow should understand in depth the nature of exponential technologies, and in particular the way to design organizations to create high impact. This enables powerful actions for dealing with societal challenges, in particular exploring key actors', such as social entrepreneurs', roles and motivations for driving high impact, as suggested by Surie (2017).

Technology and innovation ecosystems can be considered as organizational structures aimed at enabling research, development and production of technology towards the development and growth of companies, as supported by Clarysse et al. (2014). Furthermore, Giugliani et al. (2014) argue about the importance of ICT to support the governance and development of innovation ecosystems (e.g., Bogers et al., 2017), in particular considering the complexity involved in the ecosystems after the worldwide financial and social crisis, and the fact that current organizations are working at worldwide levels and with multicultural teams, which requires new models of entrepreneurship (van Loon, 2017).

Following this line of thought, Battisti (2014) argues that collaboration between companies, universities, research centres and society towards addressing the most pressing issues must be a key driver, and he suggests the creation of living labs as the main mechanism to foster innovation for high impact creation in academia, in the business arena, as well as in society. This could be useful for supporting ecosystem managers (Borgh et al., 2012), in particular, when companies are exploring the context-based experience provided by the key people in such ecosystems (e.g., Almirall and Wareham (2011).

The knowledge-intensive companies play a crucial role in the success of innovation ecosystems and creation of high impact, as supported by Chiaroni et al. (2008), Battisti (2012) and Borgh et al. (2012). Aiming at extending the value creation of knowledge-intensive organizations, Pompermayer et al. (2016) and Battistella et al. (2017) argue about the importance of creating the mechanisms (for example, business accelerators) that enable the launch of global-born companies, which use exponential technologies and organizational models (Ismail et al., 2014) that potentially can create disruptive platforms for long-term competitive advantage.

In this sense, Gulati (1999) argues that network resources accessed by each company could be directly related to their performance, and Gulati et al. (2000) argue that the organizational network's configuration could be used to access learning and know-how to improve innovation capacity and performance. Furthermore, Brass et al. (2004) suggest that actors are embedded within networks to obtain opportunities and overcome constraints; and Gulati et al. (2009) argue that competitive advantage derives from identifying the contingent role of partnering experience.

From this perspective, Laursen and Salter (2006) found that in early stages of the product life cycle, when the state of technology is in flux, innovative firms need to draw deeply from a small number of key sources of innovation, such as lead users, component suppliers or universities. Linking competitive advantage with innovation, Bell and Zaheer (2007) suggest that knowledge could be accessed across the organizational boundaries, using networks of partners aiming at the production of innovation. In order to develop a better competitive performance, networks must have a company leader acting as a kind of catalyst hub of knowledge and coordination.

Given that social proximity could be considered a key factor for the success of innovation development because of socially embedded relations between agents, Boschma (2005) suggests that these relations between actors are socially embedded when they involve trust based on friendship. In this sense, Dhanaraj and Parkhe (2006) suggest the importance of the network position of the hub companies (that is, they could be considered the managers of the innovation ecosystem) and the ability of this hub to manage dispersed resources and capabilities of network members. Additionally, Boschma (2005) presents the five dimensions of proximity for collaboration between organizations: cognitive, organizational, social, institutional and geographical proximity.

Gaining insight from the university role inside the partnership of organizations aiming at innovation development, Laursen et al. (2011) suggest that in local territories the geographical distance between a company and a university matter. And they argue that there is a high influence of geographical proximities and quality of the universities in the decision making of companies to collaborate with universities, such as in technology transfer for innovation. Furthermore, they found that geographical proximity is a key success factor for university–firm collaboration, and they suggest that the effects of this collaboration are very significant for value creation of the company's core capabilities and competitive advantage.

Understanding the dynamics of innovation ecosystems could be a way to predict and act towards the high impact and support of launch and growth of start-ups and spin-off from research. It is particularly crucial to avoid the high number of companies that failed because of a lack of integration, collaboration and knowledge flow in local ecosystems, as argued by Brown (2016). In order to address this issue, Ghallab et al. (2014) argue for the need to focus on the key actors to address technology development;

'action' in a conceptual way is a world-transformation step that can be used to perform a task (that is, a specific action that affects the process of solving needs). Furthermore, this specific action could change based on the environmental dynamicity of the place where this task is performed, an argument supported by Pistore et al. (2006). It is also supported by van Loon (2017), who argued that reality is unpredictable because of the high growth of new technologies and their societal impact.

This chapter takes as reference the definition of Davis et al. (2009), who stated that dynamic environments are characterized to present four main variables: velocity – the rate at which new opportunities emerge; complexity – the number of features of an opportunity that must be correctly executed to capture an opportunity; ambiguity – the lack of clarity such that it is difficult to interpret opportunities; and unpredictability – the amount of turbulence in the flow of opportunities such that there are less consistent patterns.

Dynamic environments require rapid developments within innovation processes and quick innovation outcomes of specific projects or joint collaborations. It is a requirement to deal with stakeholder needs while exploring the advantages of technology evolution, in particular, due to the nature of temporary advantage of products launched in the markets by small and medium-sized organizations (e.g., Battisti, 2013). Furthermore, Ghallab et al. (2016) argue that current mainstream literature is strong on dealing with some project constraints, such as time, resources, continuous change in the requests of society, the need to manage the request of multiple stakeholders, and uncertainty. Moreover, Prikladnicki et al. (2017) suggest that teams should be temporary, so as to perform better on high-scale software development; and Ebert et al. (2016) argue that successful software products are developed by globally distributed teams.

The need to create new collaborative planning, in order to handle time and uncertainty properly, is a key factor (Ghallab et al., 2016), in particular when considering the dynamics of the environment (e.g., Pistore at al., 2014). Moreover, Schweitzer et al. (2011) suggest that open innovation is more beneficial for companies in dynamic, rather than stable conditions; and Prikladnicki et al. (2003) argue that global open software development can increase the competitive advantage of companies, which is also empowered by the phenomenon of exponential technologies (e.g., Ismail et al., 2014; Hellebrand, 2017).

METHODOLOGY

This chapter applies 'action research methods', considering the dynamicity of the phenomenon under study. It focuses on clinical inquiry research (Schein, 2008), which is the most appropriate method to describe and analyse the collaboration between the actors and their ecosystems. In particular, clinical inquiry research enables researchers to collect data from the empirical field in the most actionable way, obtaining more in-depth and detailed information when compared with other research methods.

This research also leveraged the case study methodology principles proposed by Yin (2009) and Eisenhardt and Graebner (2007). In particular, they suggest that single case studies can enable the creation of emerging theories, because in single cases the researcher can apply their theory exactly to the particular case, and as whole inductive research is a good tool to develop, measure and create new research propositions. In the same way, as suggested by Edmonson and McManus (2007), our research focused on the creation of new avenues of research in the field of innovation ecosystems, and it was based on the high diversity of materials collected from the empirical field, which enabled the researchers to develop new positive recommendations for the managers of the innovation ecosystems.

The data were collected in the period between January 2013 and June 2017. The main sources of data were the direct observations at the workplaces of TECNOPUC and FBK, and interactions of the researchers with key actors inside the two innovation ecosystems. Furthermore, the data include in-depth information from public and private organizations involved, as well as citizens in the cities of Porto Alegre in Brazil and Trento in Italy. Furthermore, secondary data from the websites of the innovation ecosystems, as well as internal archives, were used to enrich the study.

The main motivation for the case selection is the fact that the researchers were actively working in the two institutions during the research period, having in-depth access to confidential information that was crucial for the case analysis and findings. Furthermore, it was necessary to have day-by-day interaction with the middle and top management of the two ecosystems, in order to understand the key public and private institutions that interact with TECNOPUC and FBK, and the way they collaborate towards innovation and high impact.

CASE ANALYSIS

This research analysed the collaborative model of innovation developed by TECNOPUC, the Science and Technology Park of Pontifical Catholic University of Rio Grande do Sul (PUCRS) in Porto Alegre, Brazil and Fondazione Bruno Kessler (FBK) in Trento, Italy. This model was defined as the TECNOPUC-FBK Joint Lab. TECNOPUC is a technology and science park with more than 120 companies and 6000 people, working on creativity and innovation projects in strong collaboration with PUCRS. The main actors, resources and individual innovation models have been mapped in a recent study by Lamb et al. (2016b), which proves the potential impact of this ecosystem. Their goal is to create a community of interdisciplinary people from a research and innovation background, that is, built on academic, industrial and government collaborations, which is capable of improving the competitive position of TECNOPUC in the world and enhancing the quality of life of citizens. In the perspective of business growth and societal impact, TECNOPUC introduced two new initiatives: the GLOBAL TECNOPUC, as a convergence hub for sharing and co-creation of ideas and projects; and the Strategic Resource Mapping programme, as a platform for promoting synergy among resident and non-resident stakeholders (Lamb et al., 2016a).

Furthermore, PUCRS is recognized as an entrepreneurial university towards the regional economic growth, recently recognized as the first medium-level postgraduate programme university in Brazil. In terms of internationalization, an important partner of PUCRS is UK Trade & Investment (UKTI), an agency from the United Kingdom (UK) responsible for supporting the international exchange of key projects. Moreover, TECNOPUC is recognized as the best technology park and environment for innovation experience in Brazil and Latin America.

FBK is an internationally recognized research foundation with 7 research centres, 410 researchers, 2 specialized libraries and 7 laboratories. FBK conducts scientific research in the areas of information and communication technology, advanced materials and microsystems, theoretical and nuclear physics, and mathematics research. FBK has joint PhD programmes with first-class universities in Italy, Luxemburg, the UK and the United States. The focus of FBK is to conduct excellent research and to foster the realization of software systems, experimentation in realistic settings, validation in the field by living labs, industrial applications and high impact on the market and society, which prove the high commitment to addressing societal impact. In addition, FBK carries out its mission by disseminating and publishing results, and transferring technology to companies and public entities.

From this perspective, and towards combining the two innovation ecosystems for the creation of impact in entrepreneurial education, business growth and in society, the Joint Lab performed the following actions:

- Special projects: development of research and technology projects for private firms, local governments or other public agencies to design tools to foster better organizations and societies, leveraging fundraising from European and Brazilian funding agencies; considering project complexity as a key factor.
- Education: creation, development and operational support of joint PhD programmes and post-master's courses in entrepreneurship, business administration, innovation management, knowledge management and interdisciplinary studies, which are strongly connected with the fields of engineering, and computer science.
- Consultancy: this action is related to consultancy services to public and private organizations, addressing the intersection between innovation management, knowledge management and other interdisciplinary areas.
- Social innovation: development of ICT-based social innovation projects. The lab explores this paradigm to research, develop, deploy and test new technologies, to improve organizations, cities, and societies, in order to help in solving social issues in Brazil and Italy, bridging interdisciplinary fields.
- Exchange of people: exchange of students, researchers and faculty staff between the ecosystems, in order to promote the exchange of knowledge, joint teaching activities and seminars, and face-to-face collaborations in strategic projects.
- Co-creation: development of creativity and co-creation activities for new processes and services based on design thinking for understanding needs, and agile methodologies to implement technologies that cope with stakeholders' needs.
- Business acceleration: synergy for the acceleration of new business opportunities combining companies and final customer needs, as well as technology transfer from the research to the entrepreneurs incubated inside the ecosystems.
- Go-to-market: support the launch and growth of highly scalable start-ups around the innovation ecosystems (for example, exponential technology-based innovation platforms), in order to enhance technology and business developments towards the go-to-market actions.

From the analysis of the activities performed by the Joint Lab, the main similarities and complementarities of the lab can be categorized, towards

Table 12.1 Joint lab similarities

Topic	Description
Co-working	Companies are launched and scaled up in specific physical spaces that are co-located in close collaboration with researchers, professors and other entrepreneurs.
Labs with corporations	Special laboratories with key companies in FBK (e.g., TIM, Engineering and FCA Group) and in TECNOPUC (e.g., HP, Dell, Stefanini and Microsoft).
Industrial PhD students	Students that are co-funded by the companies for the development of state-of-the-art research to address practical problems of the companies.
Research field	TECNOPUC and FBK's main research field is ICT, which is also the domain that enables the majority of opportunities for joint research that enables innovation.
Territorial level	There is strong synergy with regional and local governments in Trento and Porto Alegre, as well as strong synergy with other innovation actors: FBK with HIT (Hub Innovazione Trentino); and TECNOPUC with the Hub of Science and Technology with UFGRS (Federal University of Rio Grande do Sul).

the identification of the main drivers of success. Thus, the main observed similar characteristics are presented in Table 12.1.

This research observed the main complementary characteristics between the ecosystems, which can be considered very useful for understanding the importance of collaboration between FBK and TECNOPUC, as presented in Table 12.2.

DISCUSSIONS AND CONCLUSIONS

The main contribution of this research to the fields of entrepreneurship and innovation is the empirical classification of the TECNOPUC-FBK Joint Lab actions into four drivers of success. These drivers proved to be crucial to keep the strong collaboration of the two innovation ecosystems towards the high impact on business, research and society, as presented in Table 12.3.

Towards entrepreneurial success, the universities, research centres, and the innovation ecosystem as a whole must address the support of start-ups to achieve global markets. In this way, the managers of the innovation ecosystems are considering the unpredictability of exponential technolo-

Table 12.2 Joint lab complementarities

Pillars	FBK	TECNOPUC
Research towards innovation	High productivity and citation impact of researchers with a good potential for innovation	Transfer of research into business opportunities
Management of innovation	Expertise in capturing financial resources from THE EU's Horizon 2020 Framework Programme for Research and Innovation	Provides experience of managing projects in an agile way
Marketing opportunities	Develops high-quality technology to transfer to Brazilian companies	Offers a hub to access Latin America market
Education	Receives international students from TECNOPUC	Provides PhD students to join the international PhD programme of FBK

gies, and they manage innovation 'under uncertainty', a fact that must be taken as a key driver for the selection of the most prominent start-ups for the acceleration of businesses.

The top management of the two ecosystems seems to take into consideration the management of innovation under uncertainty as a critical factor, considering it as the main issue that is pressuring Italy and Brazil under the current economic, social and political scenarios. On one hand, the Italian economy is not growing, and the unemployment rate is increasing. This is also caused by the fact that European Union is changing its economic and social models, and the phenomenon of public referendums towards the separation of frontiers (that is, such as Brexit) of some European countries in relation to the European Union is growing fast. On the other hand, the forecast Brazilian economic growth seems to be far from the expectations of the financial markets, thus not following the BRIC (Brazil, Russia, India, China) results in terms of economic development.

By understanding joint lab activities, this research identified four drivers for the success of sustainable collaborations in research and innovation, expanding open innovation theory such as the research of Bogers et al. (2017). Furthermore, these drivers extend the fields of living labs (e.g., Katzy et al., 2012) and innovation platforms (Gawer and Cusumano, 2014), in particular by confirming that the elimination of bottleneck connections among actors is a key success factor of innovation ecosystems, as argued by Oh et al. (2016).

Table 12.3 Four drivers of success

Driver	Description
1. Consultancy: public and private funding support to address business and social needs	Carry out external consultancy for developing and managing strategic projects, in order to understand and address the requests of public and private organizations, which includes co-creation activities between the final users of exponential technologies and knowledge-based entrepreneurs.
2. Collaboration: small and medium-sized companies are developing products with society and academia	Supporting new business opportunities between companies towards strong collaboration and knowledge creation, including soft-landing of start-ups between Trento and Porto Alegre towards the development of exponential technologies for high impact both in local ecosystems in collaboration with entrepreneurial universities, as well as with a global mindset.
3. Education: companies and society needs are empowering academics to promote joint research	Promotion of joint PhD programmes in the areas of computer science and materials engineering and technology, which is key to prepare the next generation of tech people, who should be ready to face unpredictable social challenges, being able to design, development and launch companies to create high entrepreneurial impact via the use of exponential technologies.
4. Mobility: researchers are collaborating together in specific physical places	Providing the physical infrastructure and organization model to support people to work and have a life experience abroad. It helps the growth of a new generation of entrepreneurs by focusing on understanding the critical issues of researchers, companies and society, aiming at the launch of new services and products at the market.

The practical implications for academia, companies and society are summarized as follows: intensively work together, considering the agendas of organizations; focus on narrow topics and deliver small and impactful results; apply agile methodologies to develop research and innovation; prioritize key actions to deliver impact to industry and society; satisfy stakeholders, considering the different priorities for the countries or regions.

A limitation is the analysis of two innovation ecosystems in a qualitative way, focusing on finding similarities and complementarities for the creation of high-impact drivers. This limitation opens up avenues for further research in entrepreneurial education and innovation platform fields; in particular, researchers could validate the drivers via a quantitative method, as well as create a new measurement of performance model that includes the four drivers. Furthermore, the open innovation field of research could be extended by measuring the effects (that is, short-, medium- and long-term) of the joint lab activity throughout the local territories involved, as well as the relationship between the universities and the local governments for the new generation of entrepreneurs who will lead start-ups based on exponential technologies.

NOTE

* We would like to thank the CIKI community for the feedback received during the presentation of an early version of this chapter at the International Congress of Knowledge and Innovation (CIKI) held on 11–12 September 2017 in Foz do Iguaçu/PR, Brazil, which was entitled 'High impact drivers in innovation ecosystems: the case of TECNOPUC-FBK Joint Lab'.

REFERENCES

Adner, R. (2017). Ecosystem as structure: an actionable construct for strategy. *Journal of Management*, **43**(1), 39–58.

Almirall, E., and Wareham, J. (2008). Living Labs and open innovation: roles and applicability. *Electronic Journal for Virtual Organizations and Networks*, **10**(3), 21–46.

Almirall, E. and Wareham, J. (2011). Living Labs: arbiters of mid-and ground-level innovation. *Technology Analysis and Strategic Management*, **23**(1), 87–102.

Baregheh, A., Rowley, J., and Sambrook, S. (2009). Towards a multidisciplinary definition of innovation. *Management Decision*, **47**(8), 1323–1339.

Battistella, C., Battistella, C., De Toni, A.F., De Toni, A.F., Pessot, E., and Pessot, E. (2017). Open accelerators for start-ups success: a case study. *European Journal of Innovation Management*, **20**(1), 80–111.

Battisti, S. (2012). Social innovation: the process development of knowledge-intensive companies. *International Journal of Services Technology and Management*, **18**(3/4), 224–244.

Battisti, S. (2013). Social innovation in dynamic environments: organising technology for temporary advantage. *International Journal of Social Entrepreneurship and Innovation*, **2**(6), 504–524.

Battisti, S. (2014). Social innovation in living labs: the micro-level process model of public–private partnerships. *International Journal of Innovation and Regional Development*, **5**(4/5), 328–348.

Bell, G.G., and Zaheer, A. (2007). Geography, networks, and knowledge flow. *Organization Science*, **18**(6), 955–972.

Bogers, M., Zobel, A.K., Afuah, A., Almirall, E., et al. (2017). The open innovation research landscape: established perspectives and emerging themes across different levels of analysis. *Industry and Innovation*, **24**(1), 8–40.

Borgh, M., Cloodt, M., and Romme, A.G.L. (2012). Value creation by knowledge-based ecosystems: evidence from a field study. *R&D Management*, **42**(2), 150–169.
Boschma, R. (2005). Proximity and innovation: a critical assessment. *Regional Studies*, **39**(1), 61–74.
Bramwell, A., and Wolfe, D.A. (2008). Universities and regional economic development: the entrepreneurial University of Waterloo. *Research Policy*, **37**(8), 1175–1187.
Brass, D.J., Galaskiewicz, J., Greve, H.R., and Tsai, W. (2004). Taking stock of networks and organizations: a multilevel perspective. *Academy of Management Journal*, **47**(6), 795–817.
Brown, R. (2016). Mission impossible? Entrepreneurial universities and peripheral regional innovation systems. *Industry and Innovation*, **23**(2), 189–205.
Chiaroni, D., Chiesa, V., De Massis, A., and Frattini, F. (2008). The knowledge bridging role of technical and scientific services in knowledge-intensive industries. *International Journal of Technology Management*, **41**(3/4), 249–272.
Clarysse, B., Wright, M., Bruneel, J., and Mahajan, A. (2014). Creating value in ecosystems: crossing the chasm between knowledge and business ecosystems. *Research Policy*, **43**(7), 1164–1176.
Davis, J.P., Eisenhardt, K.M., and Bingham, C.B. (2009). Optimal structure, market dynamism, and the strategy of simple rules. *Administrative Science Quarterly*, **54**(3), 413–452.
Dhanaraj, C., and Parkhe, A. (2006). Orchestrating innovation networks. *Academy of Management Review*, **31**(3), 659–669.
Ebert, C., Kuhrmann, M., and Prikladnicki, R. (2016). Global software engineering: evolution and trends. In *Global Software Engineering* (ICGSE) (pp. 144–153), 2016 IEEE 11th International Conference.
Edmonson, A.C., and McManus, S.E. (2007). Methodological fit in management field research. *Academy of Management Review*, **32**(4), 1155–1179.
Eisenhardt, K.M., and Graebner, M.E. (2007). Theory building from cases: opportunities and challenges. *Academy of Management Journal*, **50**(1), 25–32.
Gawer, A., and Cusumano, M.A. (2014). Industry platforms and ecosystem innovation. *Journal of Product Innovation Management*, **31**(3), 417–433.
Ghallab, M., Nau, D., and Traverso, P. (2014). The actor's view of automated planning and acting: a position paper. *Artificial Intelligence*, **208**, 1–17.
Ghallab, M., Nau, D., and Traverso, P. (2016). *Automated Planning and Acting*. New York: Cambridge University Press.
Giugliani, E., Selig, P.M., and dos Santos, N. (2014). Innovation parks as alternative to regional development facing the world crises: a governance model. In: Benedicto, J.L.L. (ed.), *Tipologias de regions en la Union Europea y otros estudios* (pp. 111–144). Barcelona: Publications i Edicions de la Universitat de Barcelona.
Guerrero, M., Cunningham, J.A., and Urbano, D. (2015). Economic impact of entrepreneurial universities' activities: an exploratory study of the United Kingdom. *Research Policy*, **44**(3), 748–764.
Gulati, R. (1999). Network location and learning: the influence of network resources and firm capabilities on alliance formation. *Strategic Management Journal*, **20**(5), 397–420.
Gulati, R., Lavie, D., and Singh, H. (2009). The nature of partnering experience and the gains from alliances. *Strategic Management Journal*, **30**(11), 1213–1233.

Gulati, R., Nohria, N., and Zaheer, A. (2000). Strategic Networks. *Strategic Management Journal*, **21**(3), 203–215.
Hellebrand, H.M. (2017). An exponential world: nature, patterns, and how to leverage them. In: Ellermann, H., Kreutter, P., and Messner, W. (eds), *The Palgrave Handbook of Managing Continuous Business Transformation* (pp. 95–113). London: Palgrave Macmillan.
Howells, J. (2006). Intermediation and the role of intermediaries in innovation. *Research Policy*, **35**(5), 715–728.
Ismail, S., Malone, M.S., and van Geest, Y. (2014). *Exponential Organizations: Why New Organizations are Ten Times Better, Faster, and Cheaper than Yours (and What To Do About It)*. New York: Diversion Books.
Katzy, B.R., Pawar, K.S., and Thoben, K-D. (2012). Editorial: a Living Lab research agenda. *International Journal of Product Development*, **17**(1/2), 1–7.
Kuratko, D.F. (2005). The emergence of entrepreneurship education: development, trends, and challenges. *Entrepreneurship Theory and Practice*, **29**(5), 577–598.
Lamb, C.S., Giugliani, E., Lima, L.R.R, Prikladnicki. R., and Neto, R.J. (2016a). STPs and collective thinking: the experience of TECNOPUC. In: *33rd IASP World Conference on Science Parks and Areas of Innovation*. Moscow.
Lamb, C.S., Giugliani, E., Prikladnicki, R., and Evaristo, J.R. (2016b). Strategic Planning Mapping – O Processo de Aceleração de Sinergias do TECNOPUC. In: *CIKI – Congresso Internacional de Conhecimento e Inovação*. Bogotá, Colombia.
Laursen, K., Reichsteinb, T., and Salter, A. (2011). Exploring the effect of geographical proximity and university quality on university–industry collaboration in the United Kingdom. *Regional Studies*, **45**(4), 507–523.
Laursen, K., and Salter, A. (2006). Open for innovation: the role of openness in explaining innovation performance among UK manufacturing firms. *Strategic Management Journal*, **27**, 131–150.
Oh, D.S., Phillips, F., Park, S., and Lee, E. (2016). Innovation ecosystems: a critical examination. *Technovation*, **54**, 1–6.
Pisano, G., and Verganti, R. (2008). Which kind of collaboration is right for you? *Harvard Business Review*, **86**(12), 78–86.
Pistore, M., Bettin, R., and Traverso, P. (2014). Symbolic techniques for planning with extended goals in non-deterministic domains. In: *Proceedings of the Sixth European Conference on Planning* (pp. 166–173). Palo Alto, CA: The AAAI Press.
Pistore, M., Spalazzi, L., and Traverso, P. (2006). A minimalist approach to semantic annotations for web processes compositions. In: *European Semantic Web Conference* (pp. 620–634). Berlin and Heidelberg: Springer-Verlag.
Pompermayer, L., Prikladnicki, R., Torrescasana, S., and Giugliani, E. (2016). From ideas to post incubation: Generating global-born companies at TECNOPUC and RAIAR. In: *33rd IASP World Conference*, Moscow.
Prikladnicki, R., Nicolas Audy, J.L., and Evaristo, R. (2003). Global software development in practice lessons learned. *Software Process: Improvement and Practice*, **8**(4), 267–281.
Prikladnicki, R., Perin, M.G., Marczak, S., and Dutra, A.C.S. (2017). The best software development teams might be temporary. *IEEE Software*, **34**(2), 22–25.
Ritala, P., and Almpanopoulou, A. (2017). In defense of 'eco' in innovation ecosystem. *Technovation*, **60/61**, 39–42.
Rogers, E.M. (2003). *Diffusion of Innovation*, 5th edition. New York: Free Press.
Schein, E.H. (2008). Clinical inquiry/research. In: Reason, P. and Bradbury, H. (eds), *Handbook of Action Research*, 2nd edn (pp. 266–279). London: SAGE.

Schweitzer, F.M., Gassmann, O., and Gaubinger, K. (2011). Open innovation and its effectiveness to embrace turbulent environments. *International Journal of Innovation Management*, **15**(6), 1191–1207.
Seebode, D., Jeanrenaud, S., and Bessant, J. (2012). Managing innovation for sustainability. *R&D Management*, **42**(3), 195–206.
Stewart, J., and Hyysalo, S. (2008). Intermediaries, users and social learning in technological innovation. *International Journal of Innovation Management*, **12**(3), 295–325.
Surie, G. (2017). Creating the innovation ecosystem for renewable energy via social entrepreneurship: insights from India. *Technological Forecasting and Social Change*, **121**, 184–195.
Urbano, D., and Guerrero, M. (2013). Entrepreneurial universities: socioeconomic impacts of academic entrepreneurship in a European region. *Economic Development Quarterly*, **27**(1), 40–55.
van Loon, R. (2017). The future of leadership. In: Water, B.R.S. (ed.), *Creating Organizational Value through Dialogical Leadership* (pp. 243–268). Cham, Switzerland: Springer.
van Looy, B., Landoni, P., Callaert, J., Van Pottelsberghe, B., Sapsalis, E., and Debackere, K. (2011). Entrepreneurial effectiveness of European universities: an empirical assessment of antecedents and trade-offs. *Research Policy*, **40**(4), 553–564.
Winter, J., Battisti, S., Burstrom, T., and Luukkainen, S. (forthcoming). Exploring the success factors of mobile business ecosystems. *International Journal of Innovation and Technology Management*, **15**(3).
Yin, R.K. (2009). *Case Study Research: Design and Methods*, 4th edition. Applied Social Research Methods, Vol. 5. Thousand Oaks, CA: SAGE Publications.

13. Conclusion: future suggestions for entrepreneurial universities

João J. Ferreira, Alain Fayolle, Vanessa Ratten and Mário Raposo

INTRODUCTION

There are different terms to describe an entrepreneurial university, including academic entrepreneurship, academic innovation, innovative university, university innovation and university entrepreneurship (Schmitz et al., 2017). The common theme of these definitions is the involvement of the university in disseminating knowledge for commercial or social purposes. Entrepreneurship at universities has taken on a broader meaning in recent years, as it now includes any kind of activity that is innovative, risk taking and proactive. The changing perceptions of entrepreneurship have been the result of universities creating new ways to harness knowledge made by and originating from their institutions. The move towards a knowledge society has also influenced increased attention on universities as places to exchange information. This helps to create an entrepreneurial ecosystem that enables collaboration between the university, the community and stakeholders.

Abreu and Grinevich (2013) view entrepreneurship at universities as involving activities beyond the traditional roles of teaching, research and service. Normally entrepreneurship provides a financial incentive that can occur directly via additional revenue, or indirectly through increased reputation. An important way for universities to compete in the knowledge economy is to engage in innovation through socio-economic development. This can occur via knowledge spillovers at universities that involve knowledge from education moving into related sectors of the economy. Entrepreneurship at universities involves a range of activities including consultancy arrangements, establishing new companies and service to the community (Yokoyama, 2006). In addition, there are other ways in which universities are entrepreneurial in their service agreements, such as on scholarships, funding and overheads.

The key feature of entrepreneurial universities is in their ability to find new solutions that enable more efficient use of services. This helps to build an entrepreneurial environment that places an emphasis on using knowledge for new purposes. This involves innovation such as ideas and inventions that have been discovered at a university. Knowledge exchange is part of the innovation process as it provides new applications that can contribute to economic development (Wood, 2011). There is a perception that most entrepreneurship involves a positive change, but it can have negative effects if used in the wrong way. Thus, entrepreneurship needs to be managed by universities to ensure it involves a change in social welfare. This is important, as universities contribute to the economy in both financial and non-financial ways.

This chapter provides new theoretical, practical and policy contributions to the concept of entrepreneurial universities. We provide a unified discussion of the entrepreneurial university as a way to advance theory. This also links to the practical applications of this chapter that can help universities to implement more effective entrepreneurship programmes.

This chapter is structured as follows. Firstly, the changing nature of the entrepreneurial university is discussed, which contextualizes the importance of education in society. Secondly, the new way that entrepreneurship is envisioned in universities is stated. Thirdly, future research directions for entrepreneurial universities are discussed in terms of their importance in the global economy.

ENTREPRENEURSHIP TRENDS IN UNIVERSITIES

Audretsch (2014), in a seminal article, discussed how entrepreneurial universities are shifting their focus to societal rather than just educational outcomes. This enables a better integration of universities into the social fabric of the global community. In the future, universities will have to continue promoting their knowledge efforts in terms of how they can be sustained for long-term benefit. This means focusing on the autonomy of universities in terms of leadership in their communities by promoting knowledge sharing activities. Hence, this helps to integrate knowledge into communities that enables better social development.

Entrepreneurial universities seek to be free of state control by being independent entities with the power to control their own destinies (Mainardes et al., 2011). This is important in the knowledge economy, which prides itself on the ability to meet market demands in innovative ways. Thus, the organization of knowledge by capitalizing on new strengths is an important way in which universities engage in practical activities (Etzkowitz,

2013). Universities are trying to foster entrepreneurialism on campuses by providing better infrastructure support (Jacob et al., 2003). This enables the use of research in a new way that links in with community needs and the responsibilities universities have to society. To do this, many universities are packaging entrepreneurship that enables improved financial performance through better strategic planning (Kirby et al., 2011). This is important for universities that want to evolve and create better leadership programmes that increase entrepreneurship.

There are distinctive entrepreneurial characteristics of universities, such as alliances and collaboration between government and industry (Guerrero et al., 2014). These relationships take time for universities to develop but often result in increased status of the university amongst its peer institutions. Due to increased technological change in society from mobile commerce there has been a focus on universities to develop close ties with government agencies. There are different ways in which universities are considered entrepreneurial, and these change based on the exploitation of knowledge in society. Increasingly there is specialized research and training at universities about how to be entrepreneurial. In addition, there has been substantial academic growth in entrepreneurship that has changed the organizational architecture at universities. Thus, actions towards entrepreneurship at universities tend to involve the use of innovation for the creation of new ideas.

This book provides a number of contributions to entrepreneurial university research and practice that will now be discussed. Chapter 2, about the role of university–business collaboration, contributes to developing a better understanding of the design thinking process. This is an important contribution to the literature about entrepreneurship education because it discusses an innovative teaching method focusing on entrepreneurial learning. Chapter 3 focuses on the role of entrepreneurial universities in a developing-country context. This enables a contribution to the literature about entrepreneurial universities by focusing on the role of knowledge transfer in higher education institutions. Chapter 4 discusses the importance of the knowledge-based society for universities. By stressing the academic revolution from the Internet, the chapter adds to the literature on social development and the third mission of universities. Chapter 5 focuses on entrepreneurialism in a London university, thereby contributing to the literature about the development of entrepreneurial mindsets in students. The chapter contributes to the literature on the need for curricula to evolve and take a more entrepreneurial approach. Chapter 6 discusses the role of doctoral education, including more emphasis on problem solving capacities. This enables a linkage to the literature on entrepreneurial competences. Chapter 7 focuses on the role of higher education institutions in managing innovation. The chapter contributes to the literature about entrepreneurial universities by suggesting they need to be understood from within a procedural framework. Chapter 8 discusses the role of technology-based firms in entrepreneurial universities. The findings of the chapter contribute to our understanding of politics in the emergence of entrepreneurial universities. Chapter 9 examines the role of entrepreneurial teams in entrepreneurship education. This is an important way of understanding leadership and group behaviour in entrepreneurial projects. Chapter 10 focuses on the economic and social role of entrepreneurship education. This helps to understand the effectiveness of pedagogies in developing entrepreneurial intentions. Chapter 11 discusses the role of entrepreneurship education from an engineering perspective. Therefore, the chapter contributes to our understanding of the transition by universities to become more engaged parts of society. Chapter 12 examines the growth of exponential technologies in society and their influence on innovation ecosystems. This helps us to understand the nature of entrepreneurial actions and the impact for knowledge-based start-ups.

IMPLICATIONS AND FUTURE RESEARCH DIRECTIONS

The chapters included in this book have several implications for university managers and higher education policy analysts. Firstly, there needs to be more emphasis on the entrepreneurial ecosystem as a way to communicate and collaborate. This requires more positive feedback by leadership of universities in trialling new programmes that might take some time to develop. To do this, resource funding and time allocation is needed to encourage the flow of information in the entrepreneurial ecosystem. Moreover, as the chapters in this book suggest, the cultural context of the university influences the development of entrepreneurial ecosystems.

Secondly, the chapters offer insights into different strategies about how to harness the entrepreneurial potential of universities. This helps to bridge the gap between university research and the practical implications of knowledge. To achieve more university entrepreneurship it is interesting to utilize examples from other education sectors that have utilized cross-disciplinary entrepreneurship programmes.

Finally, the chapters highlight the various ways in which entrepreneurship is understood at universities. This includes different conceptualizations of entrepreneurship, but also of innovation and creativity, as the terms can be used interchangeably. There has been a trend in defining entrepreneurship in a broad sense that is seen in the various discussions of entrepreneurial universities in this book.

Future research needs to continue looking at the role of entrepreneurial universities in society. Universities are constantly altering, based on market demands and regulatory needs. This is made more evident with online courses growing in popularity that are requiring new educational needs. Hence, research needs to keep up to date with both curriculum and research factors at universities. The topic of entrepreneurial universities is contemporary, as there has been a shift in funding models by governments to public institutions. This has caused a tension in some universities over how to be self-sufficient but at the same time maintain academic integrity. For this reason there should be more attention placed on country differences amongst universities to see how regional policy is affecting this change. Individual governments contribute to how universities function, but also demand integration with their other educational institutions. This means that it is critically important for research to focus on different levels of government policy in terms of how they are influencing universities. In addition, there is a need to understand how economic trading blocs such as the European Union are affecting entrepreneurship in universities. This is due to the emphasis on knowledge, but also regional integration and standardization of courses in universities.

The main implications of this book are to provide different ways of viewing entrepreneurial universities from an international perspective. This aligns with the global competitiveness of the university sector in education debates. Increasingly, entrepreneurship is viewed as a global education requirement in the knowledge economy. In this context, researchers need to stress the changing nature of the workforce and how this will influence entrepreneurship education. A way to do this might be to encourage research collaboration between scholars interested in artificial intelligence and knowledge management.

There are research gaps surrounding the literature about entrepreneurial universities that need to be addressed. These include the lack of research integrating disciplines apart from business in the discussion of entrepreneurial universities. Research about the holistic nature of entrepreneurship in universities from the perspective of business, engineering and science is required. This would enable a better consideration of the different ways in which entrepreneurship is embedded in course design. In addition, focus is needed on the link between urban or regional education institutions and entrepreneurship. This is important especially in cross-border regions that need to consider multiple country or state perspectives.

As indicated in the chapters of this book, there is more research needed on how entrepreneurial universities consider different cultural and social views that are often dependent on geography. Future research needs to be more international in its exploration of the literature about economic geography and entrepreneurial universities. In addition, we believe that further research could be done to analyse entrepreneurship at universities using emerging technology trends. This is necessary as universities need to capitalize on opportunities in a proactive manner.

CONCLUSION

This book focuses on entrepreneurial universities in terms of management and policies. The chapters in the book come from a number of different international perspectives that showcase the emerging trends in entrepreneurial universities. In this chapter, we have argued that there is still much research work needed on understanding entrepreneurship in universities. The variety of approaches to understanding entrepreneurship and innovation in universities were discussed as a way to integrate novel thinking. An agenda for future research was stated that focuses on the emerging areas needing more attention. We hope that this book contributes to but also extends the research on entrepreneurial universities.

REFERENCES

Abreu, M. and Grinevich, V. (2013) 'The nature of academic entrepreneurship in the UK: Widening the focus on entrepreneurial activities', *Research Policy*, **42**(2): 408–422.

Audretsch, D.B. (2014) 'From the entrepreneurial university to the university for the entrepreneurial activity', *Journal of Technology Transfer*, **39**(3): 313–321.

Etzkowitz, H. (2013) 'Anatomy of the entrepreneurial university', *Social Science Information*, **52**(3): 486–511.

Guerrero, M., Urbano, D., Cunningham, M. and Organ, D. (2014) 'Entrepreneurial universities in two European regions: A case study comparison', *Journal of Technology Transfer*, **39**: 415–434.

Jacob, M., Lundqvist, M. and Hellsmark, H. (2003) 'Entrepreneurial transformations in the Swedish university system: The case of Chalmers University of Technology', *Research Policy*, **32**(9): 1555–1568.

Kirby, D.A., Guerrero, M. and Urbano, D. (2011) 'Making universities more entrepreneurial: Development of a model', *Canadian Journal of Administrative Sciences*, **28**(3): 302–316.

Mainardes, E.W., Alves, H. and Raposo, M. (2011) 'The process of change in university management: From the "ivory tower" to entrepreneurialism', *Transylvanian Review of Administrative Sciences*, **33**: 124–149.

Schmitz, A., Urbano, D., Dandolini, G.A., Souza, J.A. and Guerrero, M. (2016) 'Innovation and entrepreneurship in the academic setting: A systematic literature review', *International Entrepreneurship and Management Journal*, **13**(2): 369–395.

Wood, M.S. (2011) 'A process model of academic entrepreneurship', *Business Horizons*, **54**(2): 153–161.
Yokoyama, K. (2006) 'Entrepreneurialism in Japanese and UK universities: Governance, management, leadership and funding', *Higher Education*, **52**(3): 523–555.

Index

'Clearly, HEIs are discovering their innovative and entrepreneurial potential to reply to the society's distinct need for them to have a more entrepreneurial role, namely in innovation. This book succeeds in discussing the theme from an interdisciplinary perspective. For that reason, this book will be of help to practitioners in university management roles and policy makers as well as anyone researching this theme and teaching entrepreneurship in HEIs.'

Nuno Fernandes Crespo, Universidade de Lisboa, Portugal

'This book offers educators, entrepreneurs, policy makers, and researchers significant and practical implications. After reading the book, we can conclude that the different experiences described by authors on the academic tools and educational methods can be generalized in many other universities around the world, in both developed and developing countries.'

Waleed Omri, EDC Paris Business School, France

'Edited by four leading researchers, Entrepreneurial Universities *provides innovative insights into how universities are contributing to the emergence of an entrepreneurial ecosystem that is both redefining universities themselves and shaping society. It is an important book for all those interested in how universities are reinventing themselves in a time of profound societal transformation.'*

Tim Marjoribanks, Swinburne University of Technology, Australia

'Universities are called to be more and more entrepreneurial – that is, innovative, proactive and risk-taking – to promote regional development and economic growth. As a Professor working in two of the most entrepreneurial Italian universities, I benefited from reading this book. I consequently recommend it to all my colleagues to guide their strategic choices and their daily activities.'

Salvatore Sciascia, IULM University and Cattaneo University, Italy

'The entrepreneurial university is an increasing phenomenon in a world where universities have to be increasingly adaptable and market responsive whilst maintaining their societal mission and balancing the needs of diverse stakeholders. A text that addresses the past, current and anticipated situation and helps us plan for a dynamic future is most welcome.'

Chris Chapleo, Bournemouth University, UK

'An Entrepreneurial University is NOT an oxymoron! After reading this book, with its examples and stories of forward-thinking universities around the world, you will be a believer that there are universities taking dramatic

steps into the future and exceeding expectations. This book is a must-read for university administrators and faculty who believe the future is now!'

Dianne H.B. Welsh, University of North Carolina Greensboro, USA

'Entrepreneurial universities are not only a hot topic in research but also in practice. This book gives a comprehensive view from an international perspective – timely and interesting!'

Alexander Brem, Friedrich-Alexander-Universität Erlangen-Nürnberg, Germany